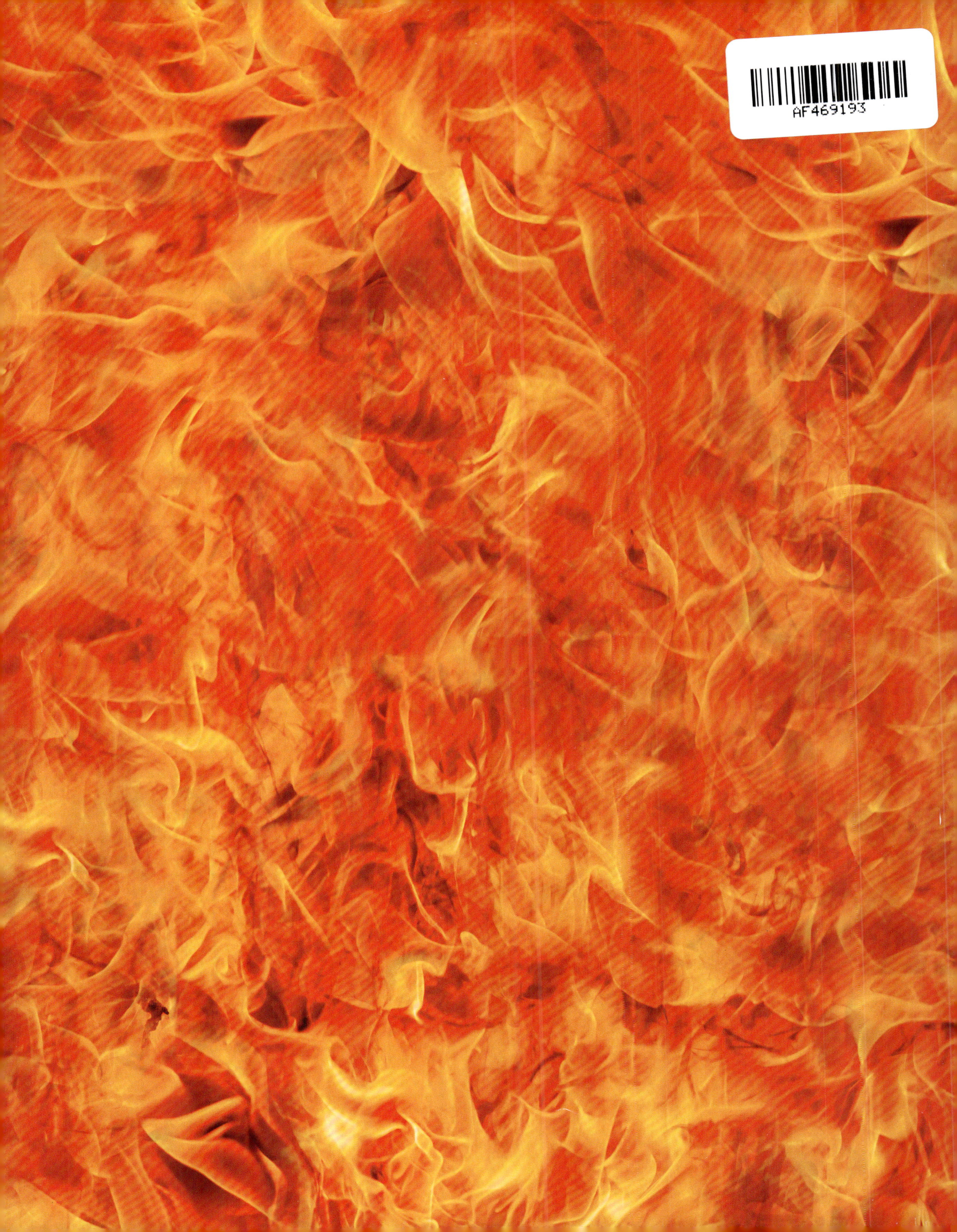

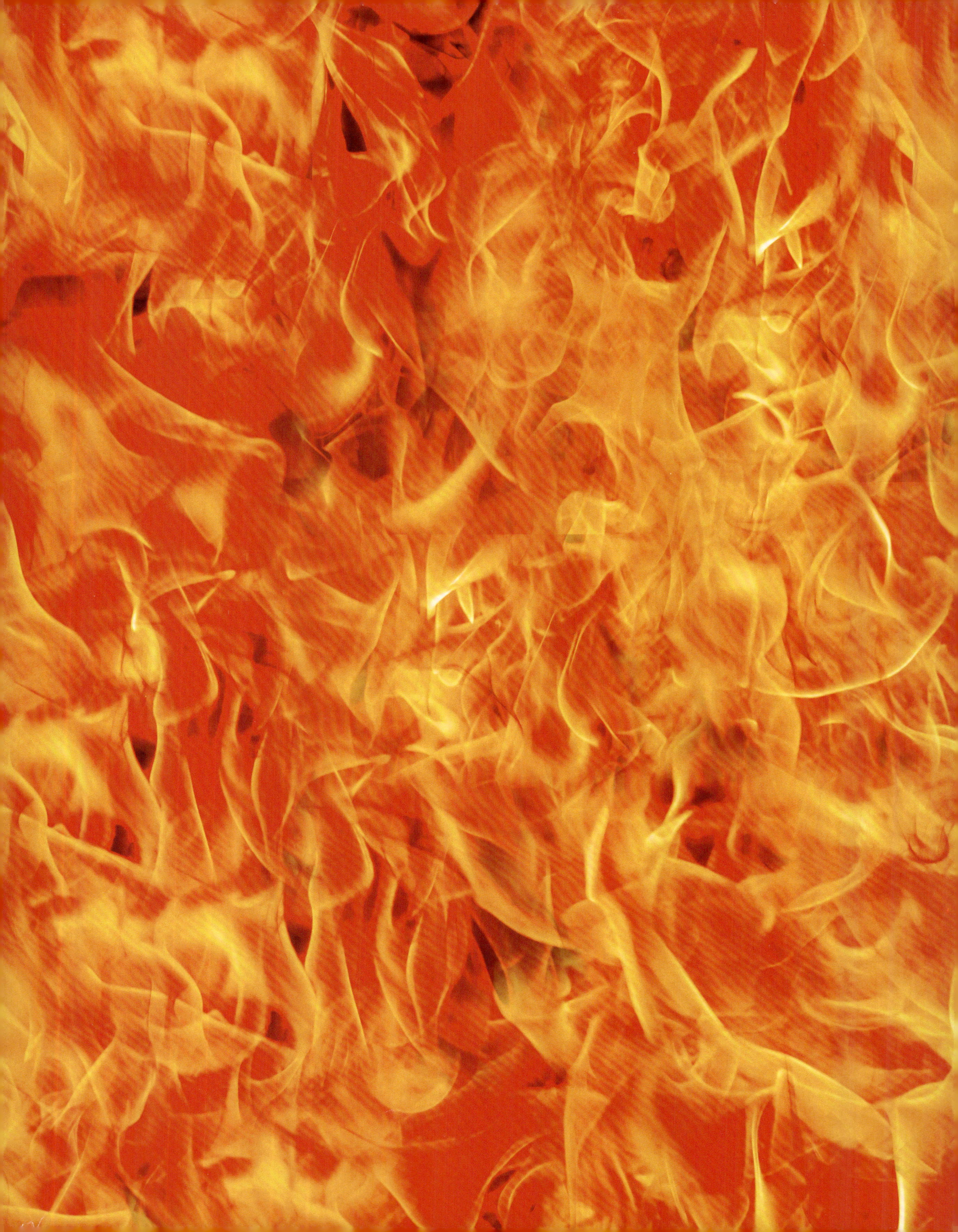

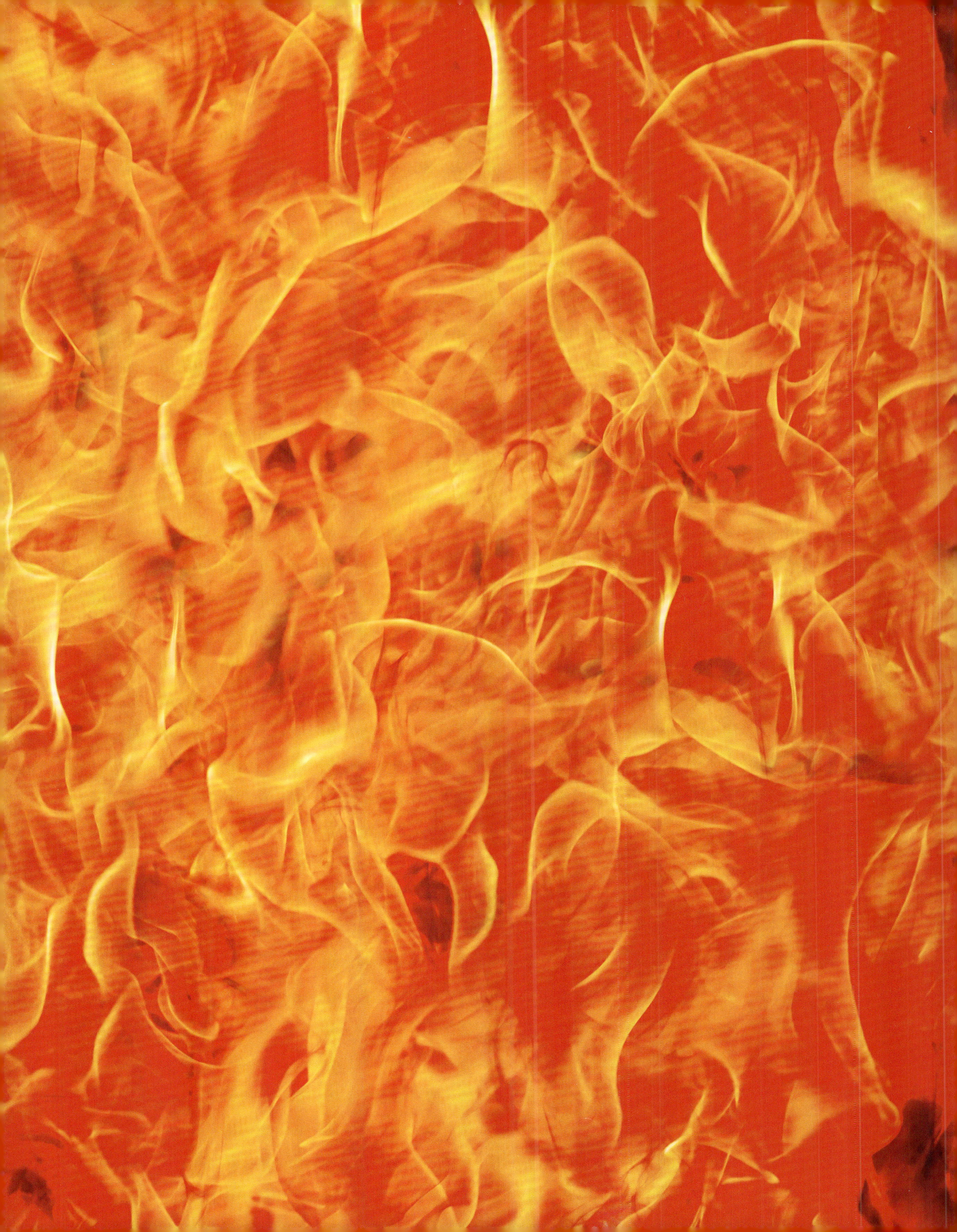

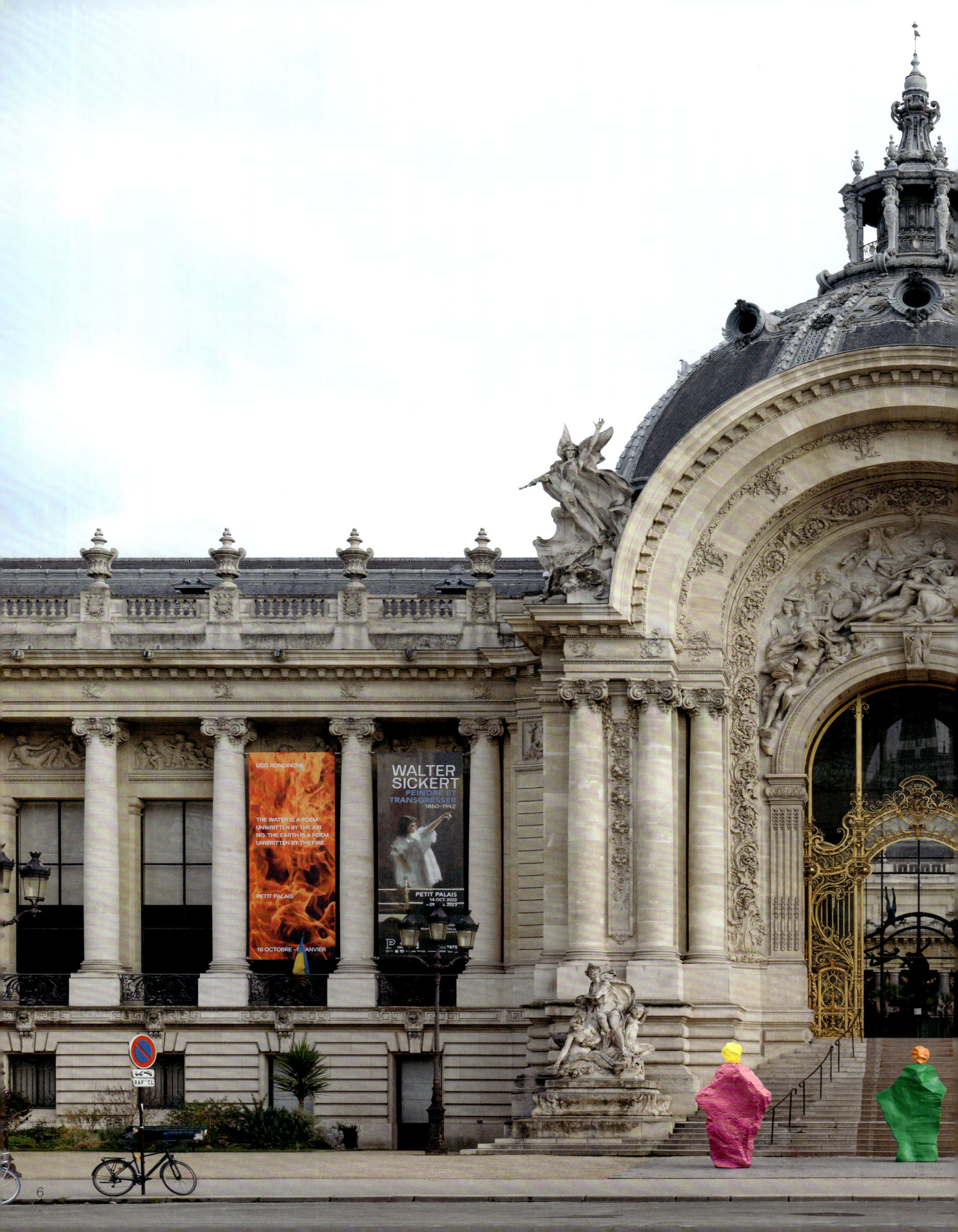
UGO RONDINONE
THE WATER IS A POEM
UNWRITTEN BY THE AIR
NO. THE EARTH IS A POEM
UNWRITTEN BY THE FIRE
PETIT PALAIS
WALTER
SICKERT
PEINDRE ET
TRANSGRESSER
1860-1942
PETIT PALAIS
14 OCT. 2022

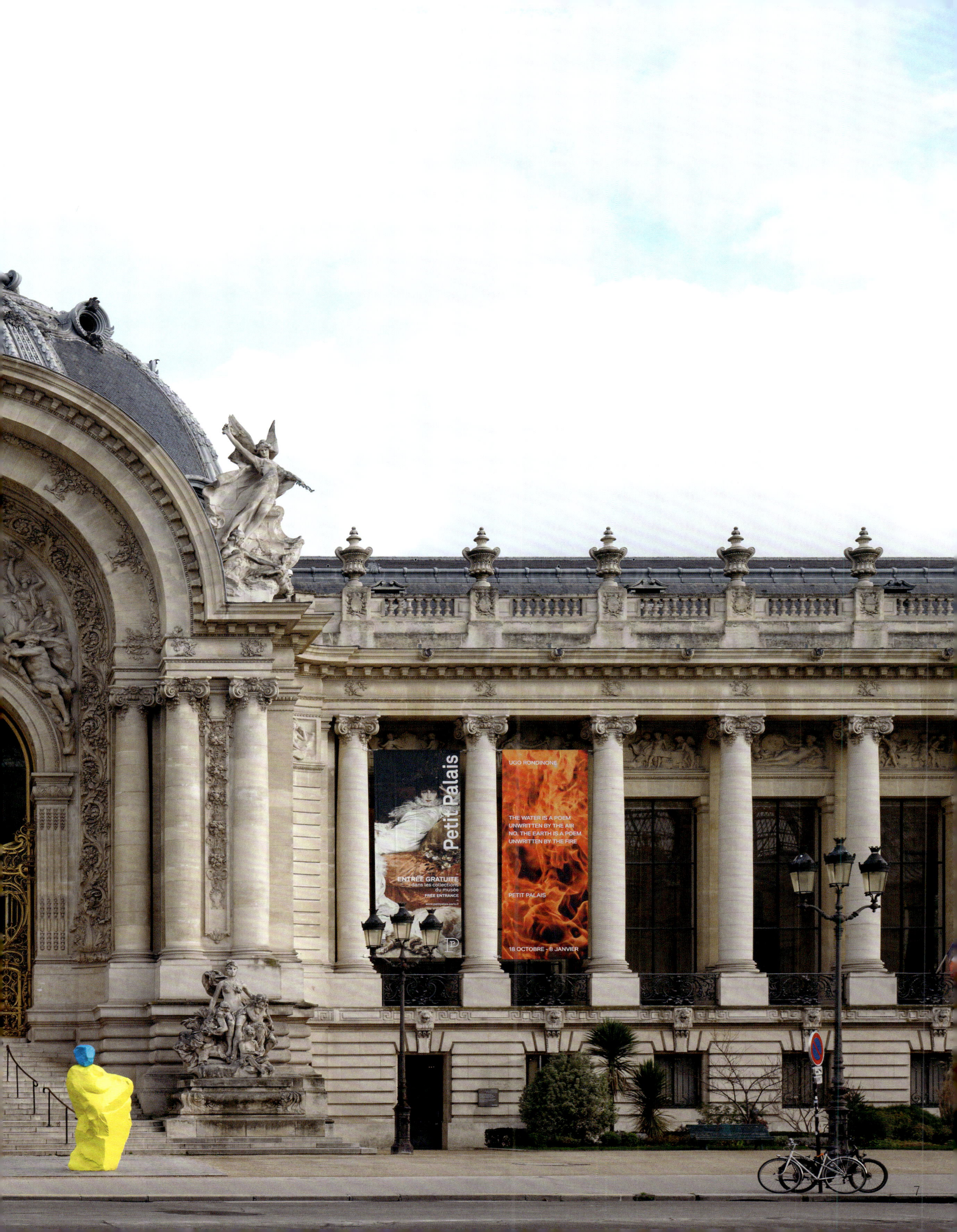
Petit Palais
ENTRÉE GRATUITE
dans les collections
du musée
FREE ENTRANCE
UGO RONDINONE
THE WATER IS A POEM
UNWRITTEN BY THE AIR
NO. THE EARTH IS A POEM
UNWRITTEN BY THE FIRE
PETIT PALAIS
18 OCTOBRE - 8 JANVIER

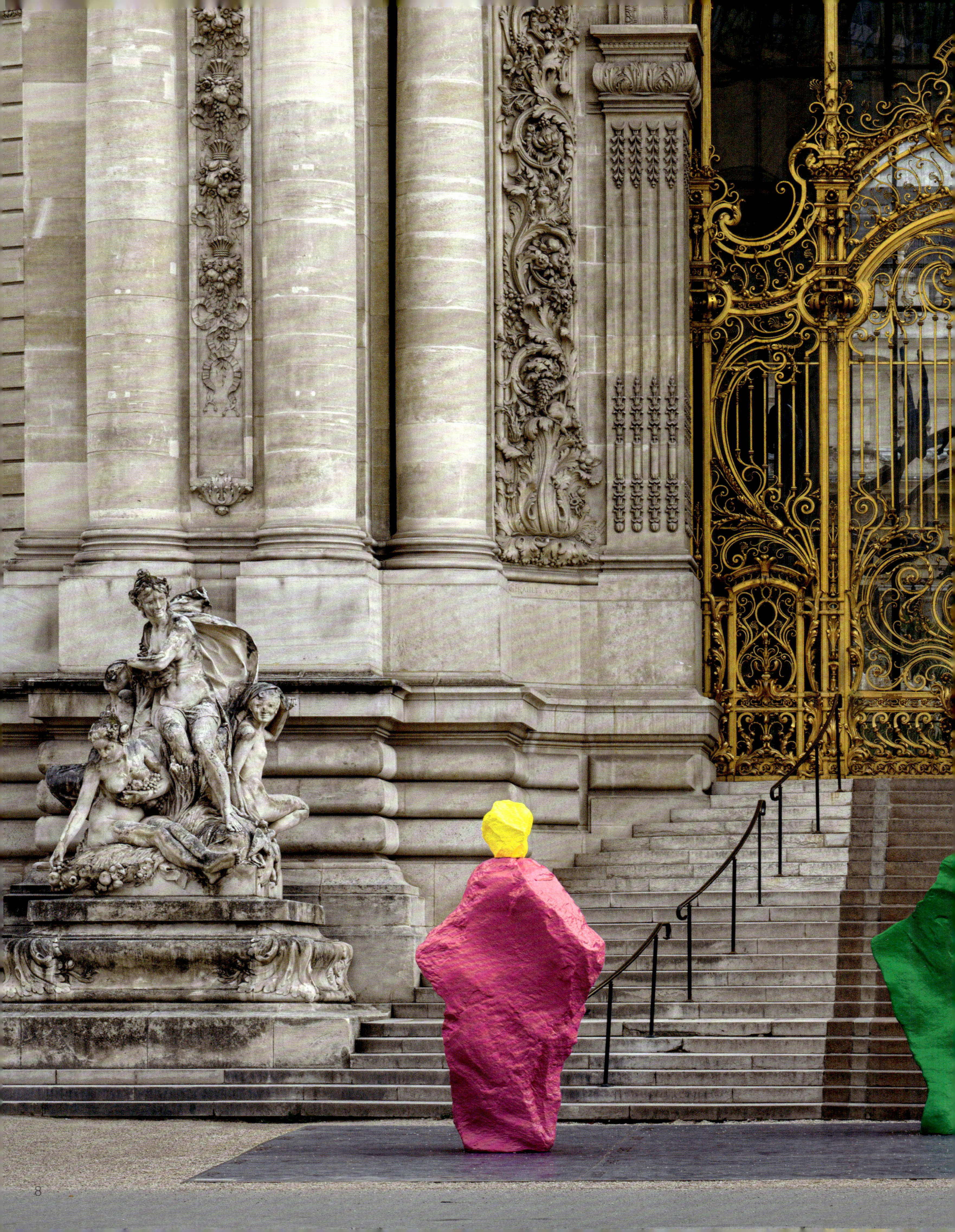

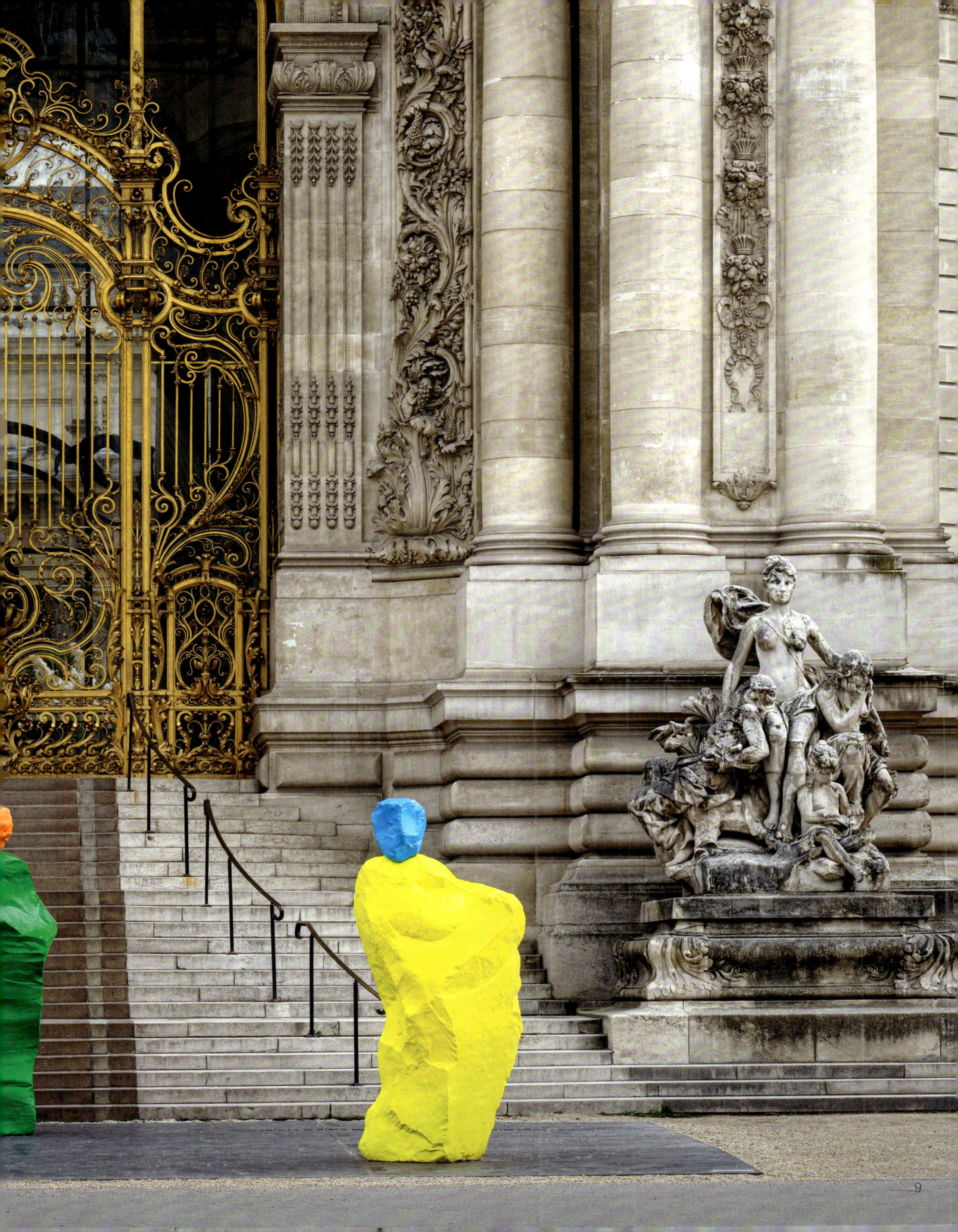

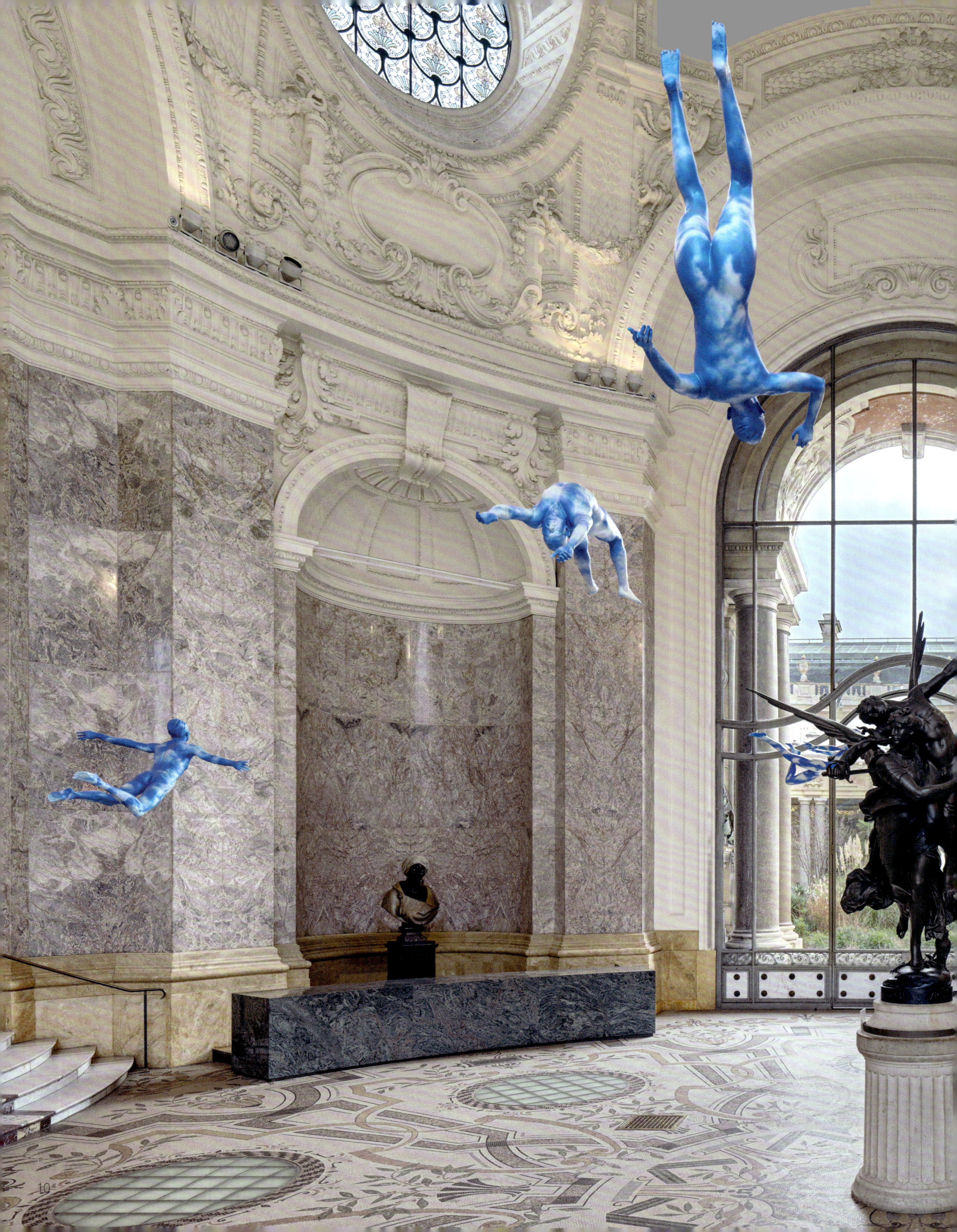

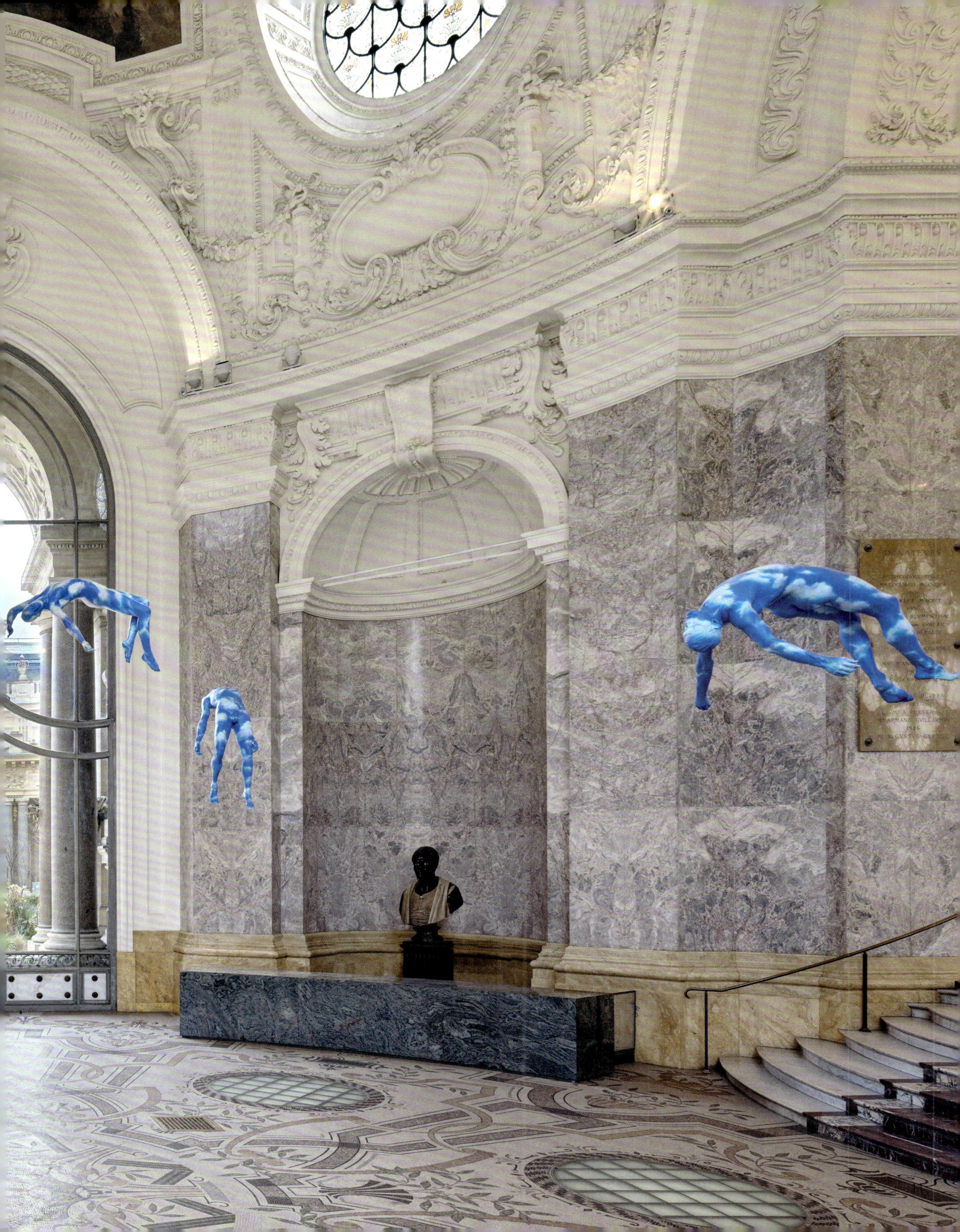

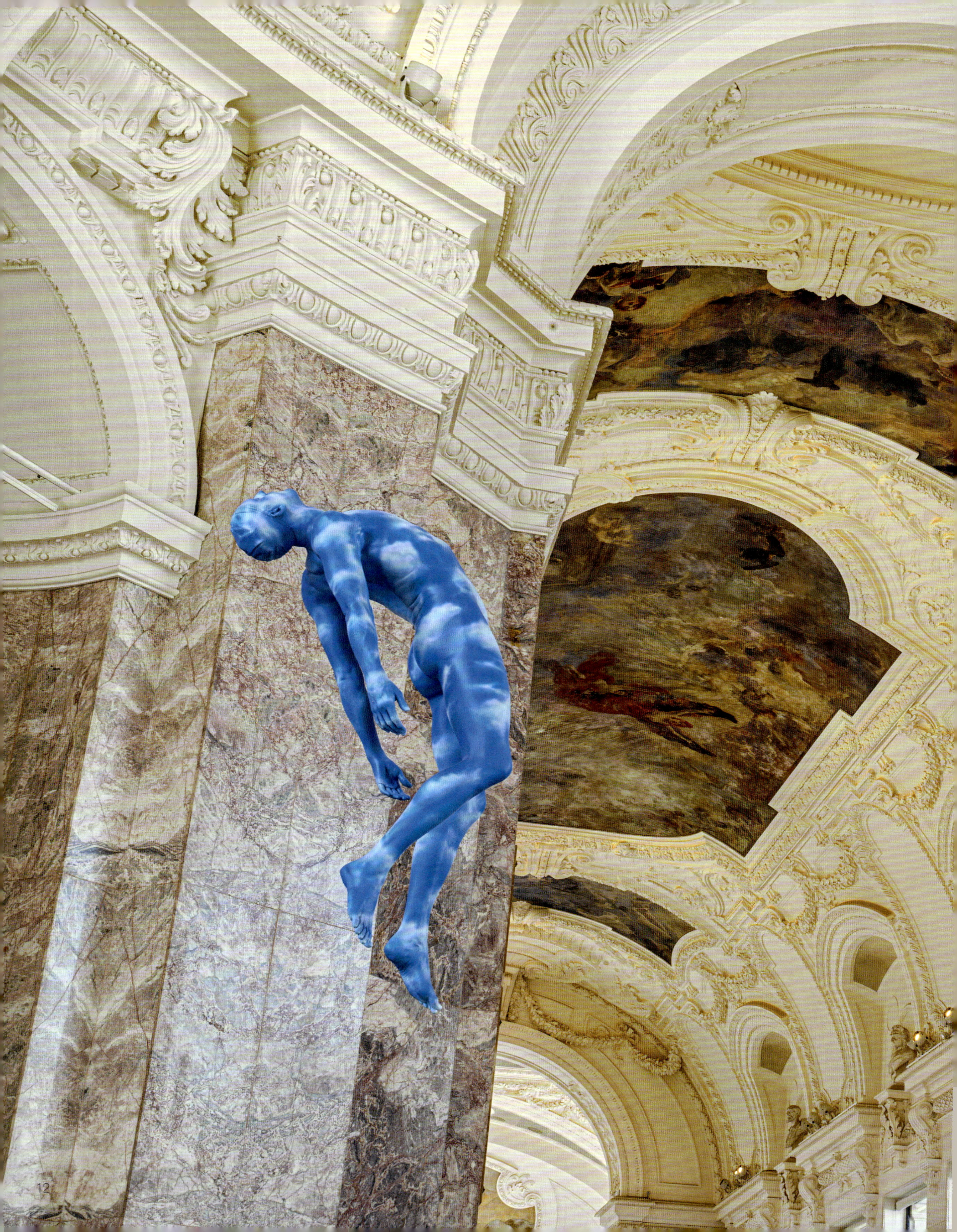

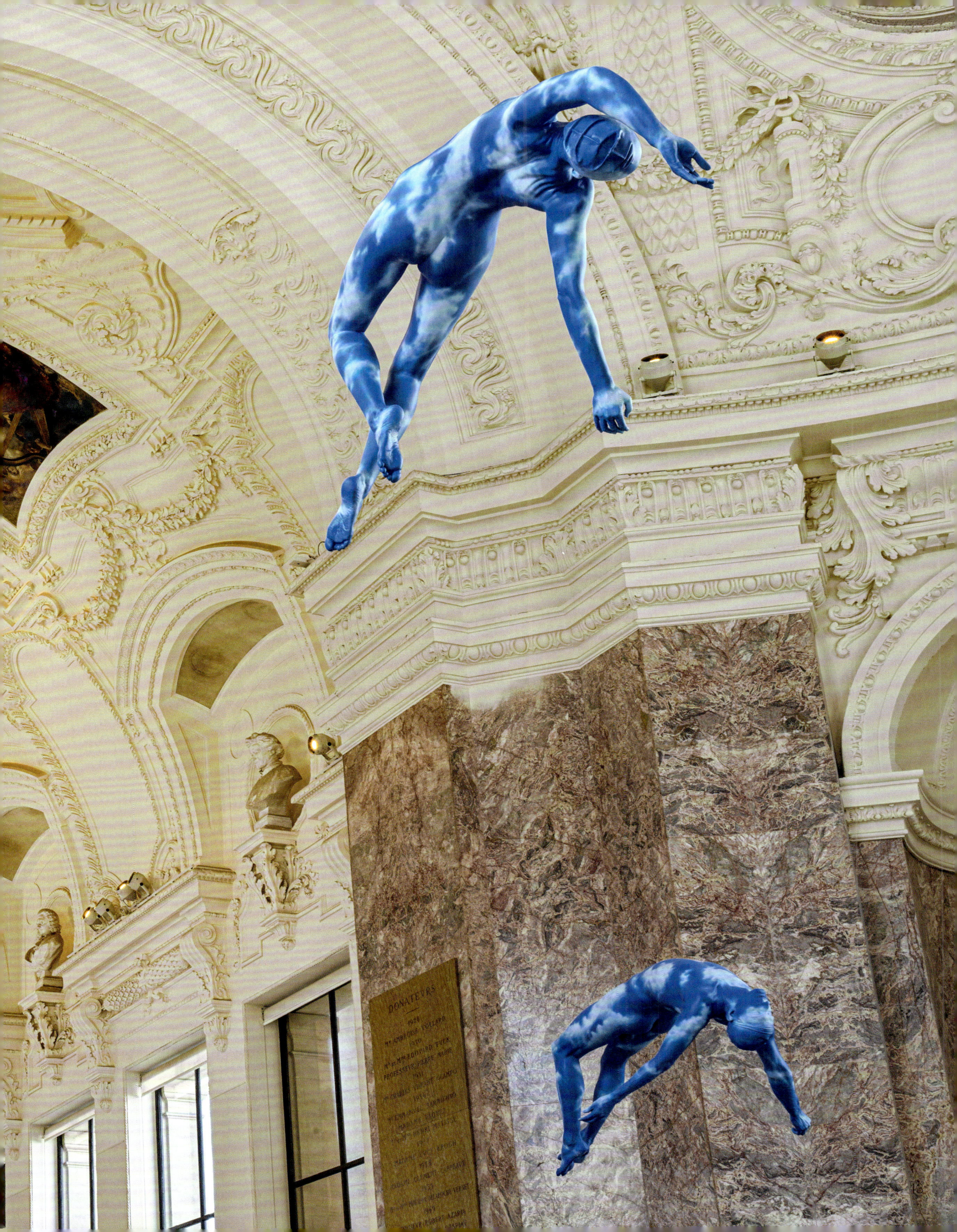
DONATEURS

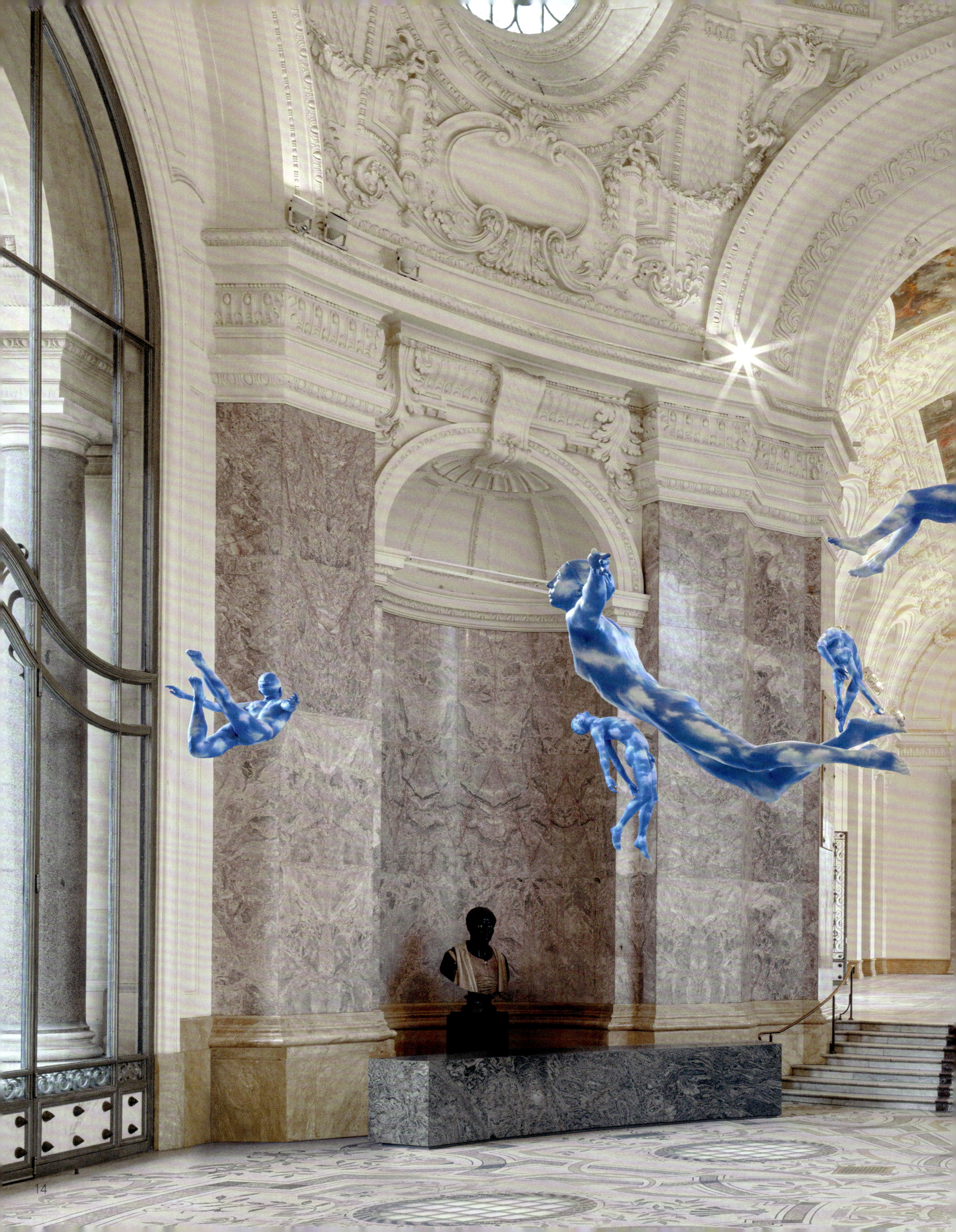

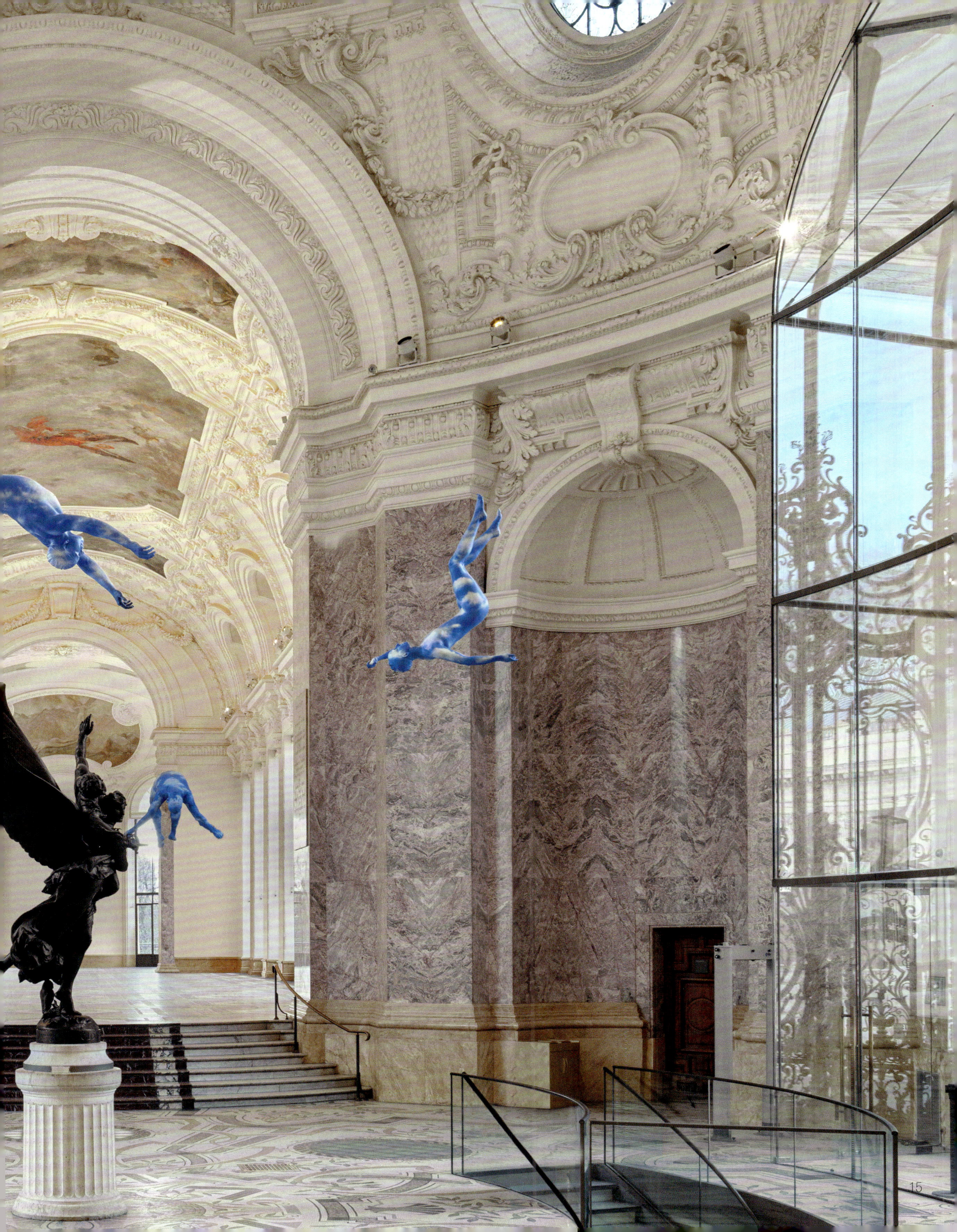

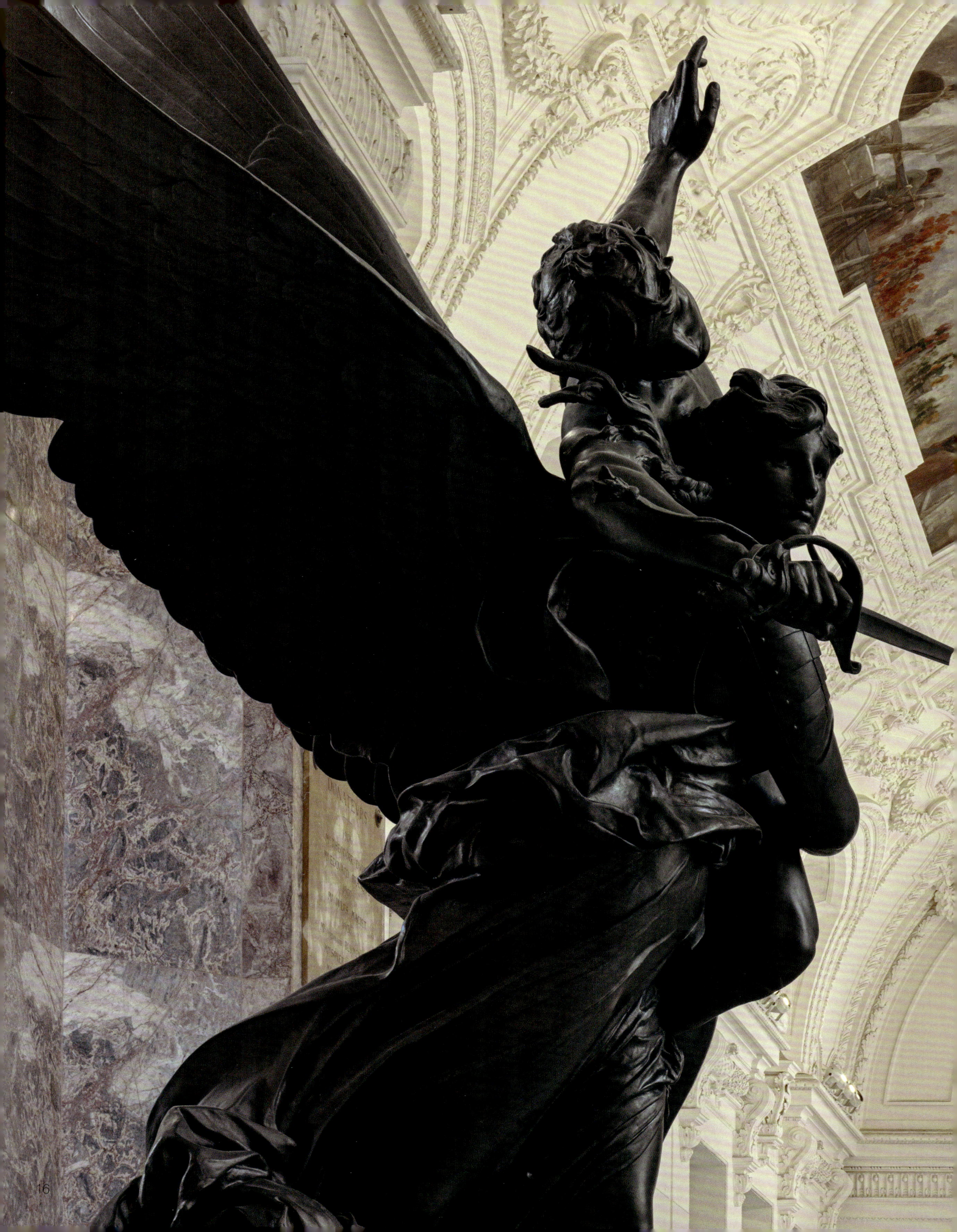

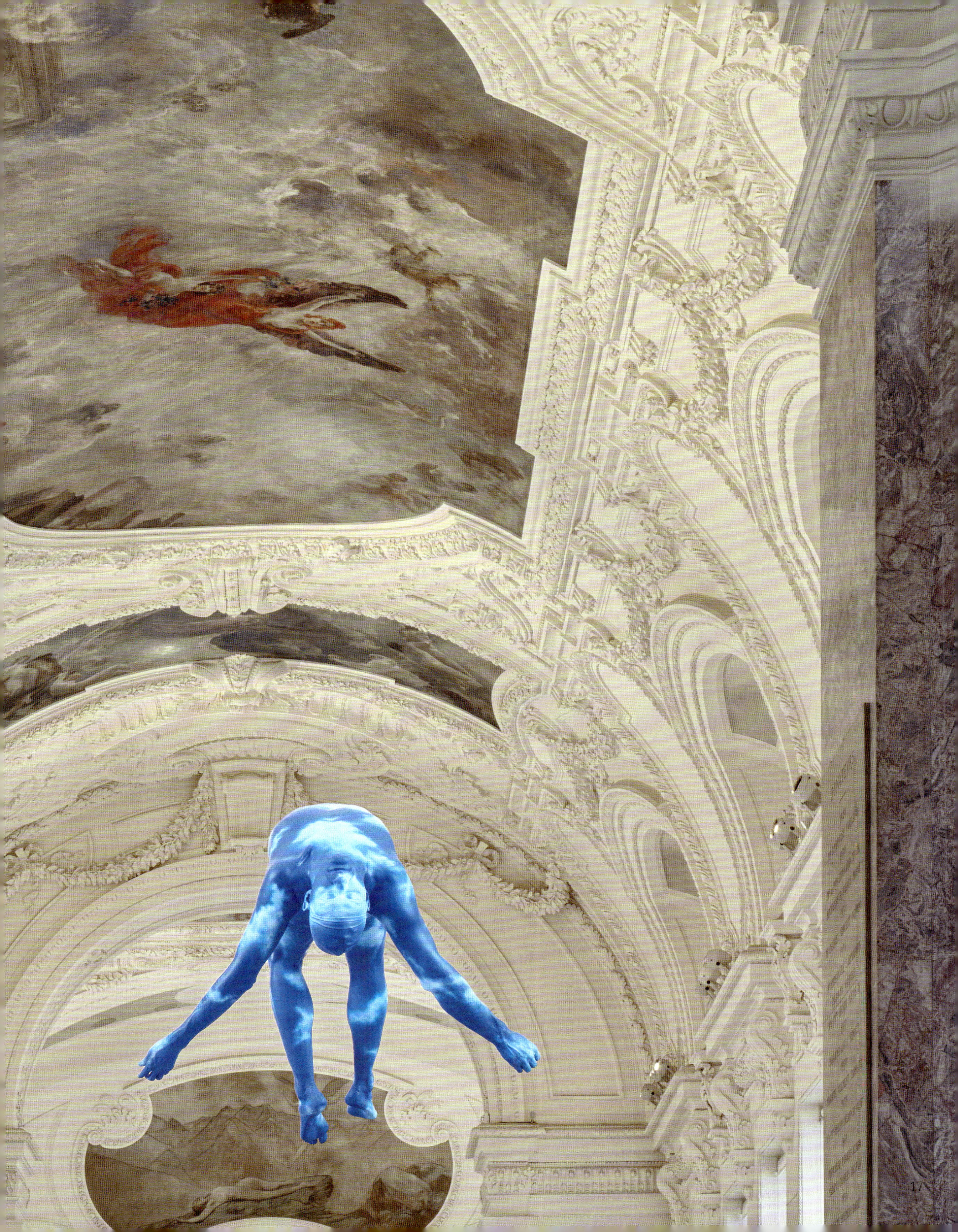

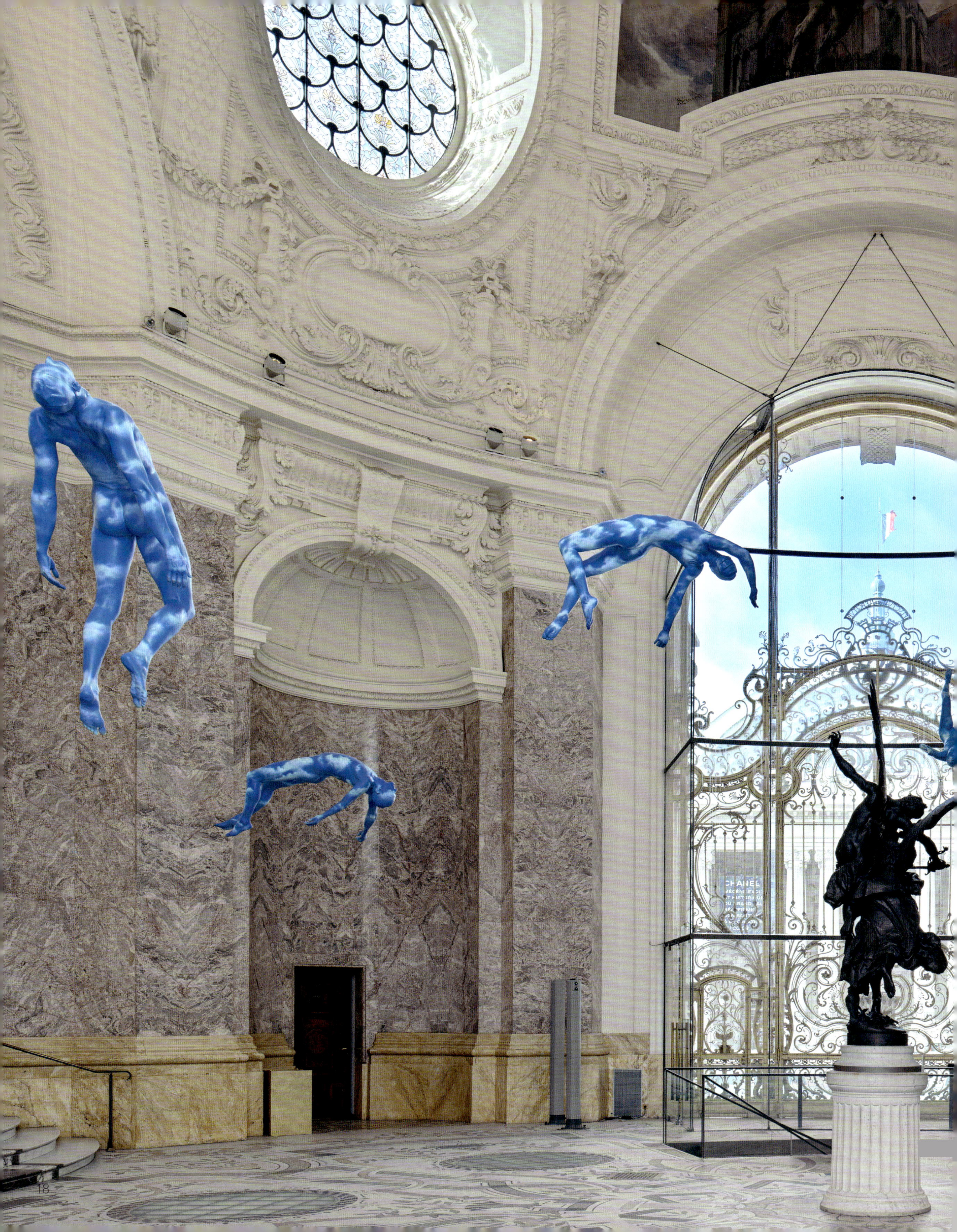
CHANEL

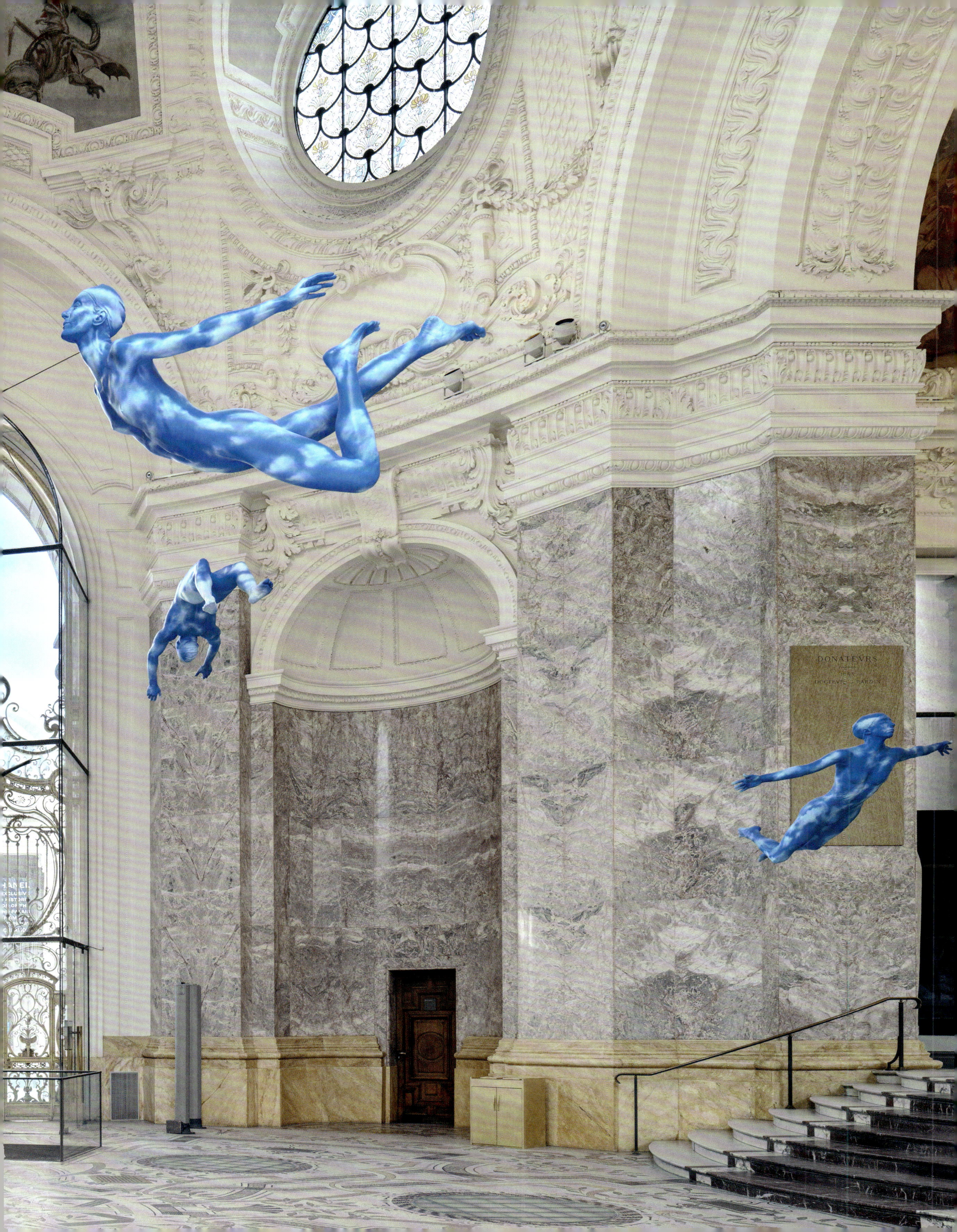
DONATEVRS

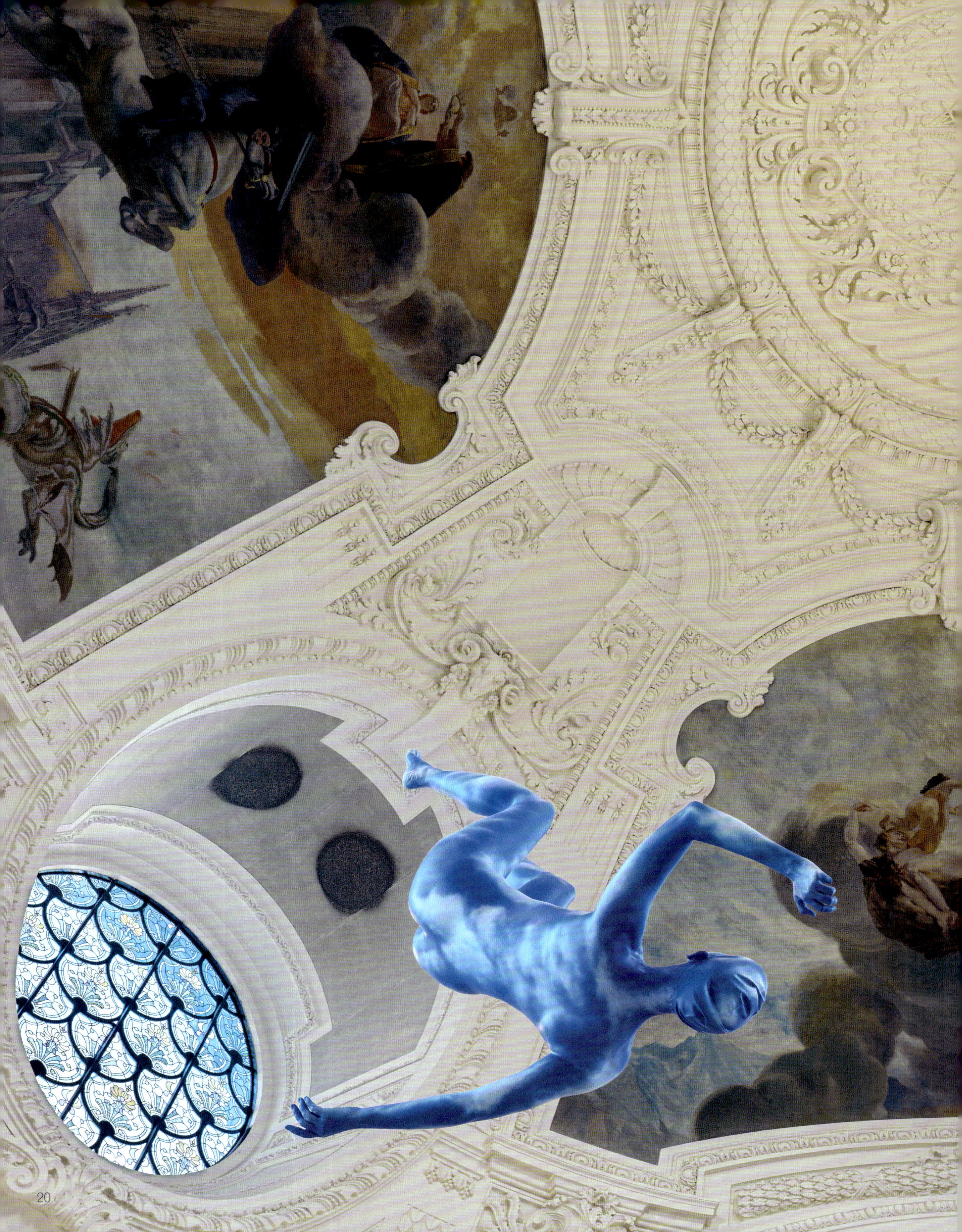

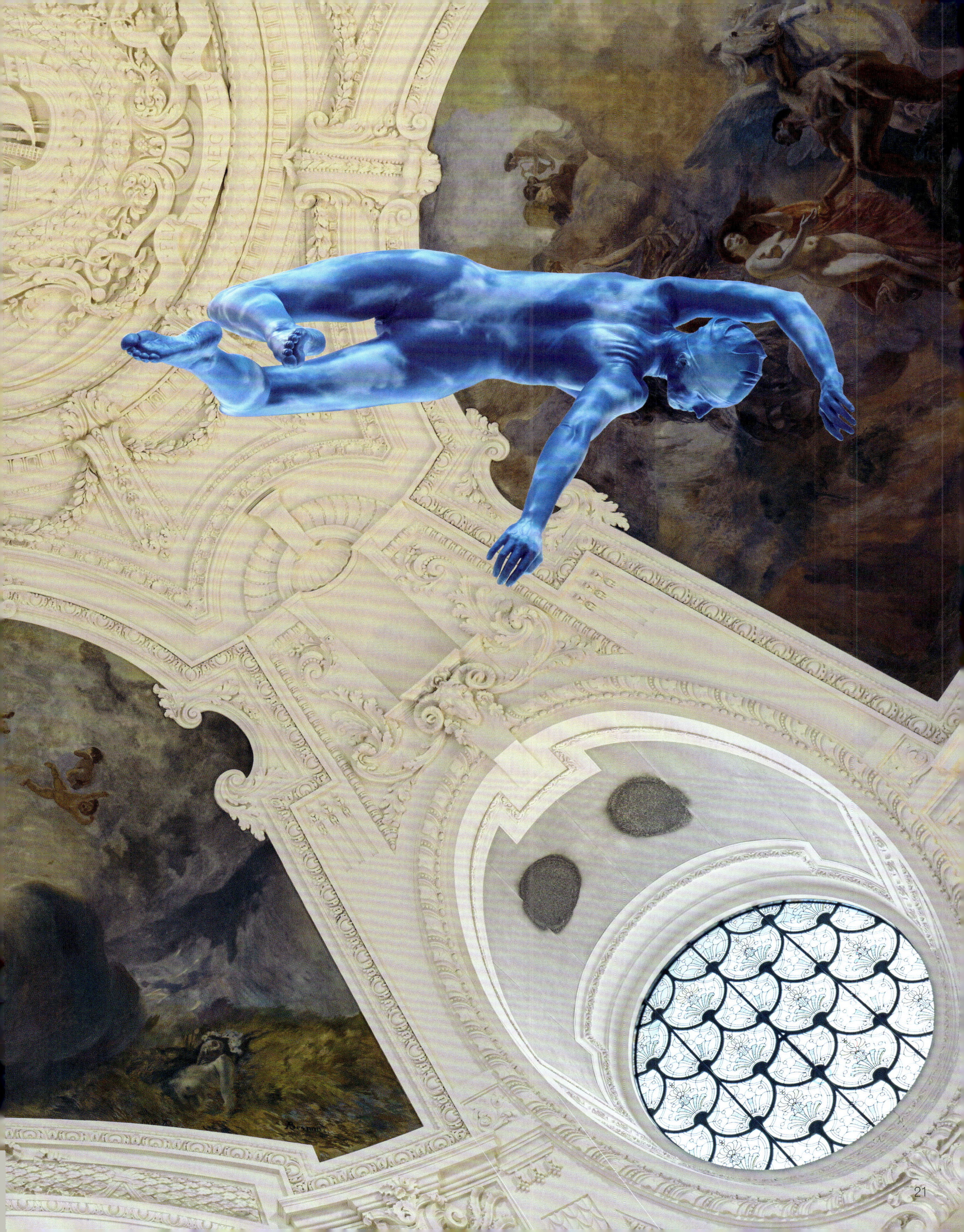

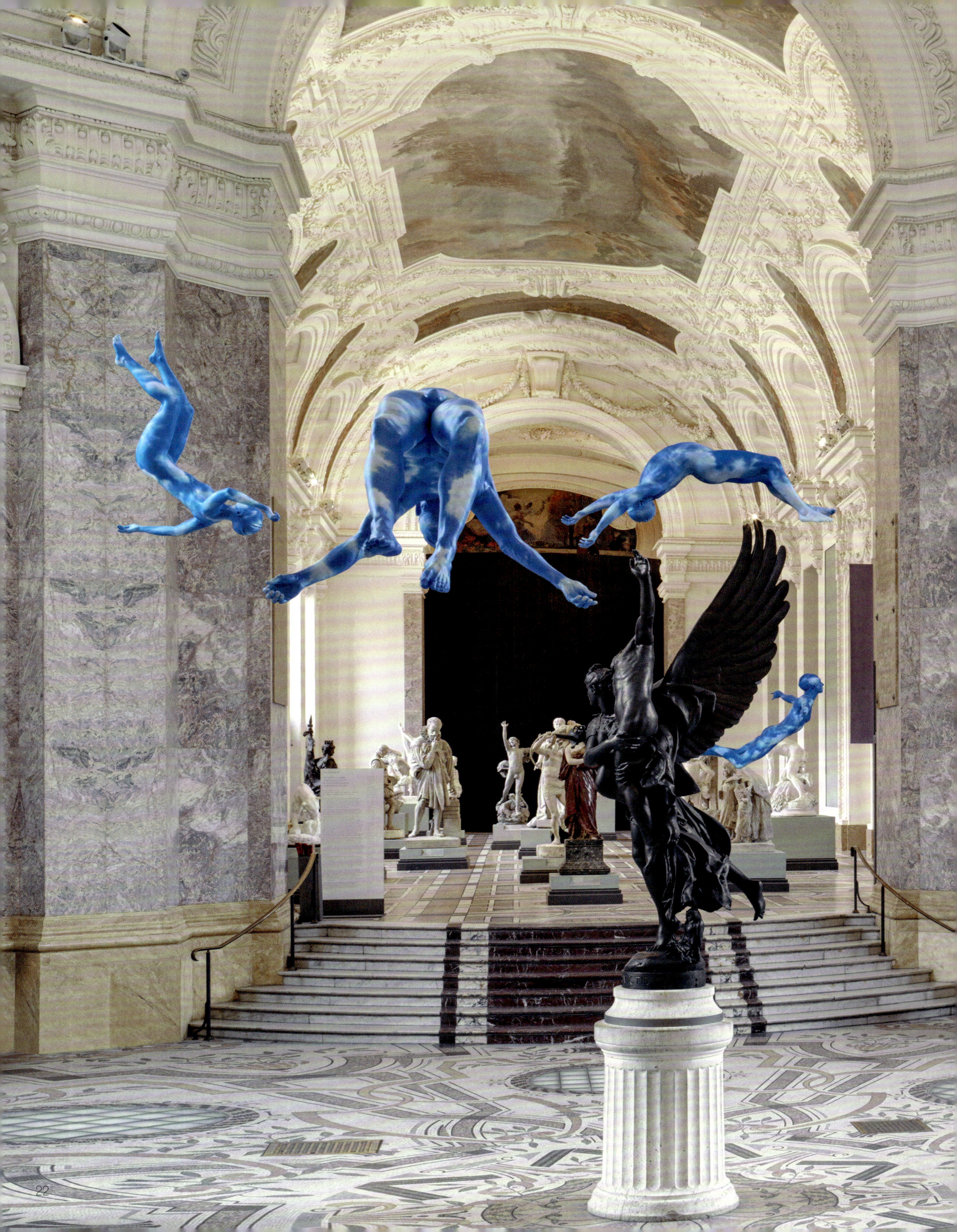

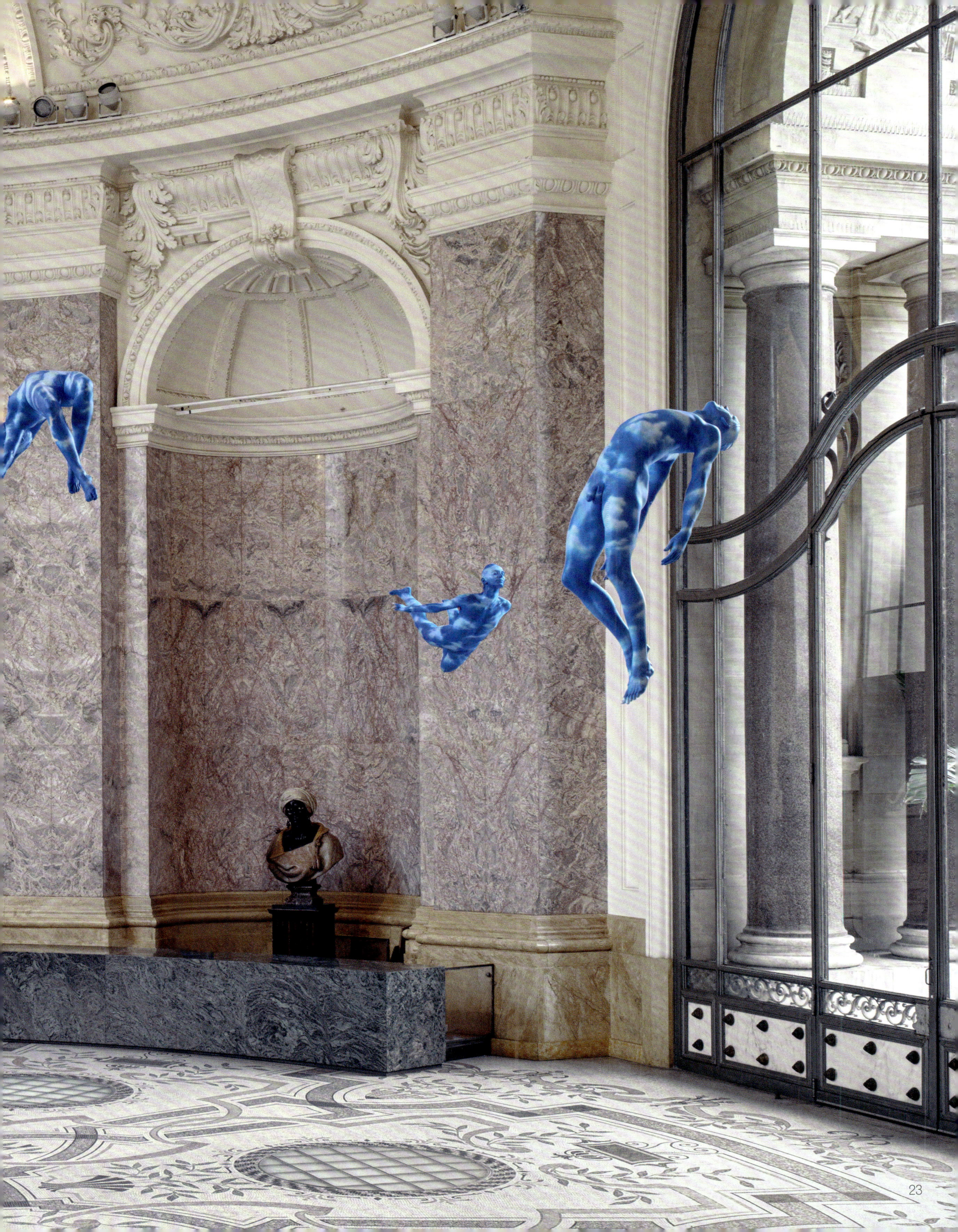

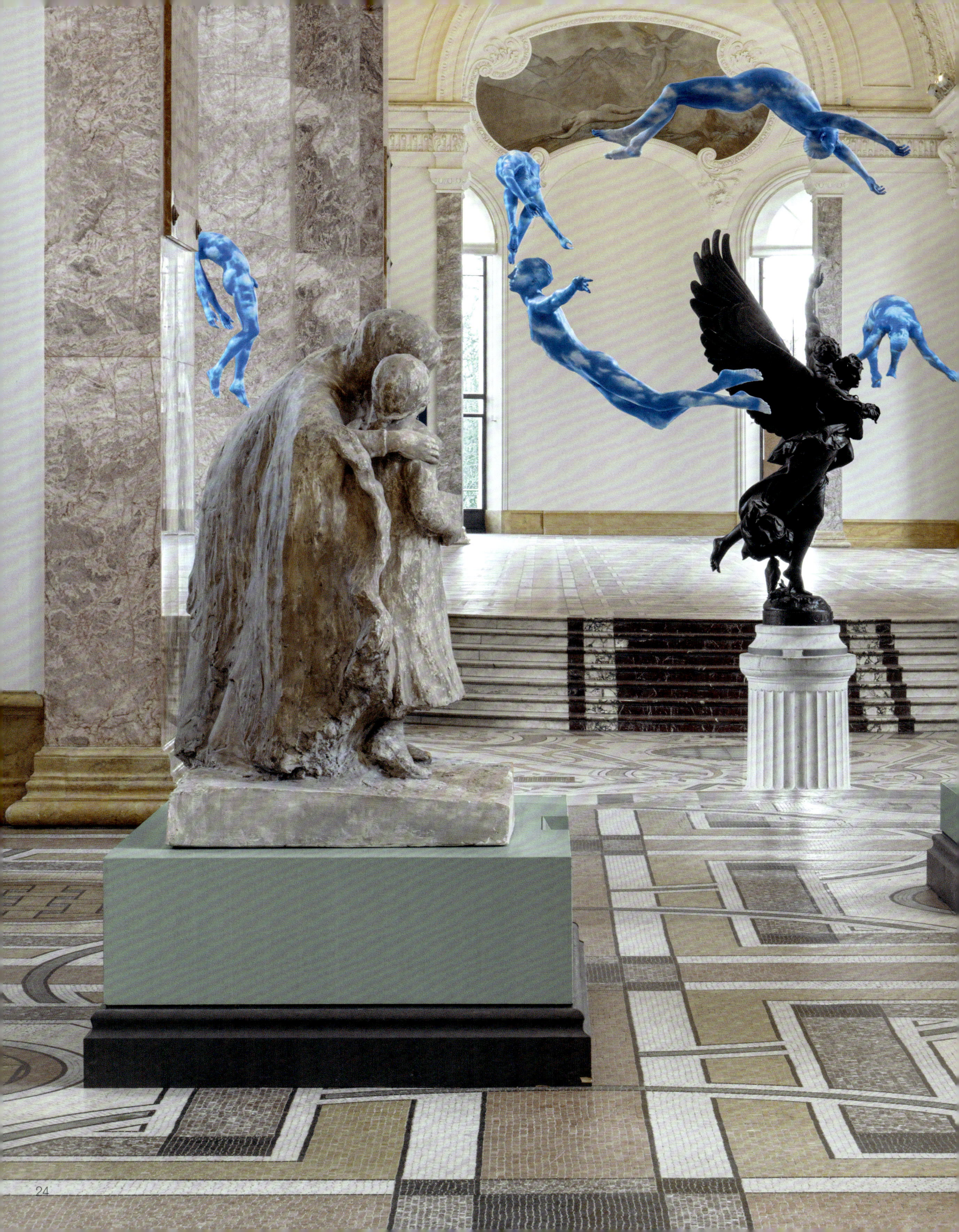

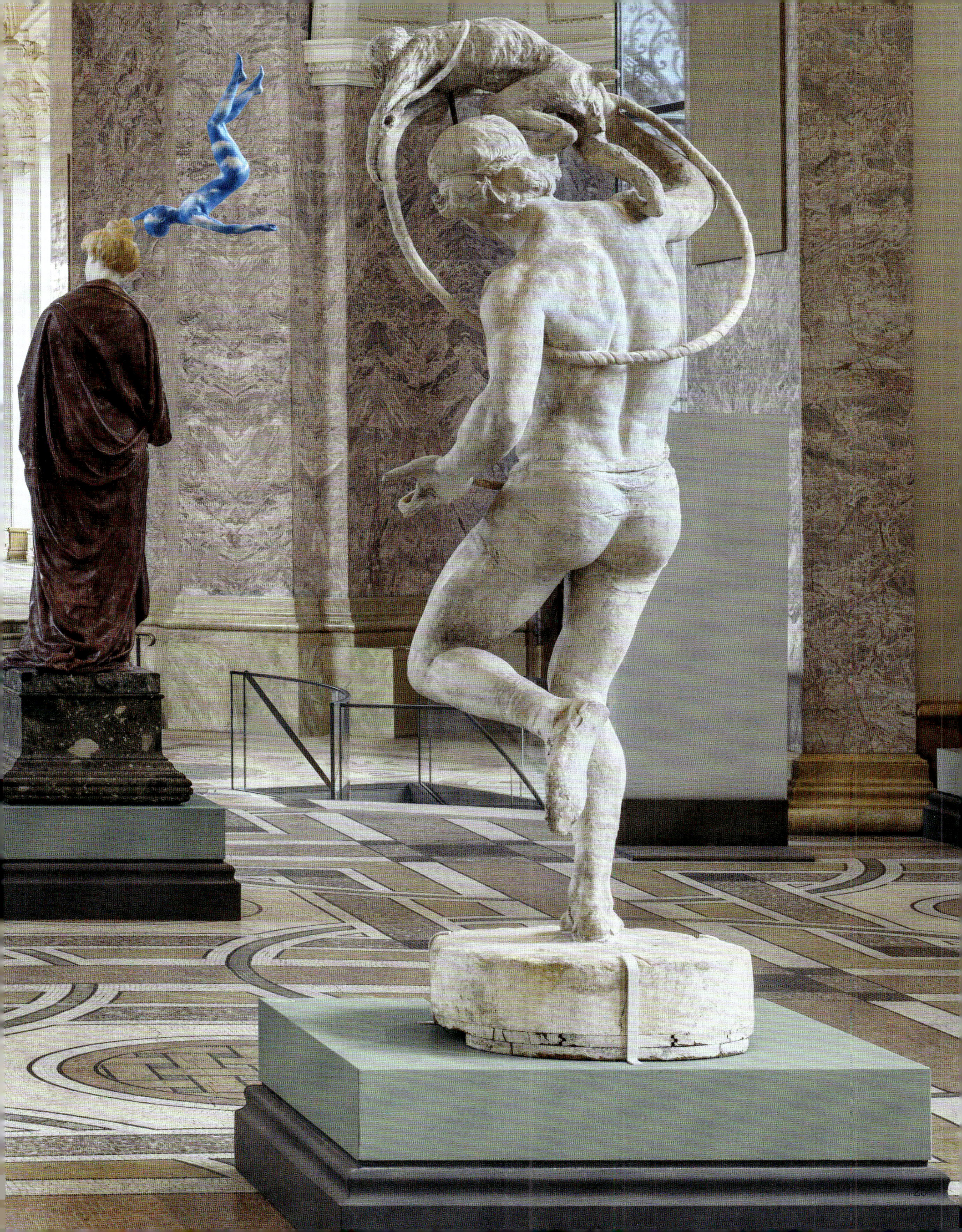

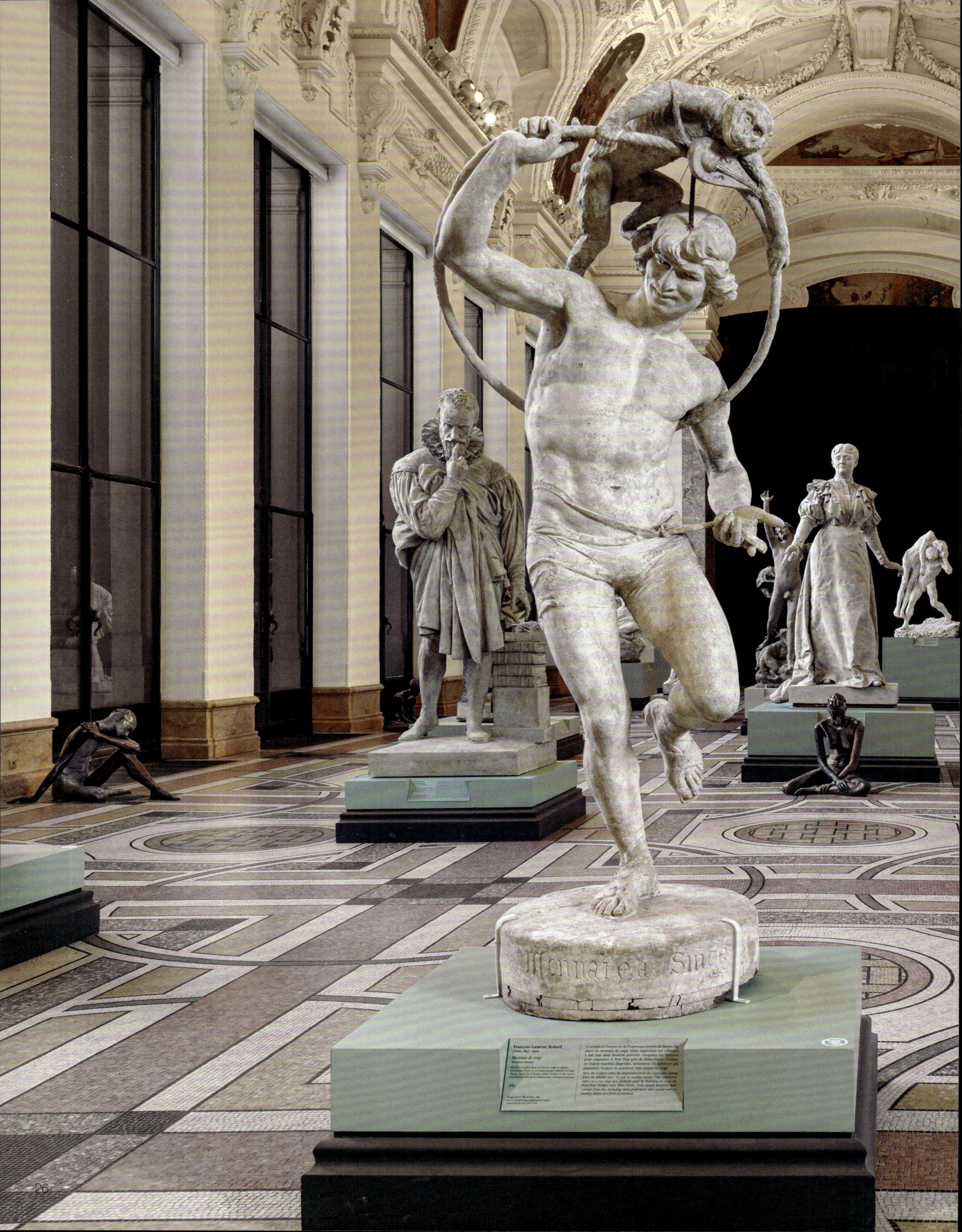
Monnaie a Singe
François-Laurent Rolard
Monnaie de singe

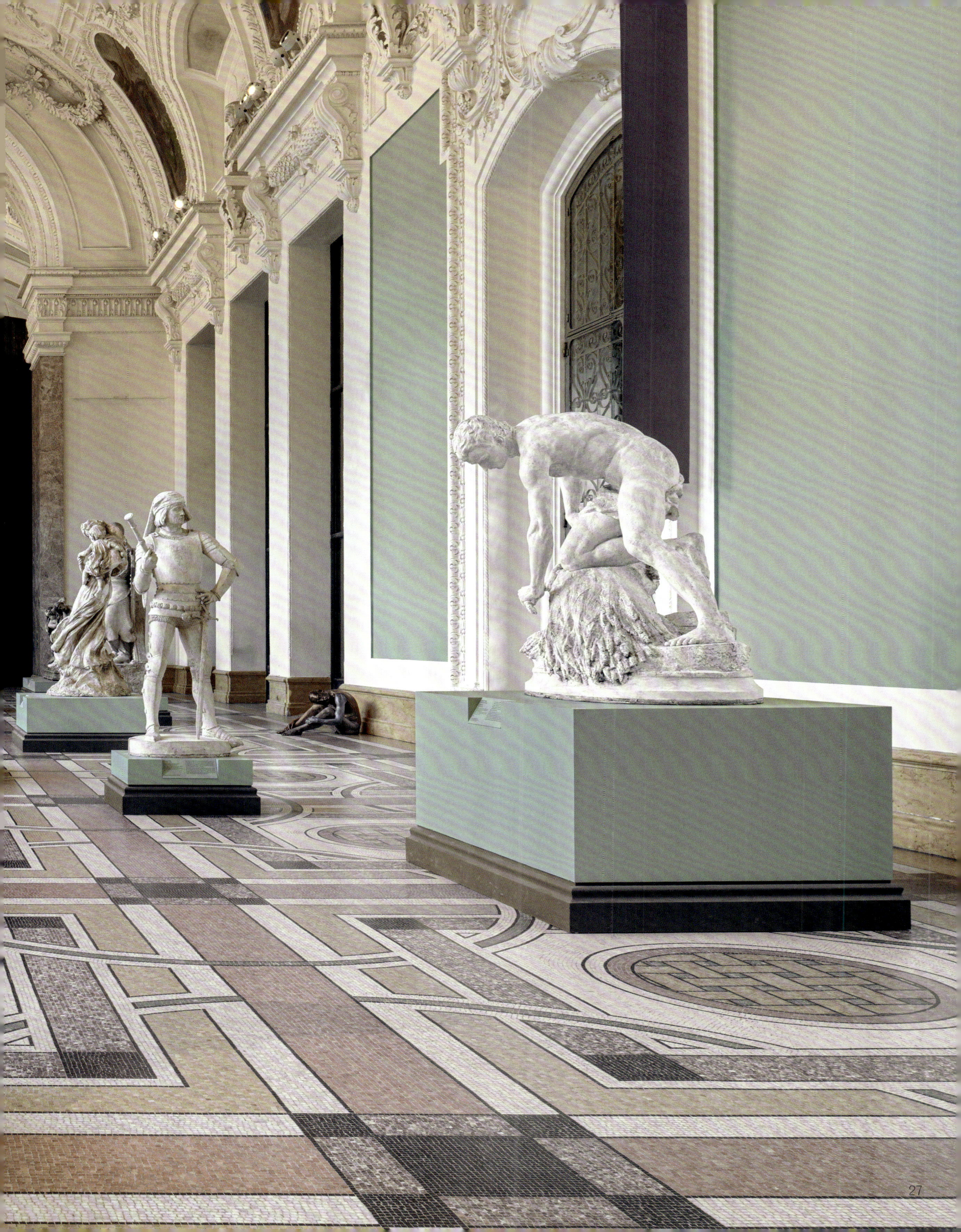

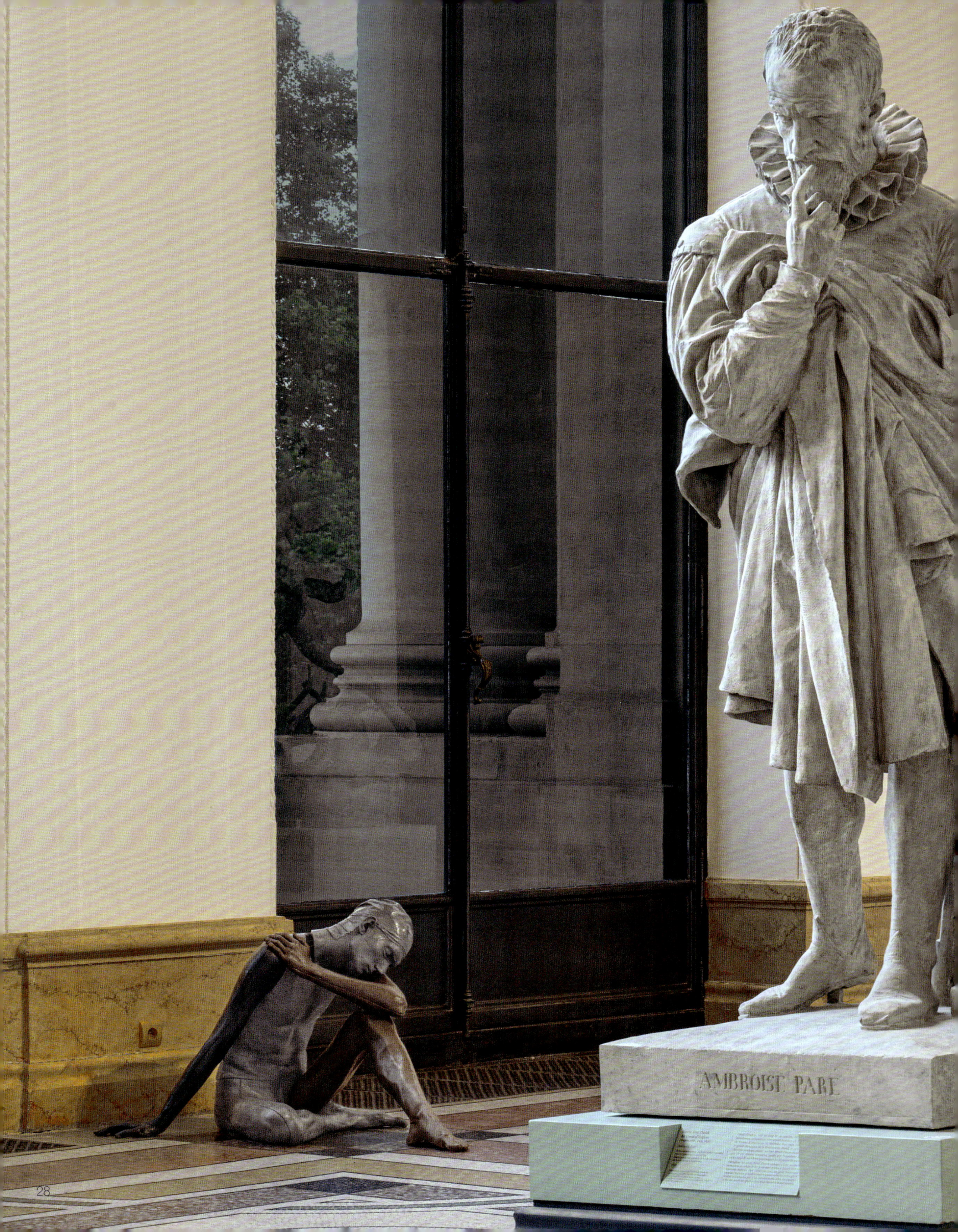
AMBROISE PARE

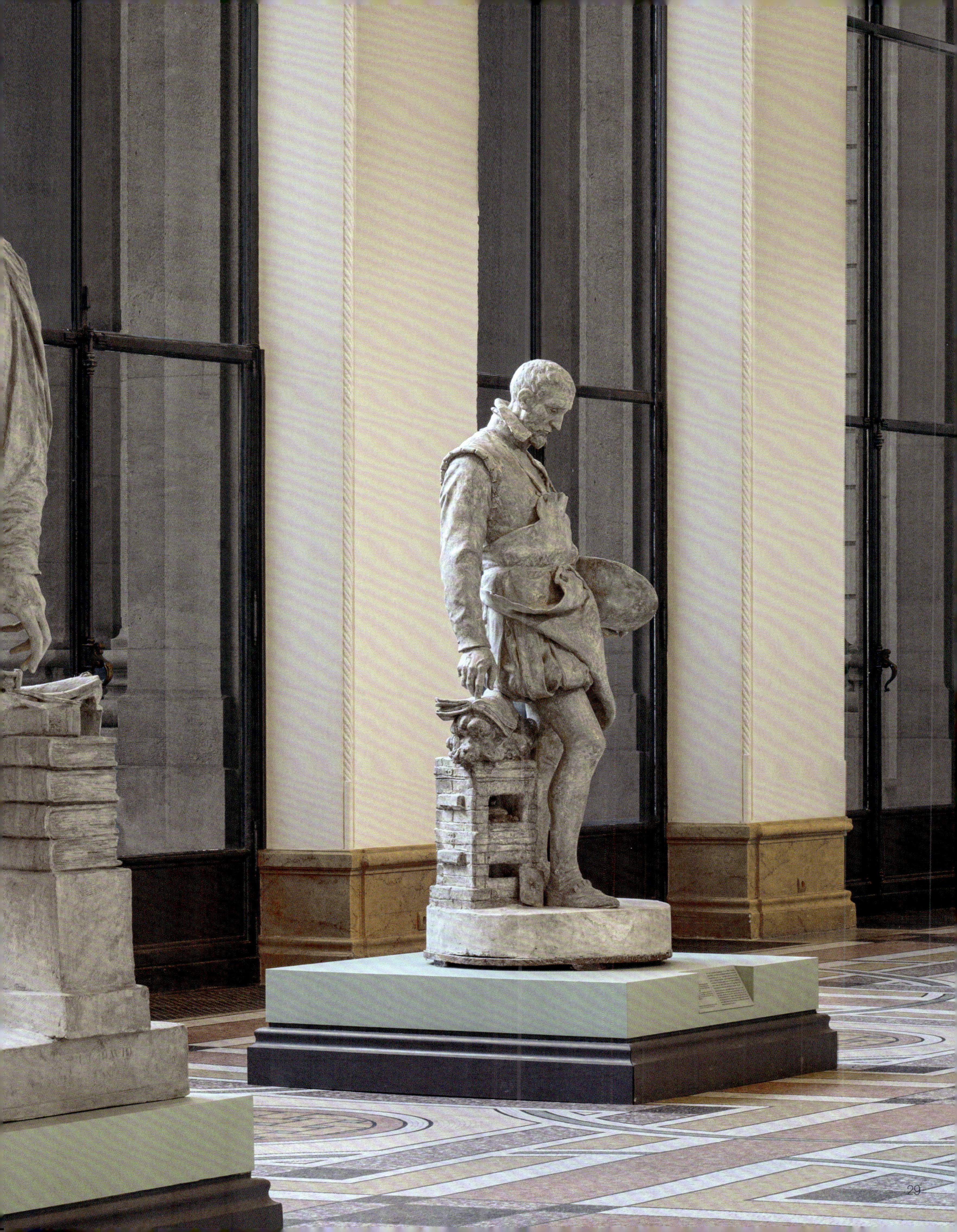

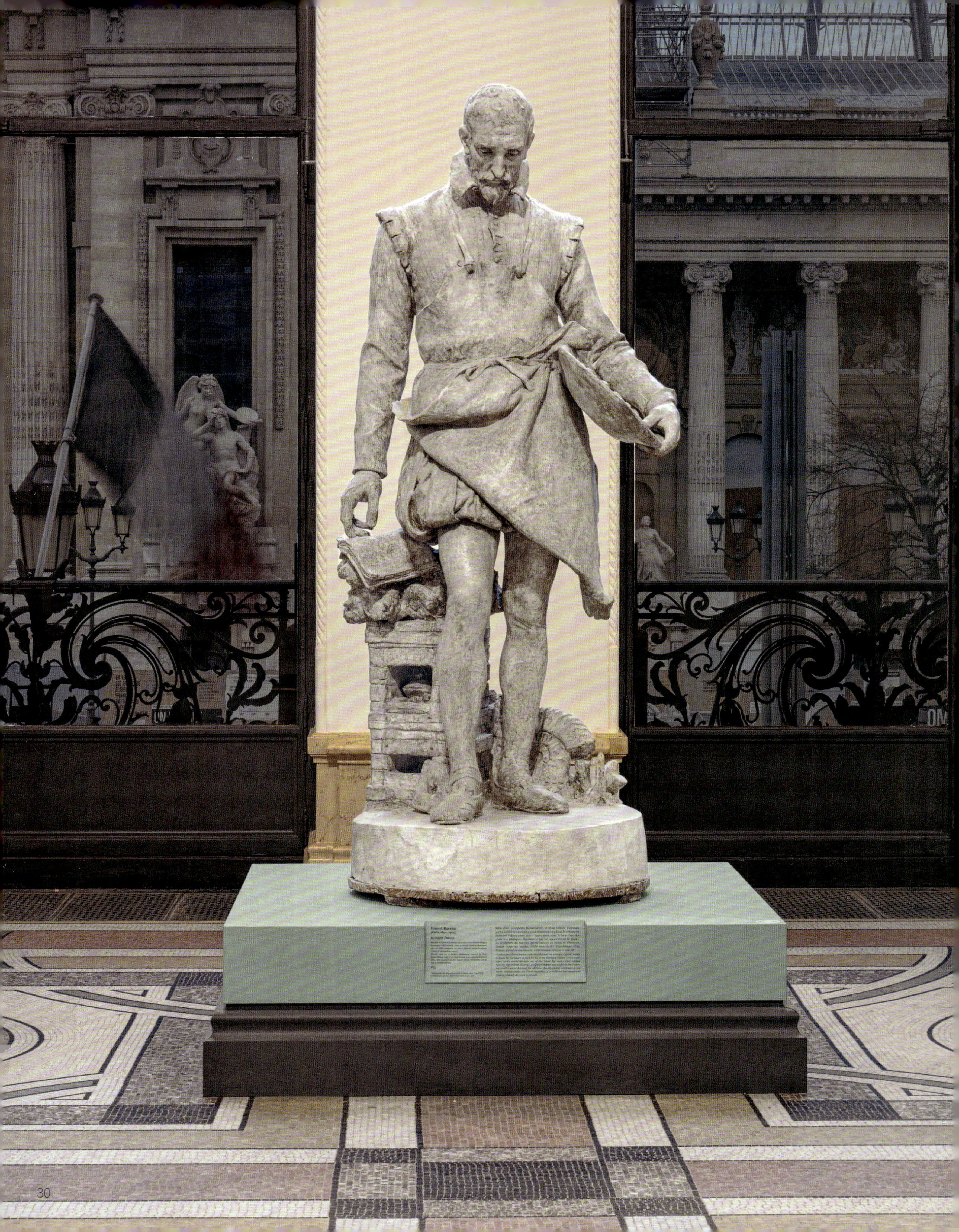

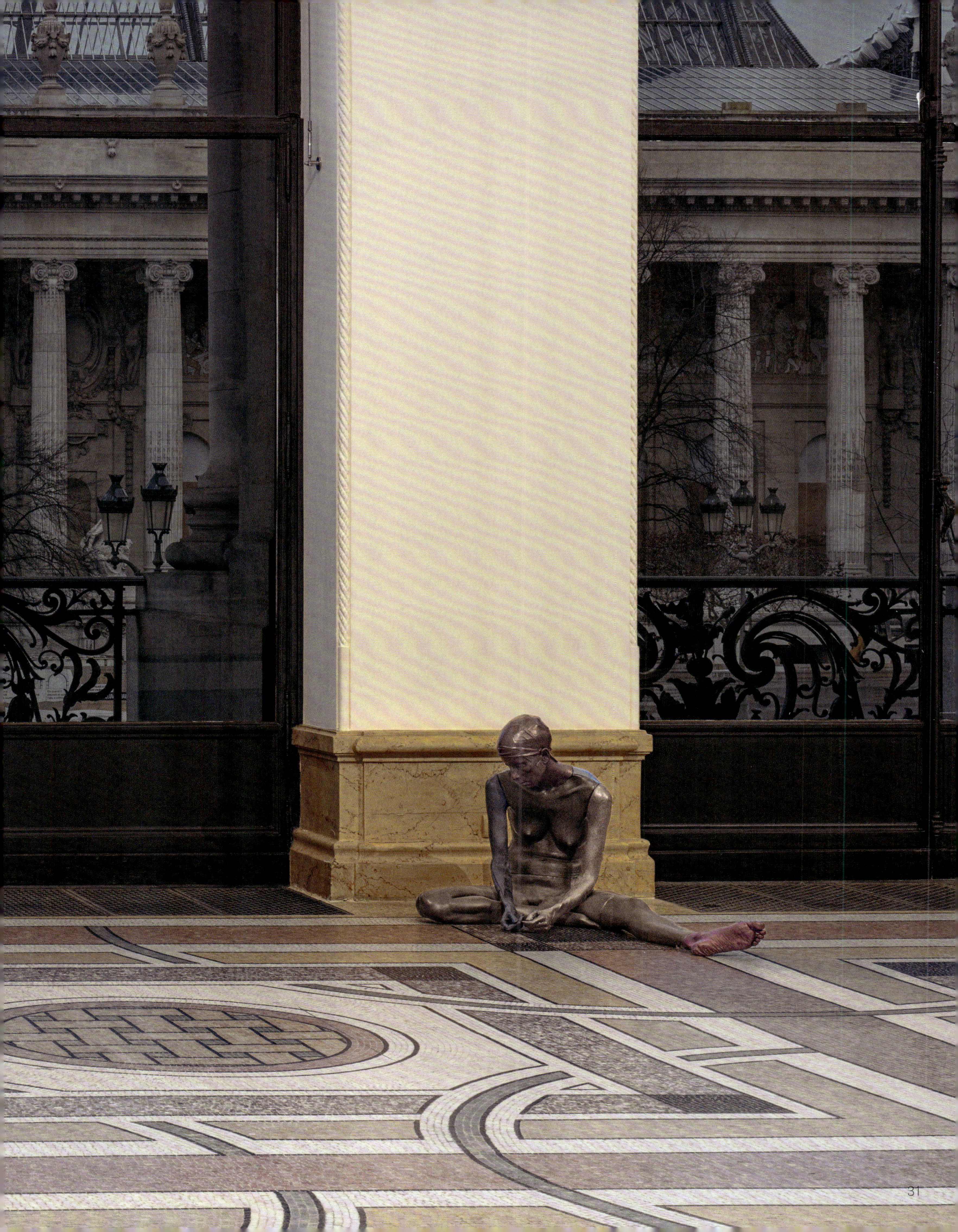

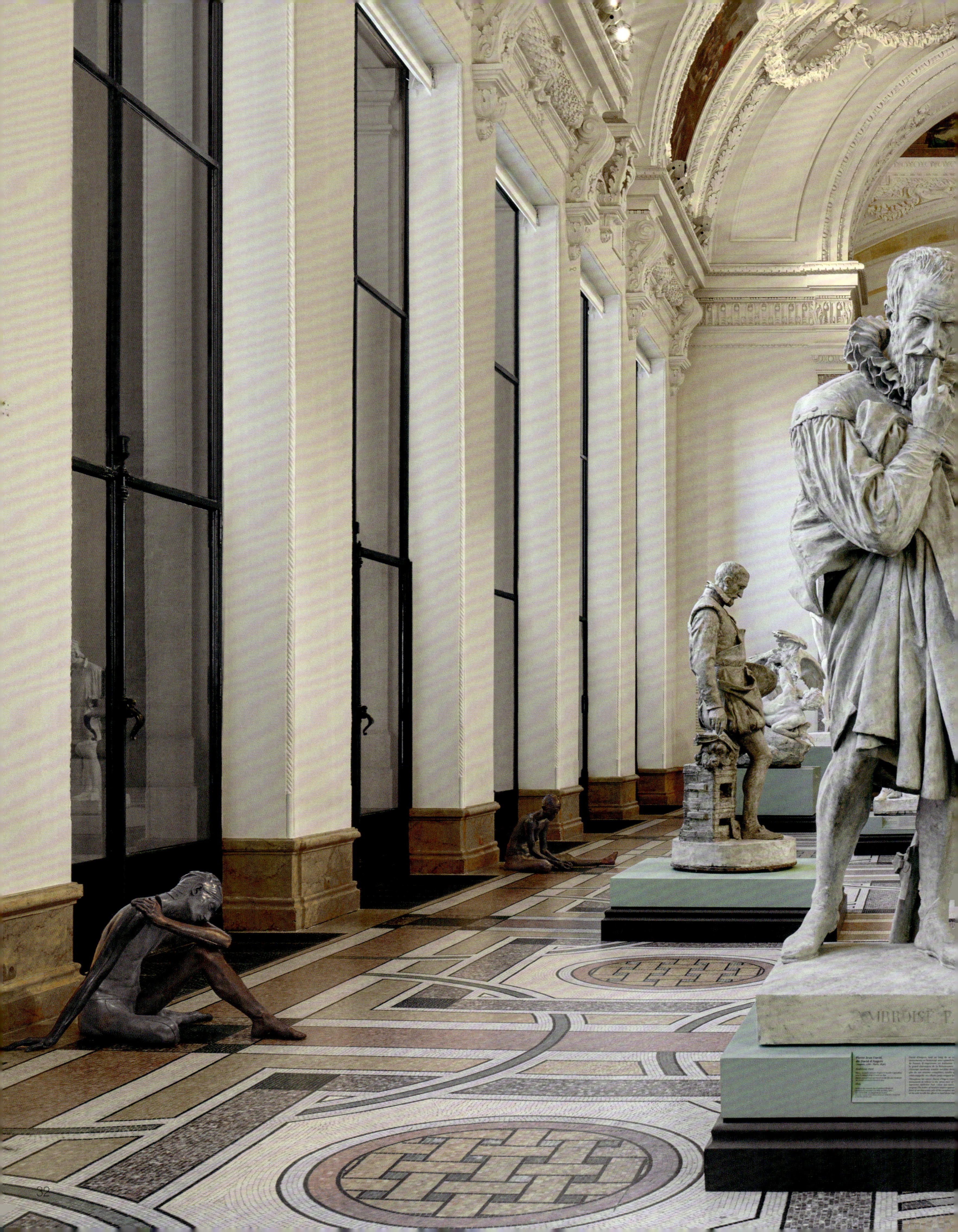

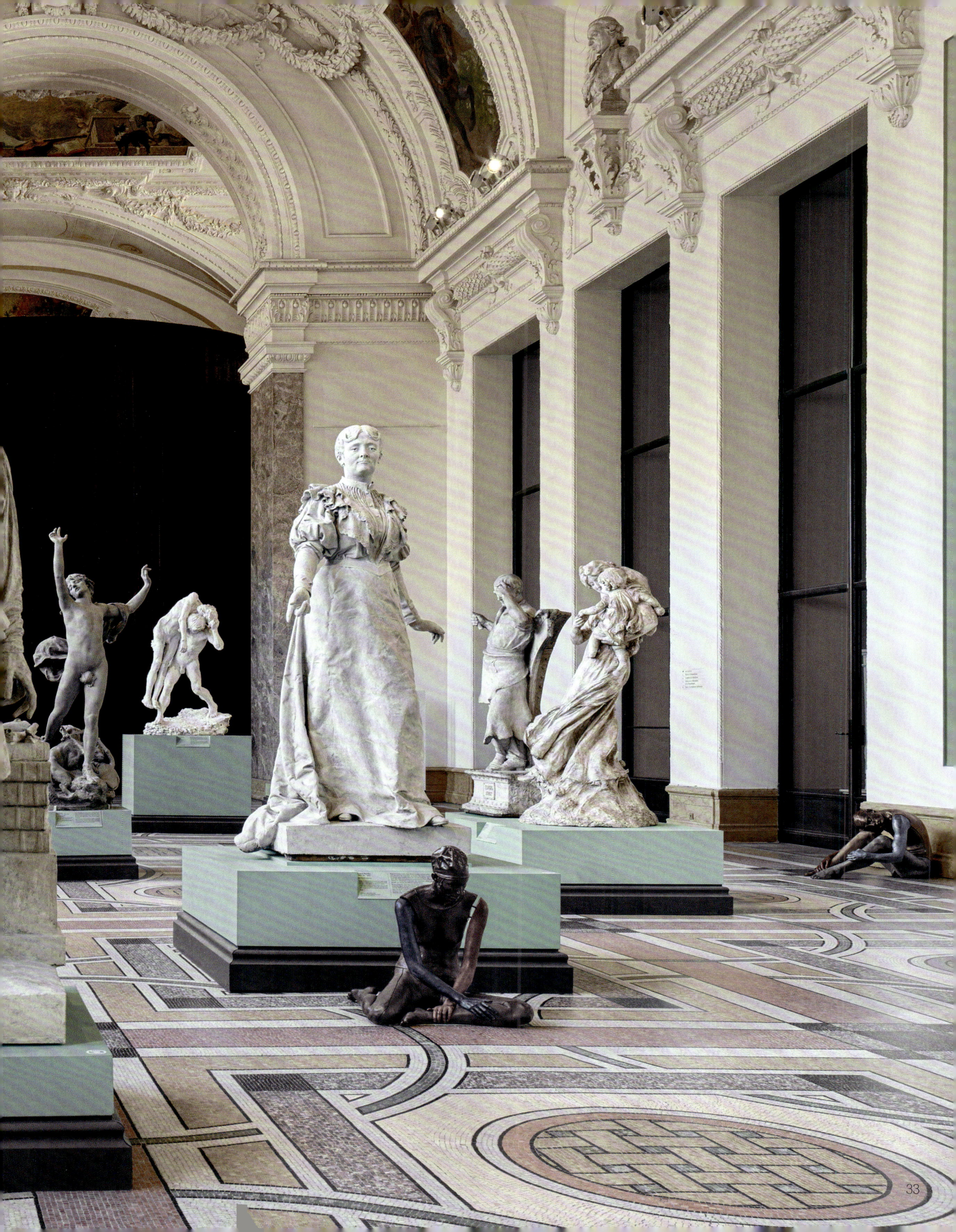

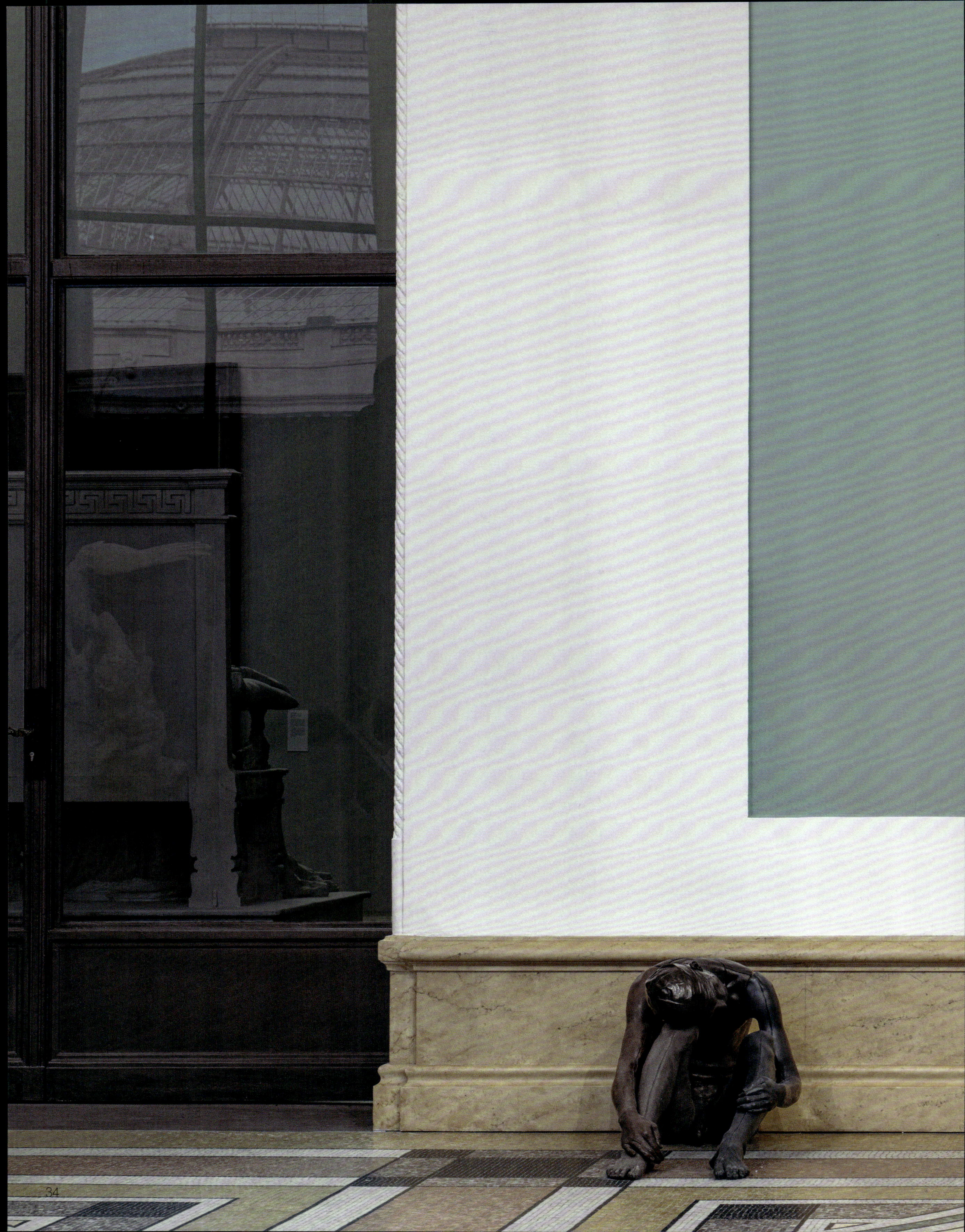

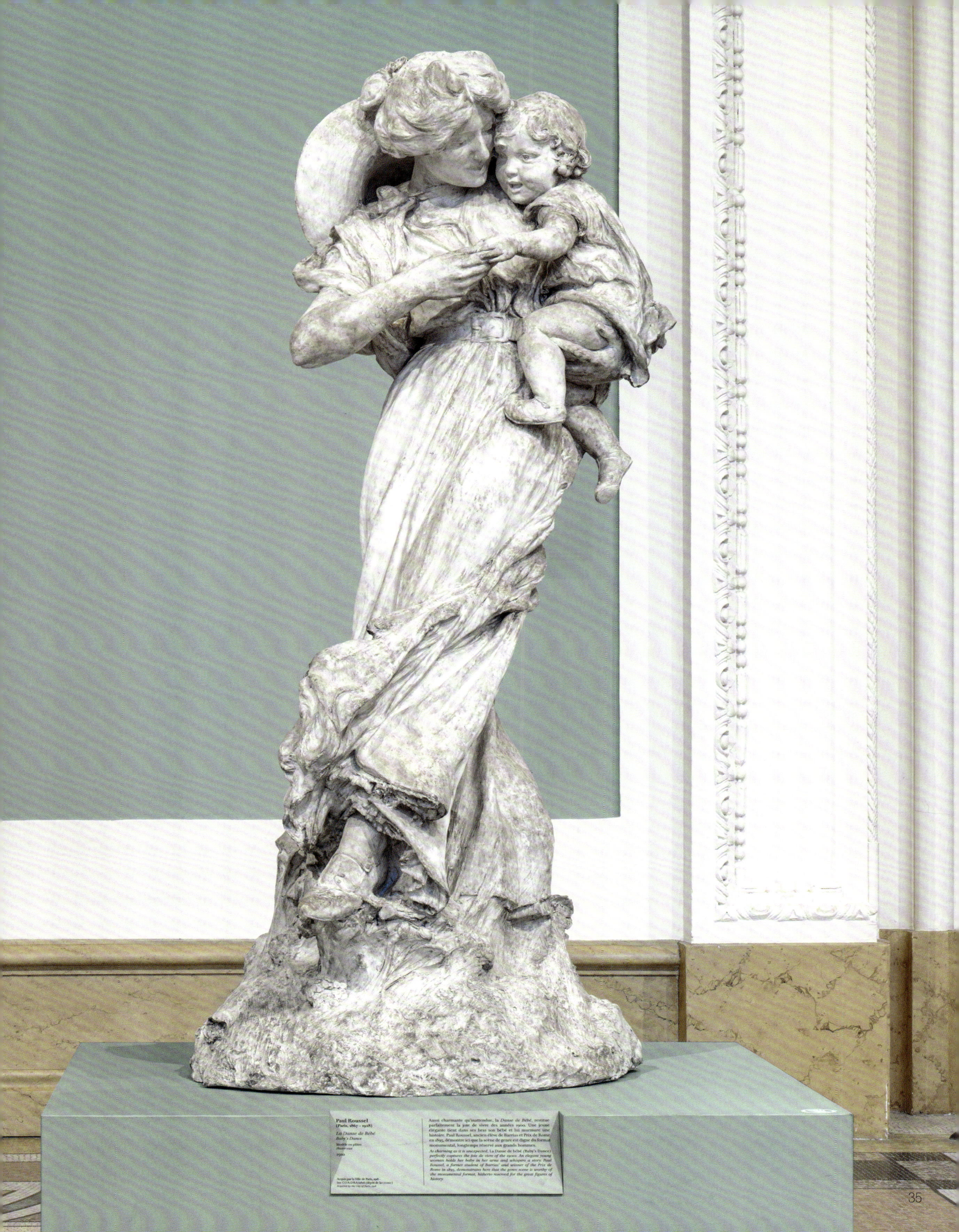
Paul Roussel
(Paris, 1867 – 1928)
La Danse de Bébé
Baby's Dance
1910
Aussi charmante qu'inattendue, la Danse de Bébé, restitue parfaitement la joie de vivre des années 1900. Une jeune élégante tient dans ses bras son bébé et lui murmure une histoire. Paul Roussel, ancien élève de Barrias et Prix de Rome en 1895, démontre ici que la scène de genre est digne du format monumental, longtemps réservé aux grands hommes.
As charming as it is unexpected, La Danse de bébé (Baby's Dance) perfectly captures the joie de vivre of the 1900s. An elegant young woman holds her baby in her arms and whispers a story. Paul Roussel, a former student of Barrias' and winner of the Prix de Rome in 1895, demonstrates here that the genre scene is worthy of the monumental format, hitherto reserved for the great figures of history.

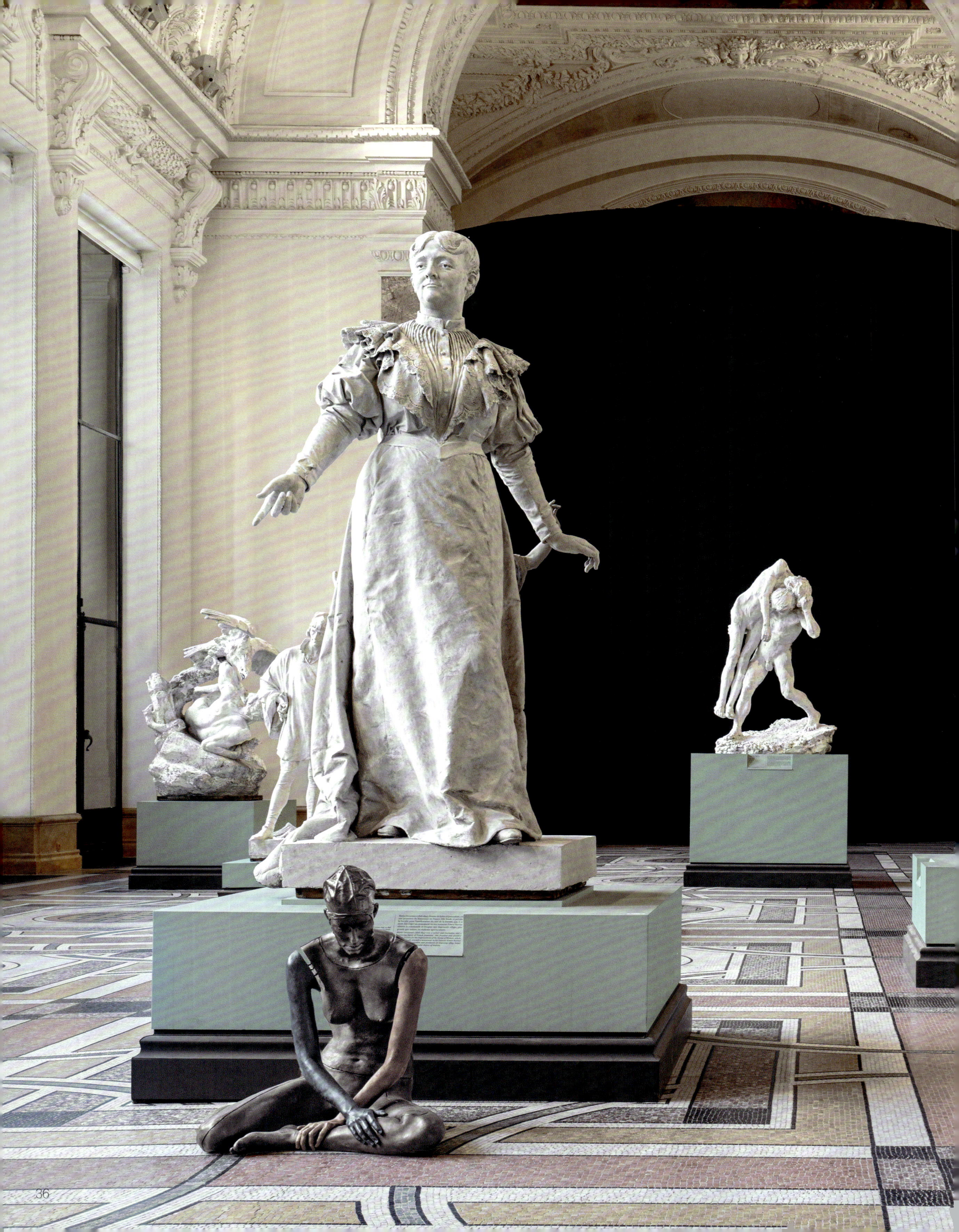

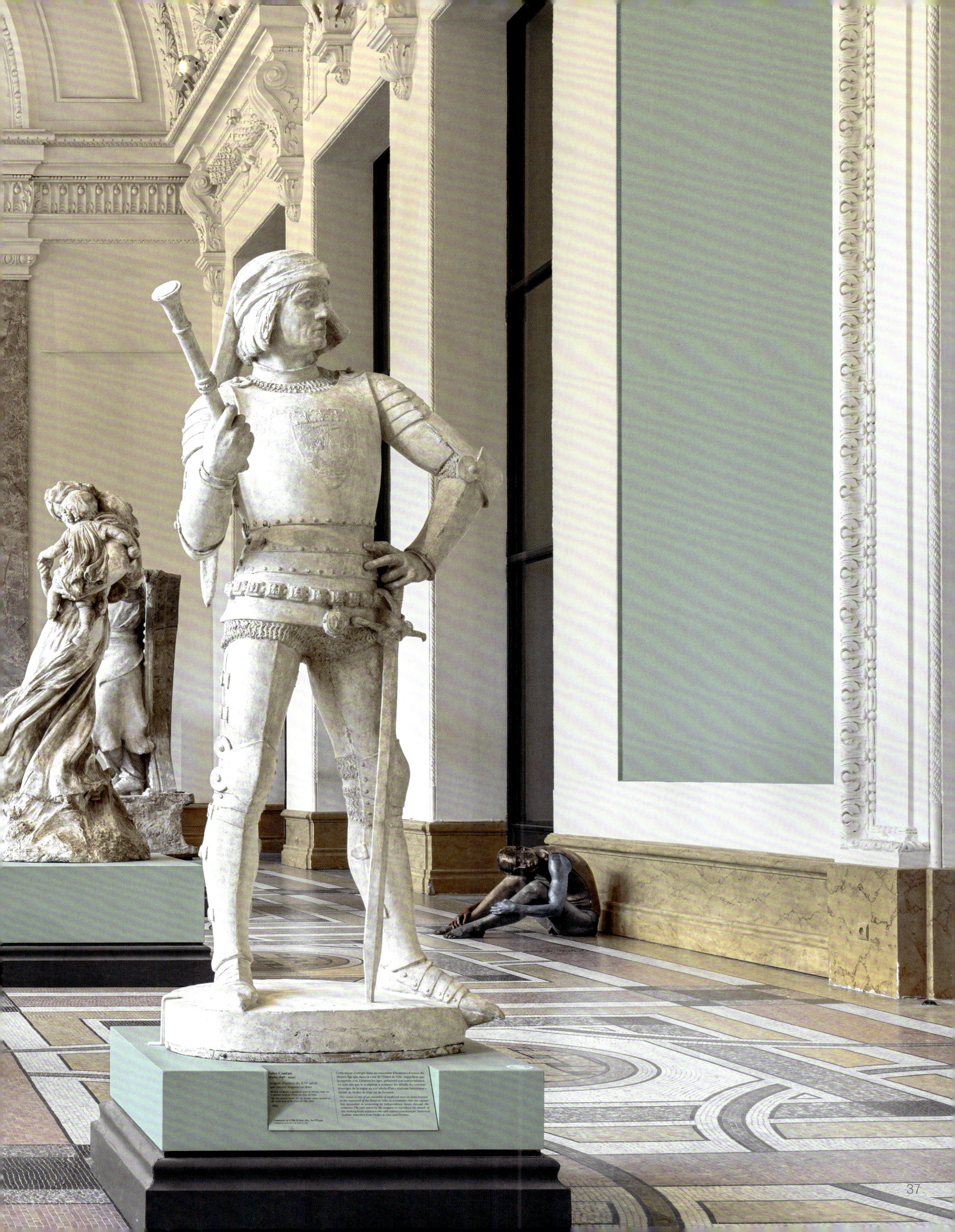
Jules Coutan

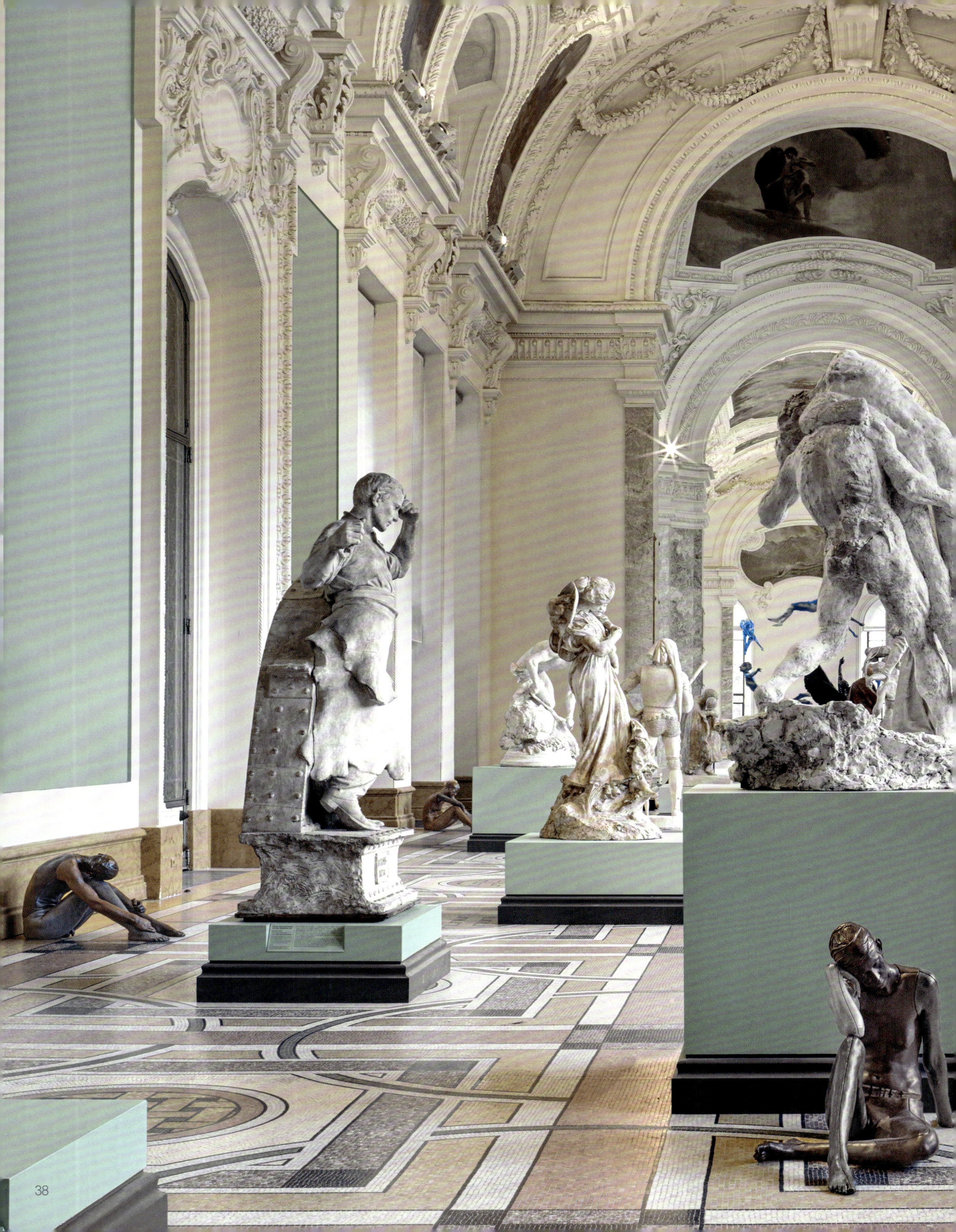

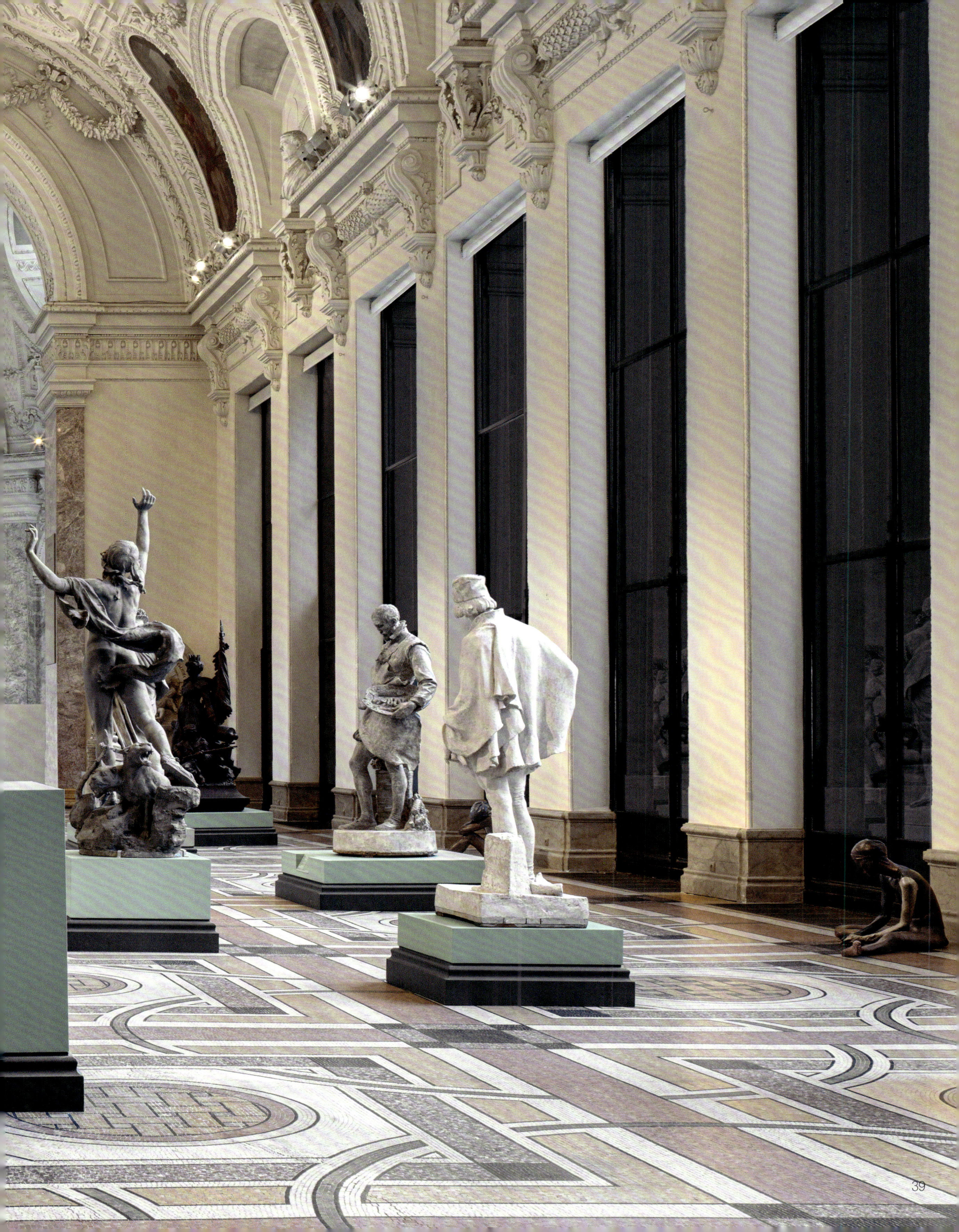

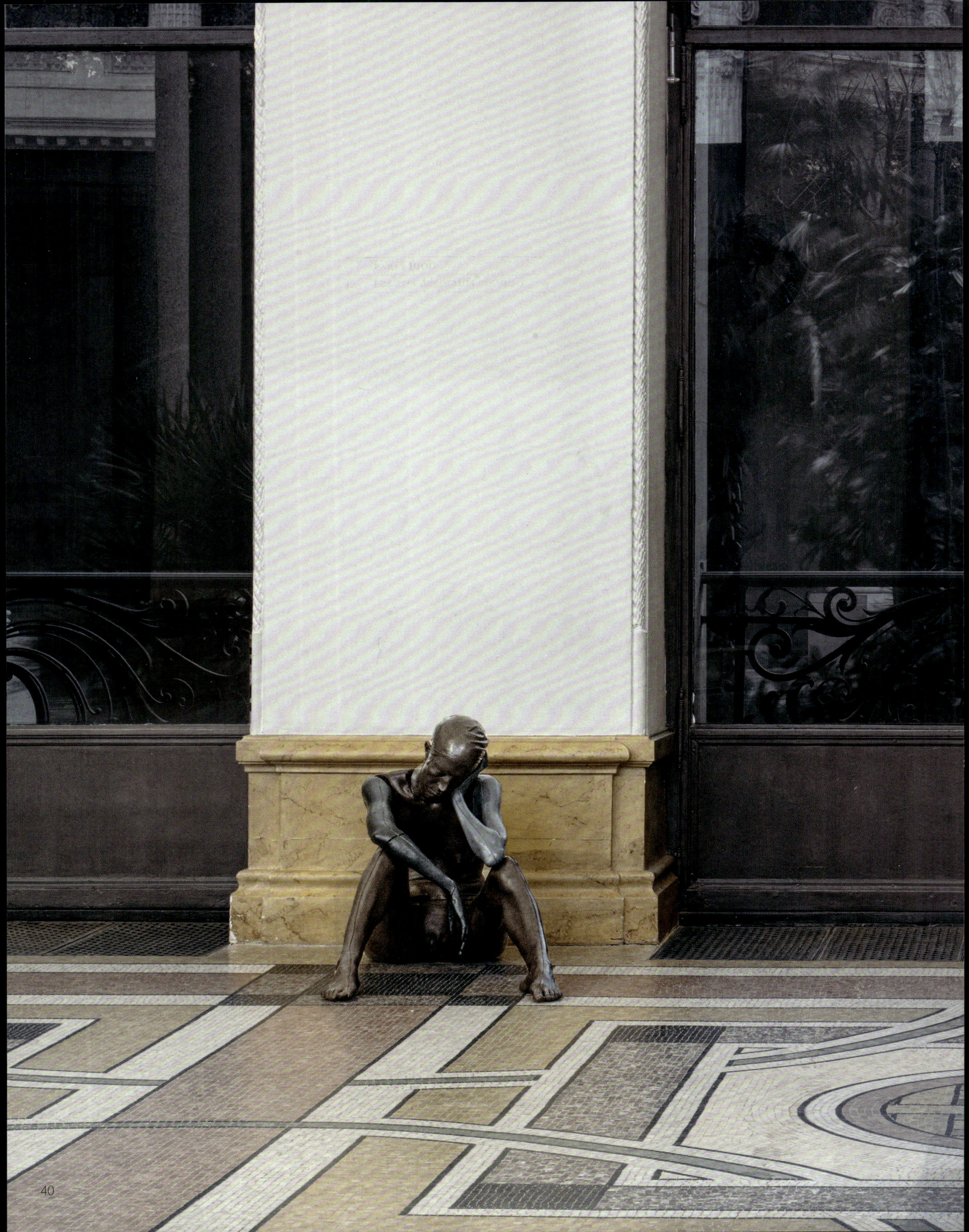

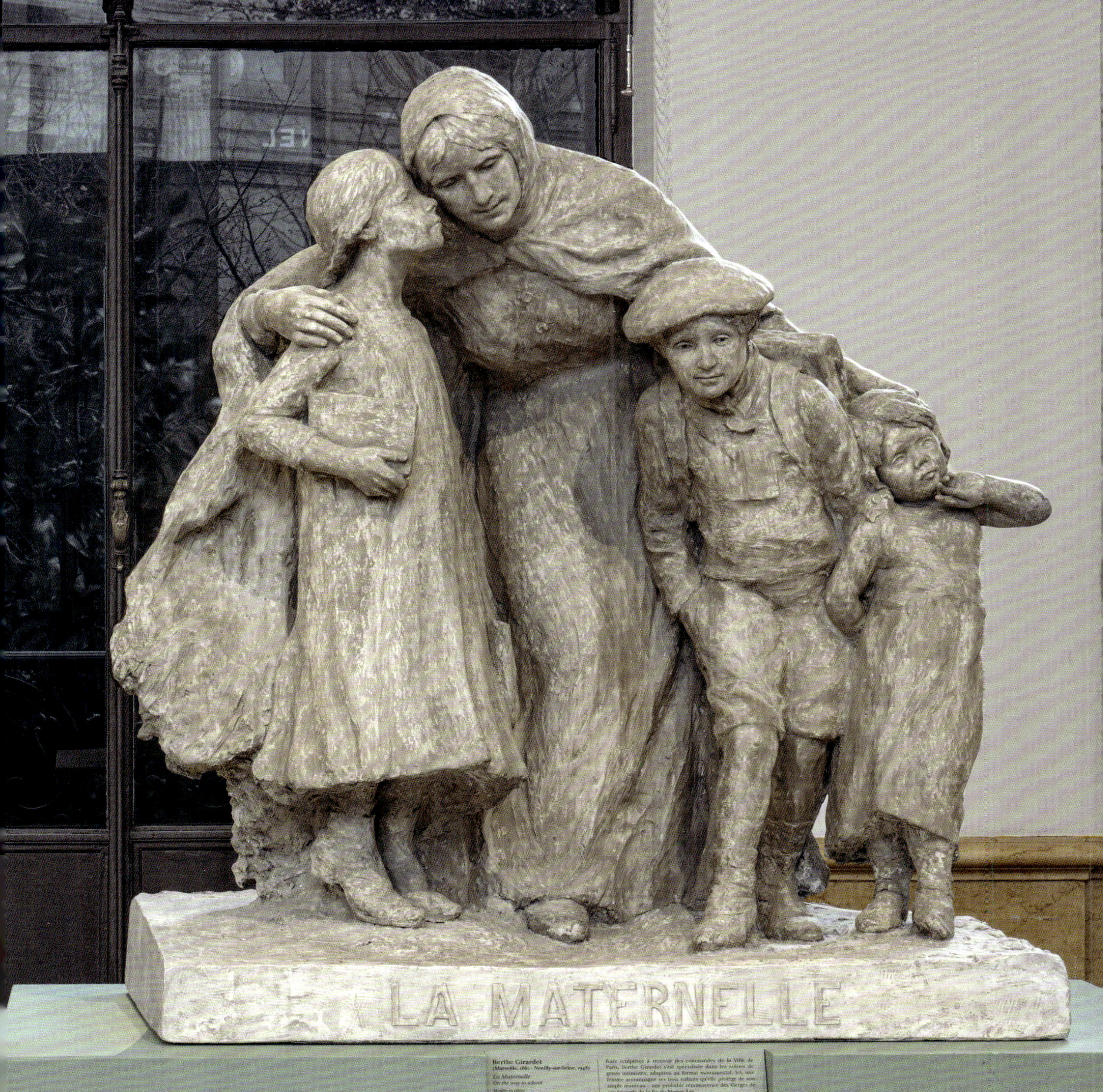
LA MATERNELLE
Berthe Girardet
(Marseille, 1861 – Neuilly-sur-Seine, 1948)
La Maternelle
On the way to school
Modèle en plâtre
Plaster model
1908
Rare sculptrice à recevoir des commandes de la Ville de Paris, Berthe Girardet s'est spécialisée dans les scènes de genre intimistes, adaptées au format monumental. Ici, une femme accompagne ses trois enfants qu'elle protège de son ample manteau – une probable réminiscence des Vierges de miséricorde de la fin du Moyen Âge.
One of the few female sculptors to have received a commission from the City of Paris, Berthe Girardet specialized in intimate genre scenes, adapted to a monumental format. Here, a woman accompanies her three children, protecting them with her ample cloak, a possible reference to the Virgins of Mercy from the late medieval period.

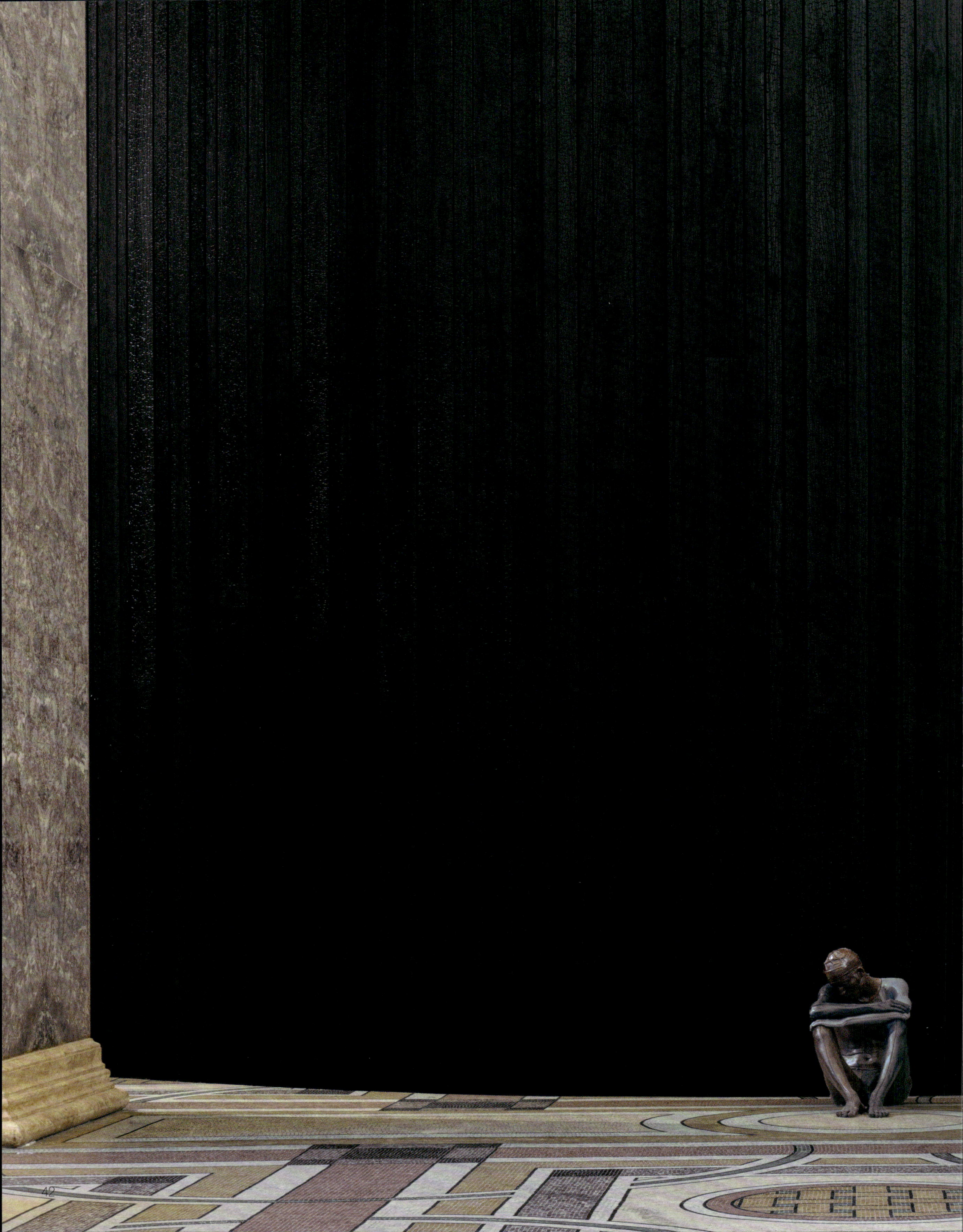

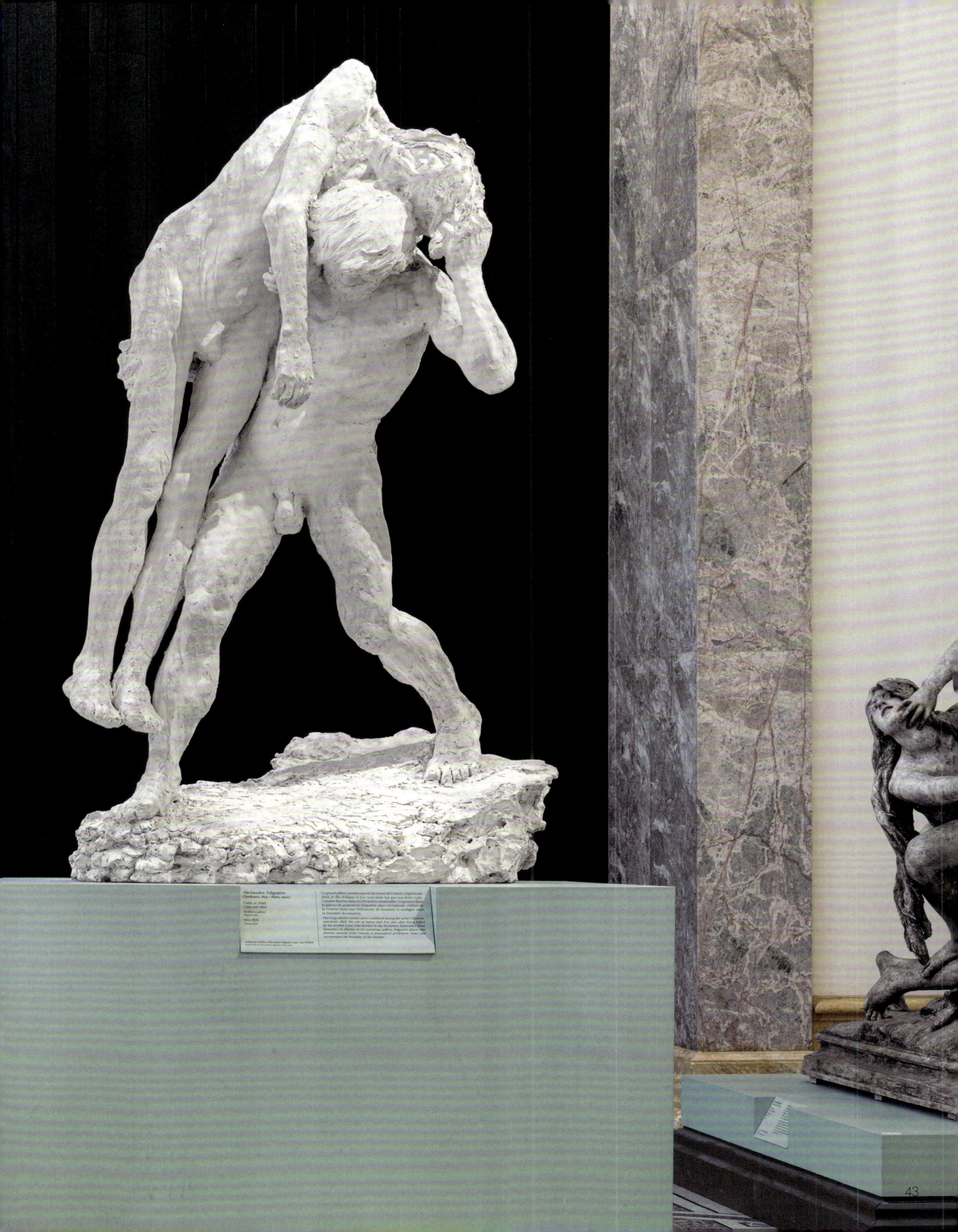
Alexandre Falguière
Caïn et Abel
Cain and Abel

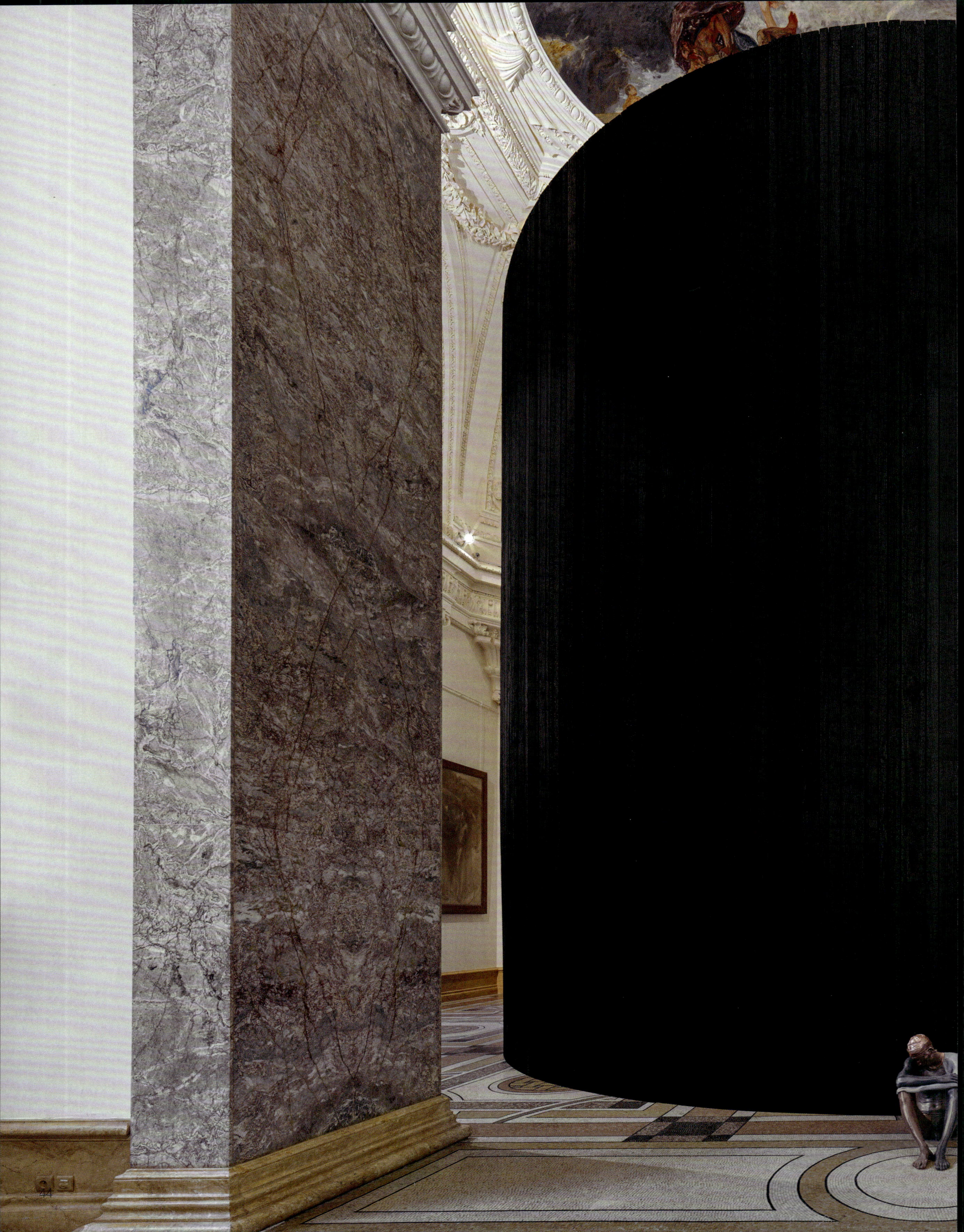

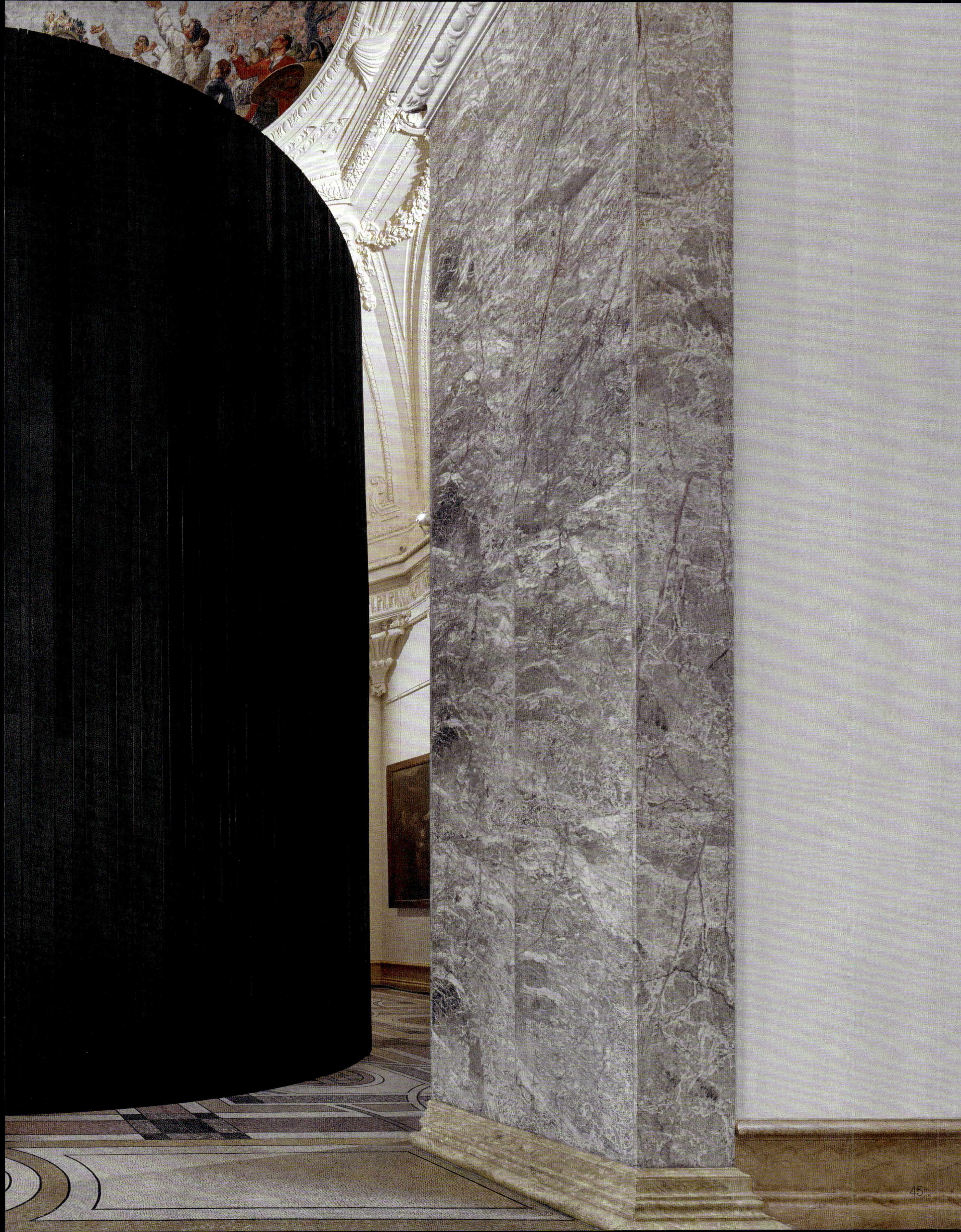

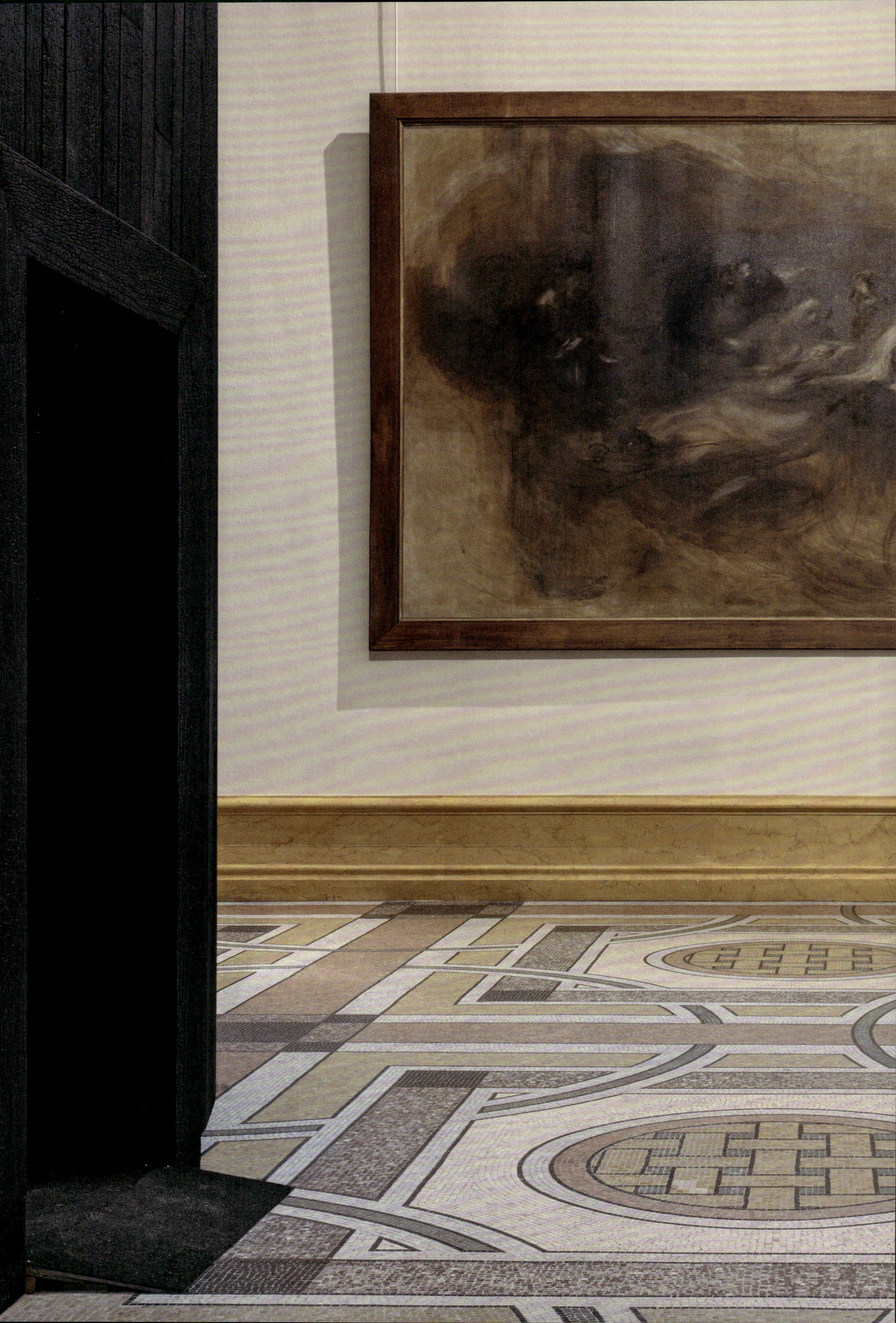

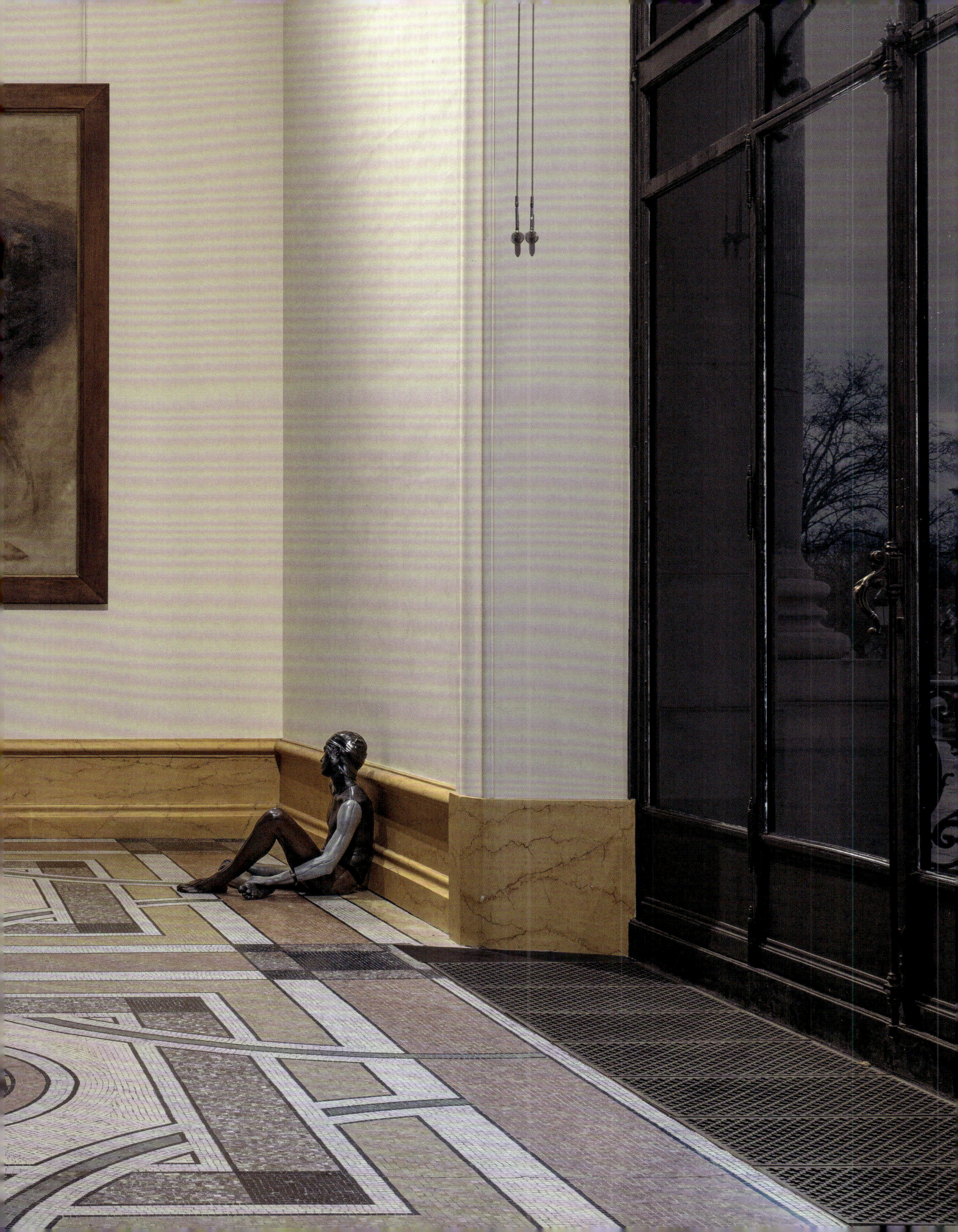

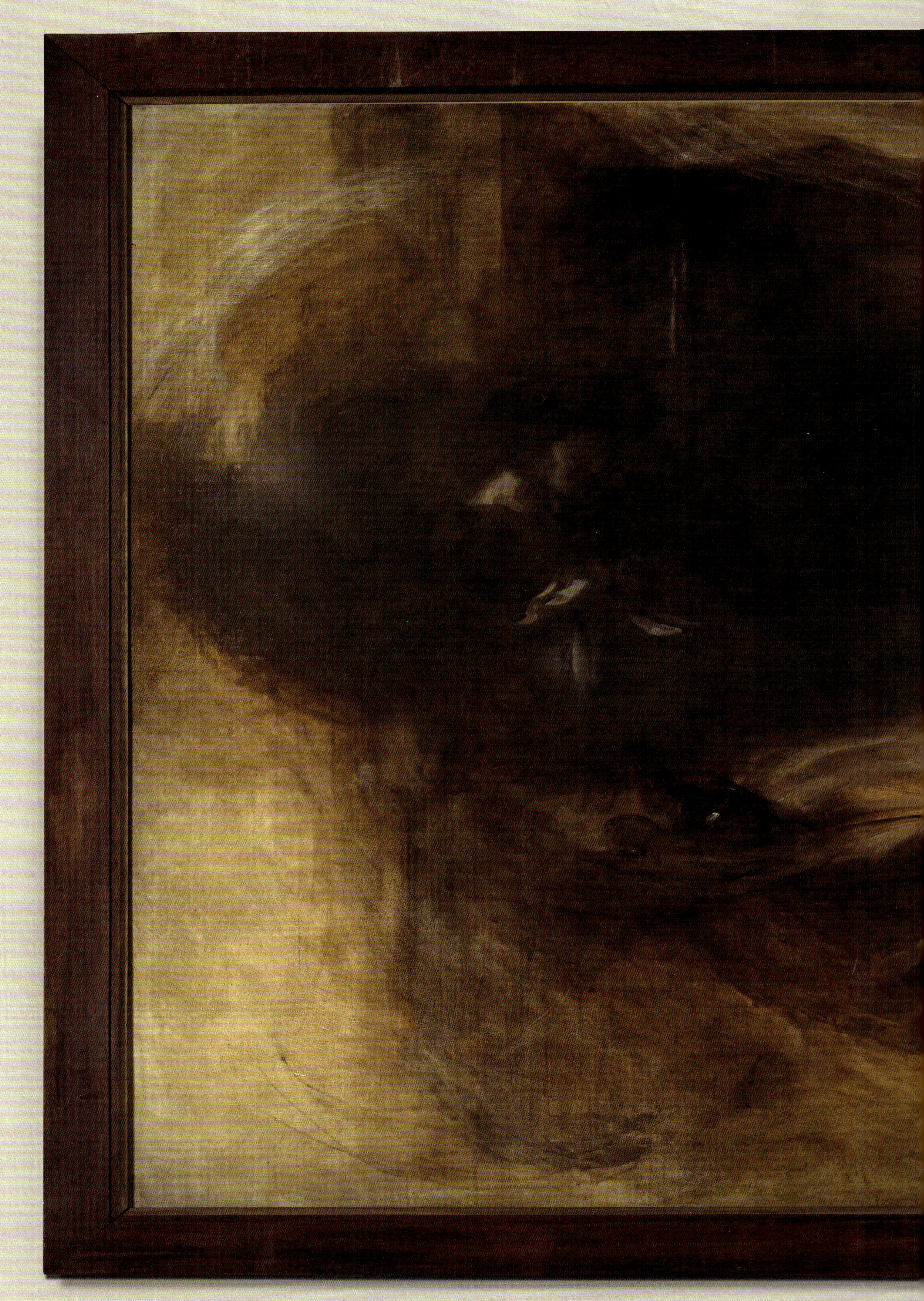

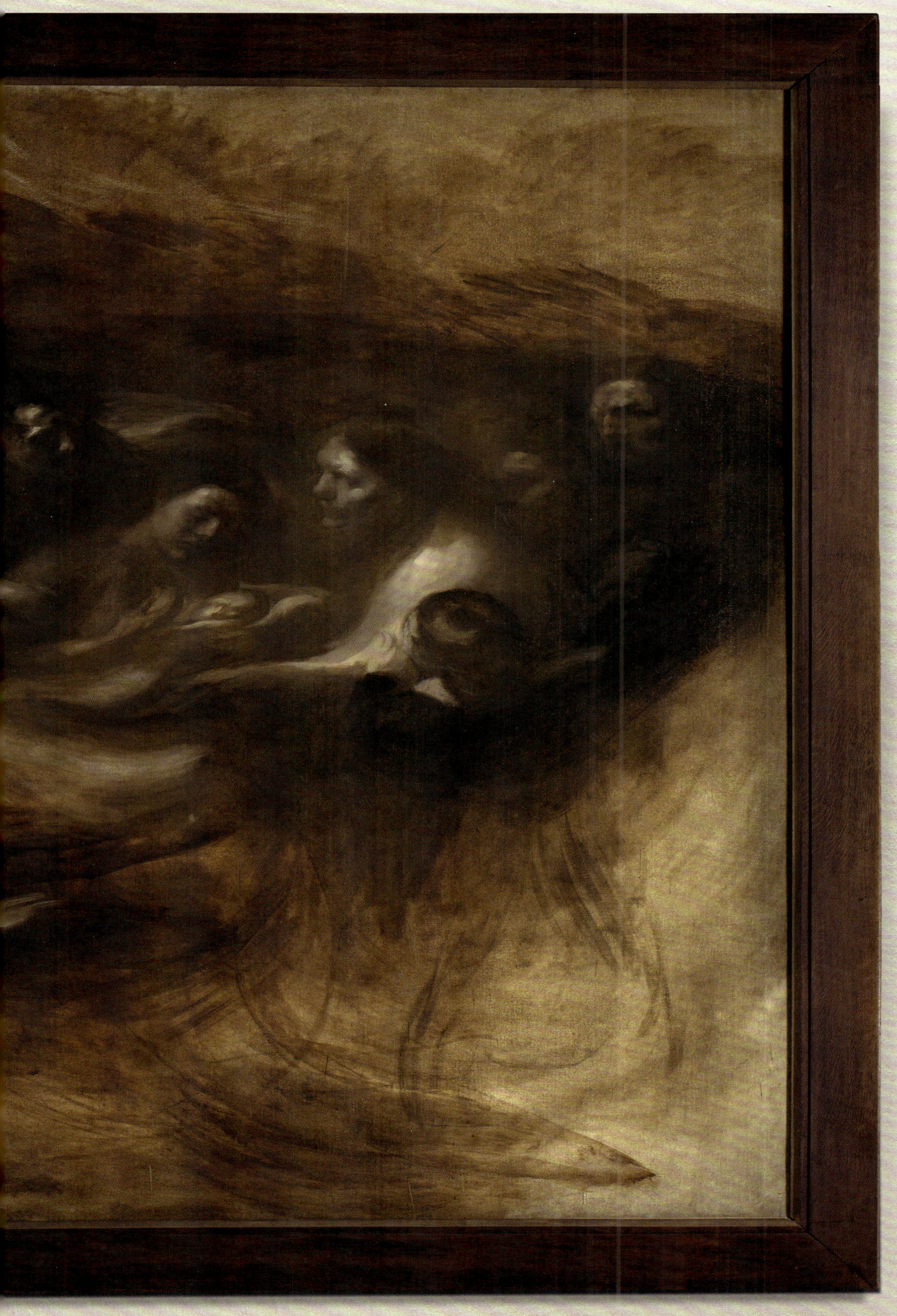

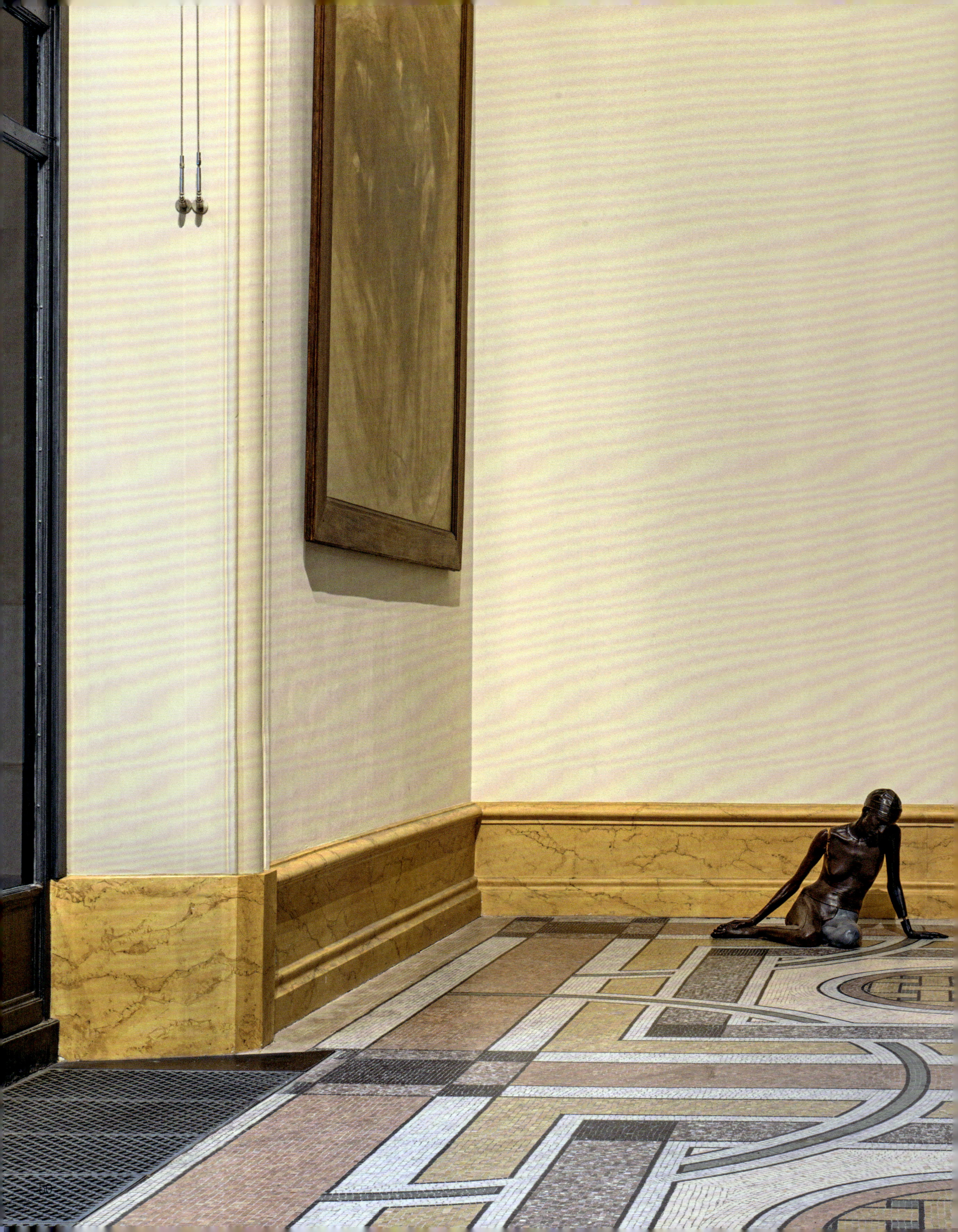

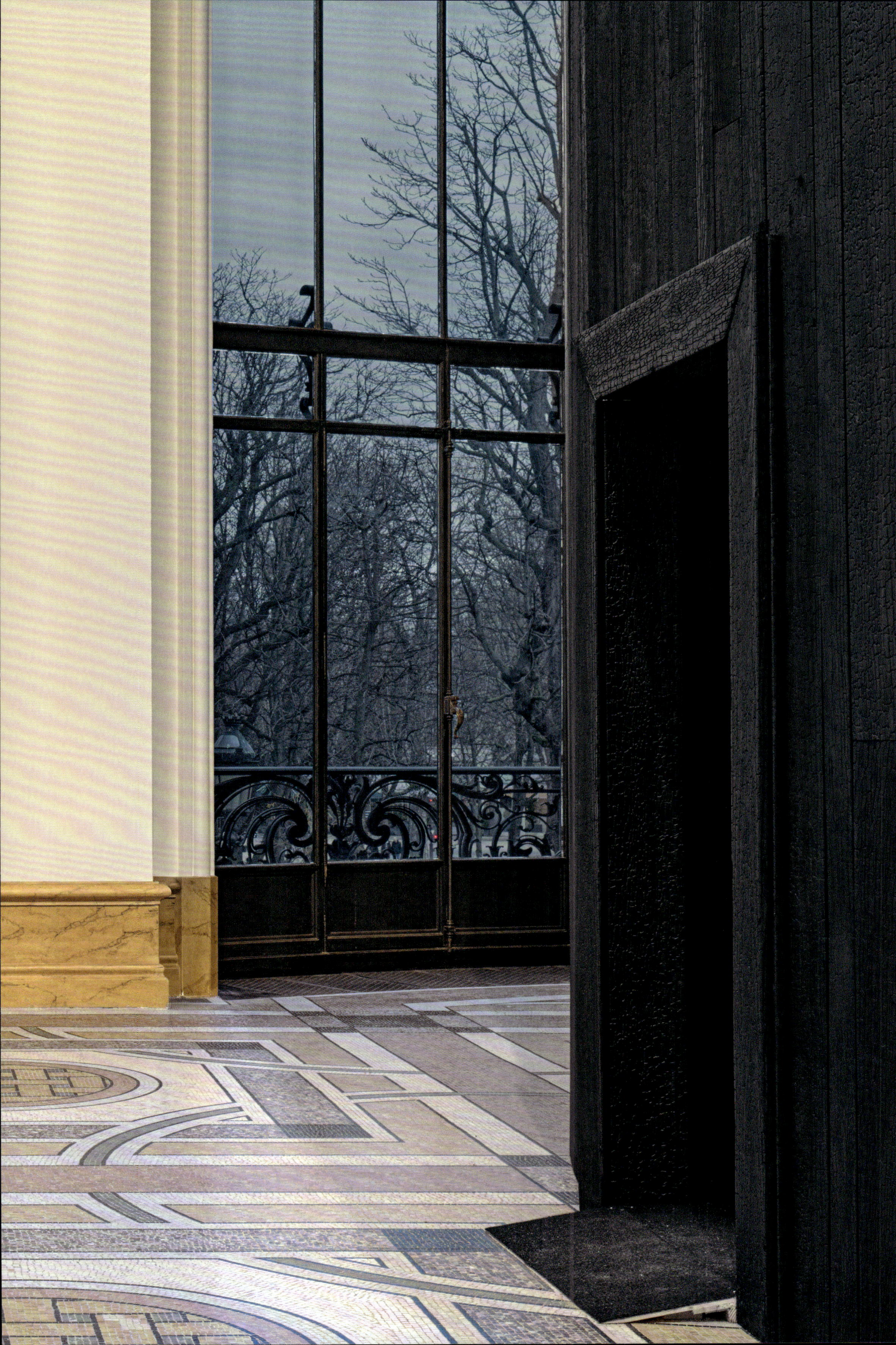

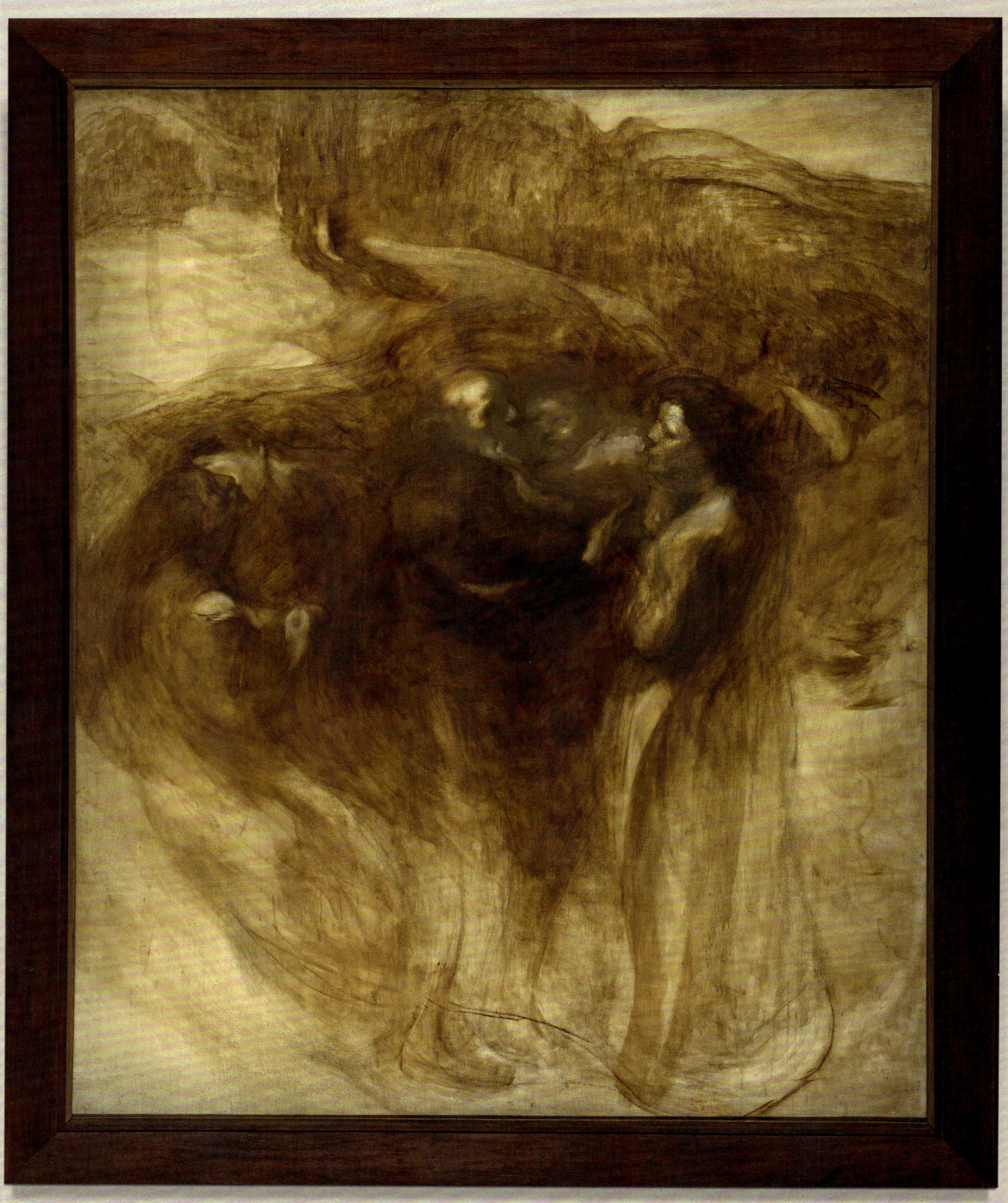

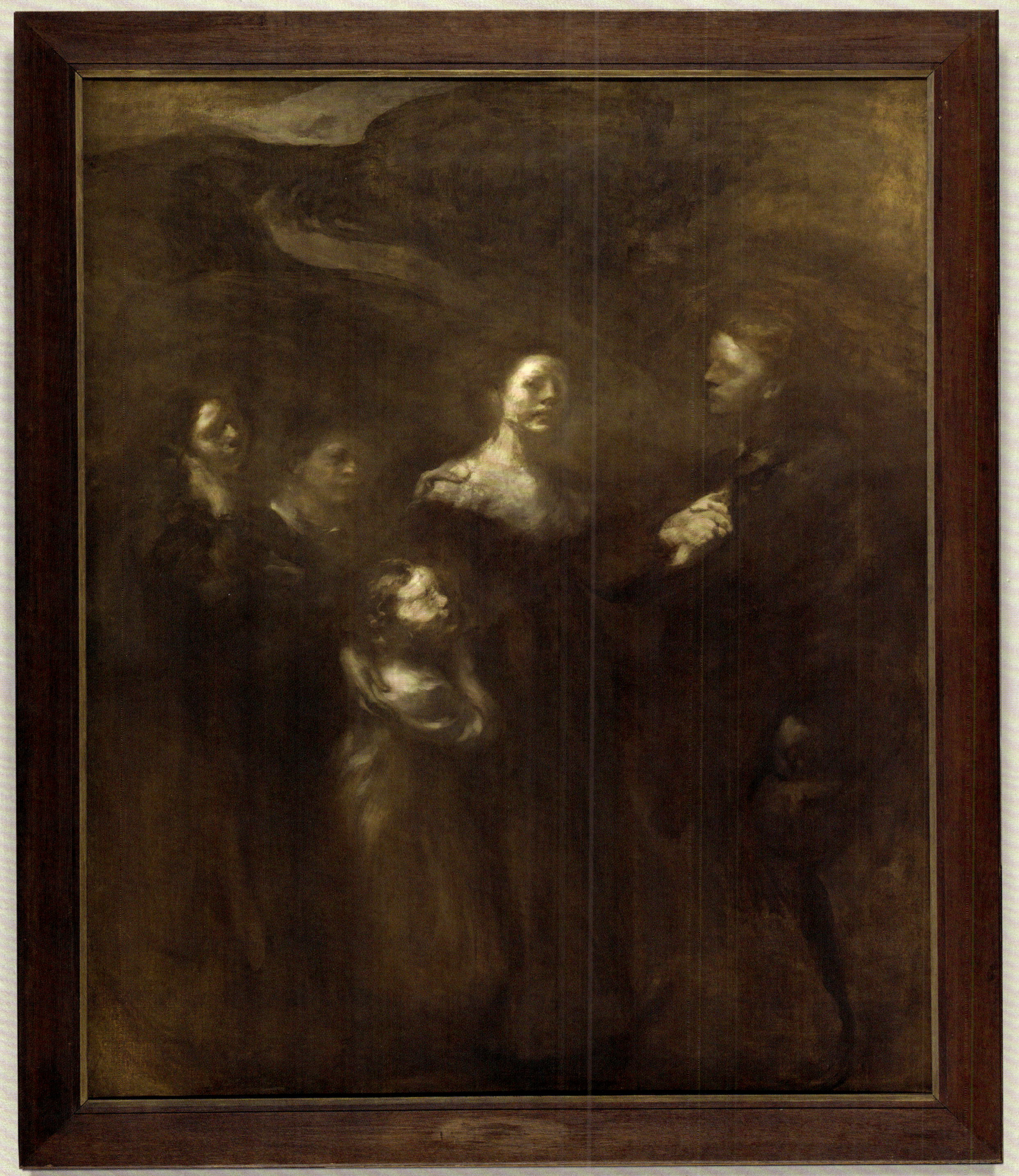

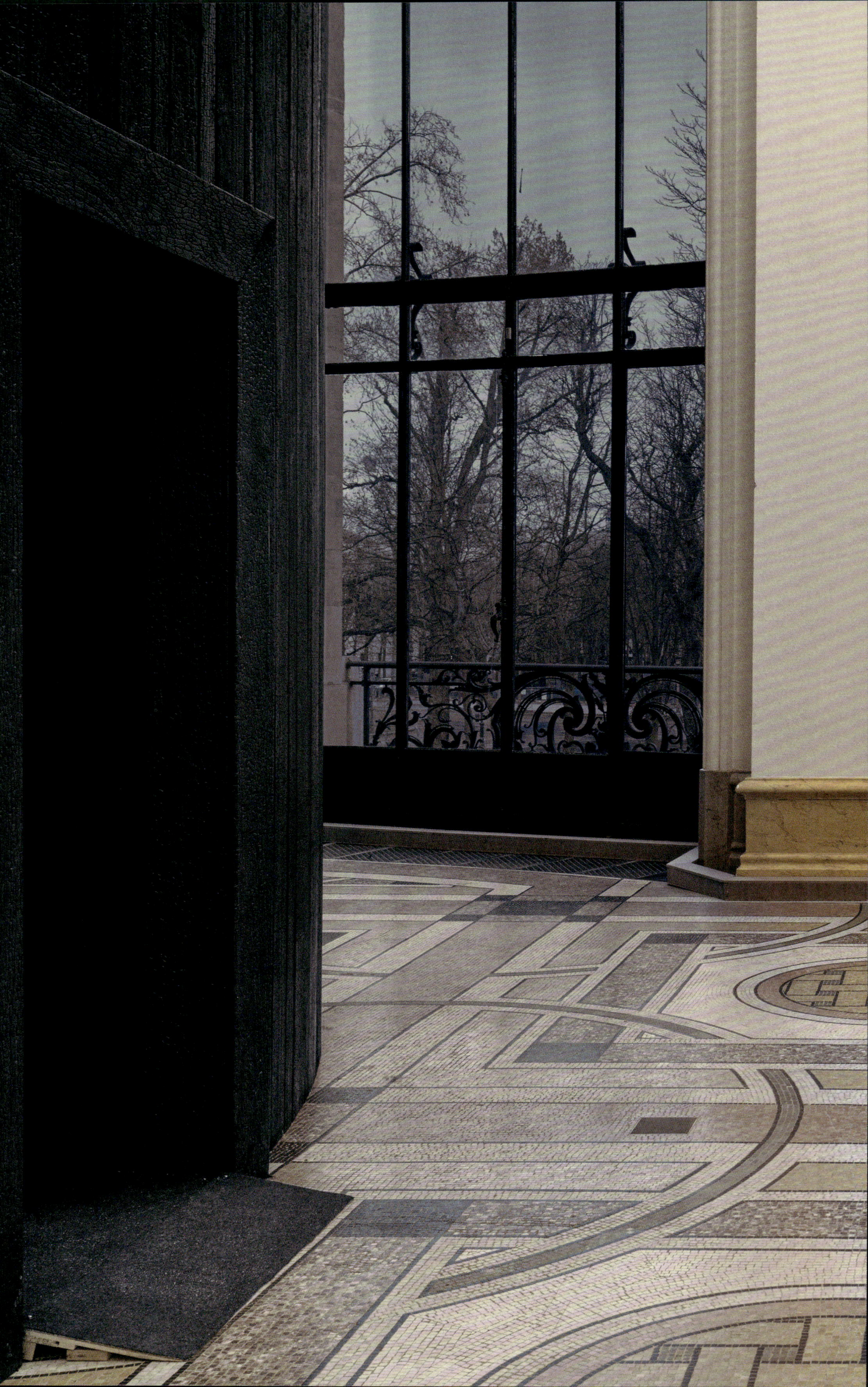

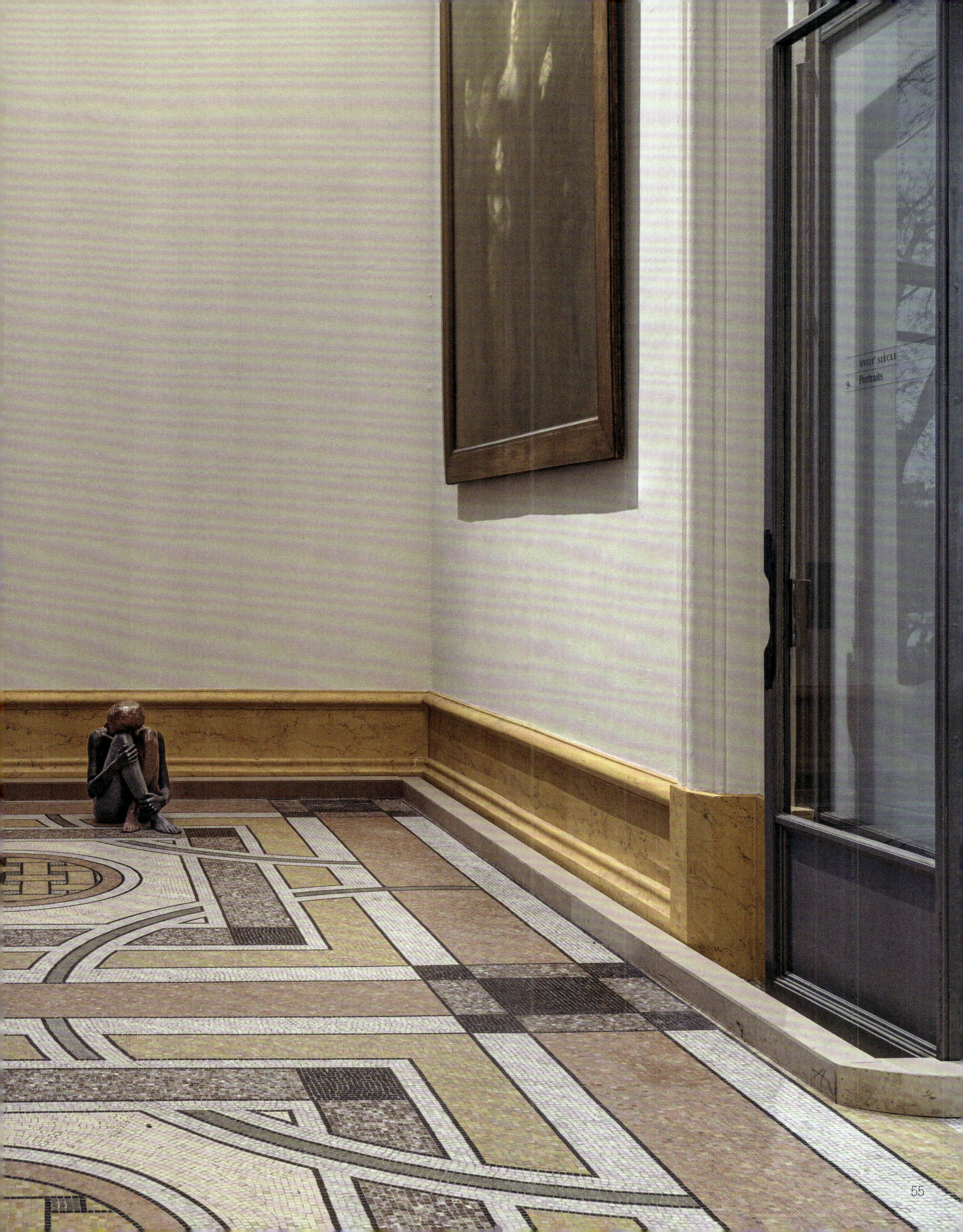
XVIIIe SIÈCLE
9. Portraits

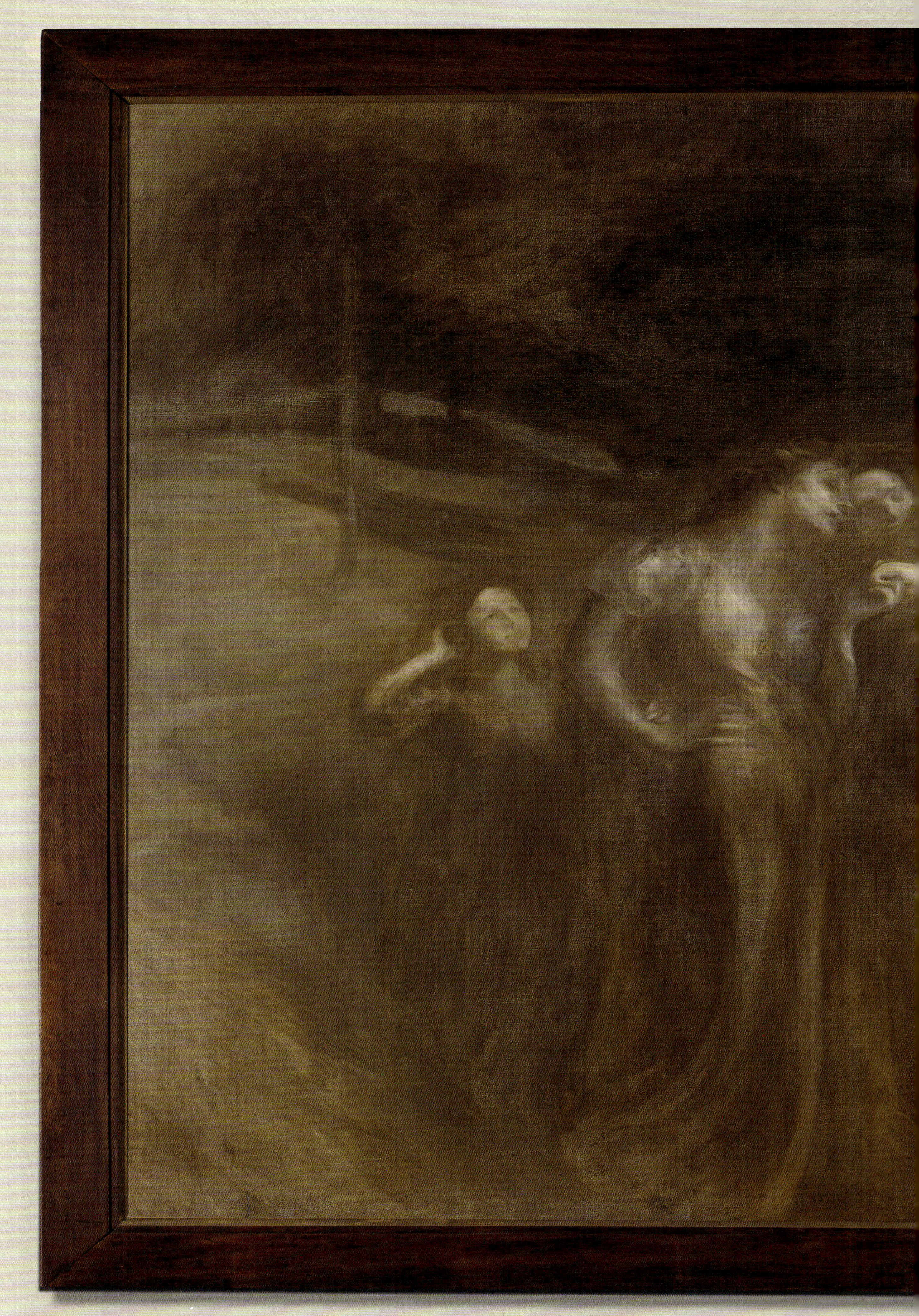

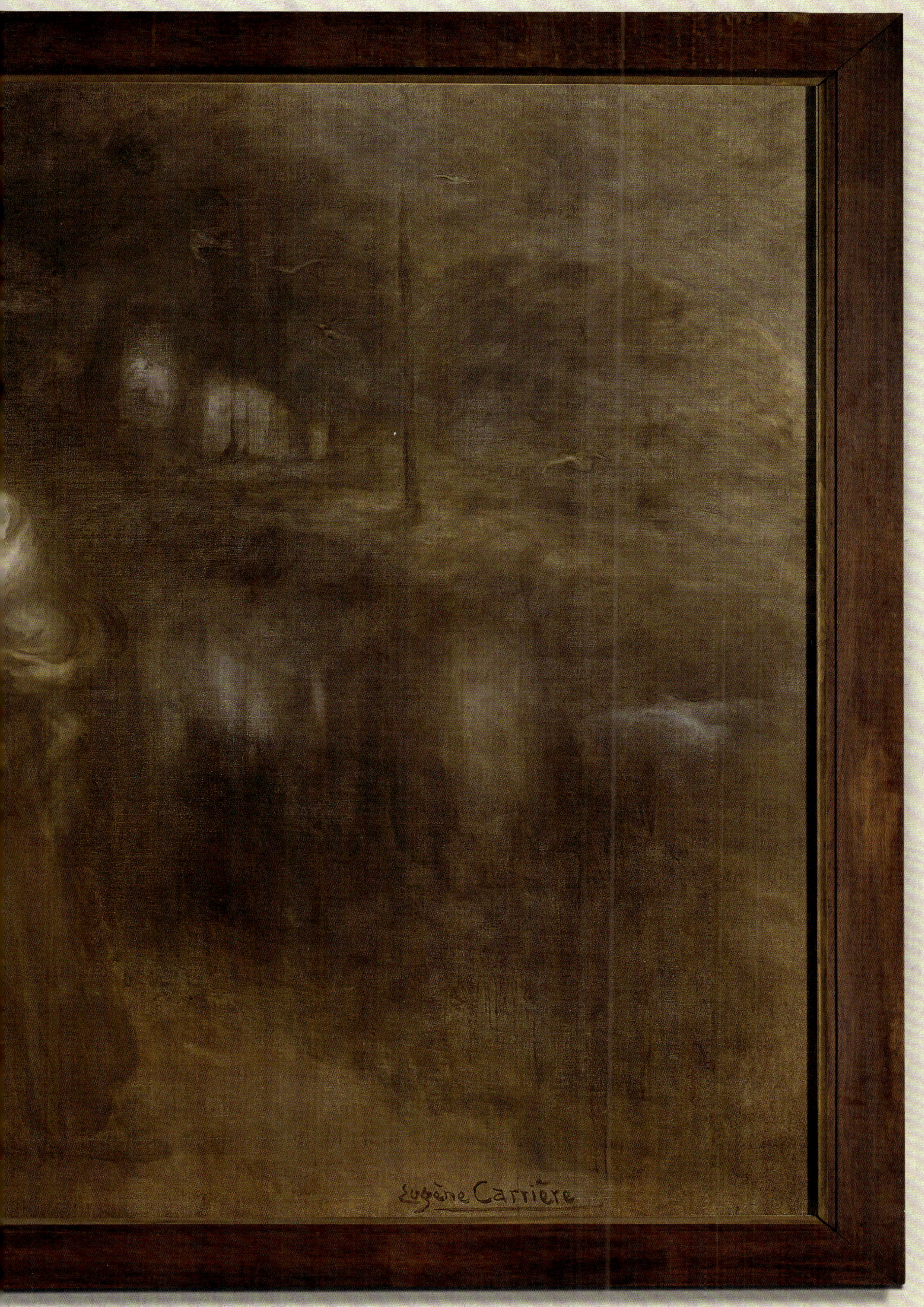
Eugène Carrière

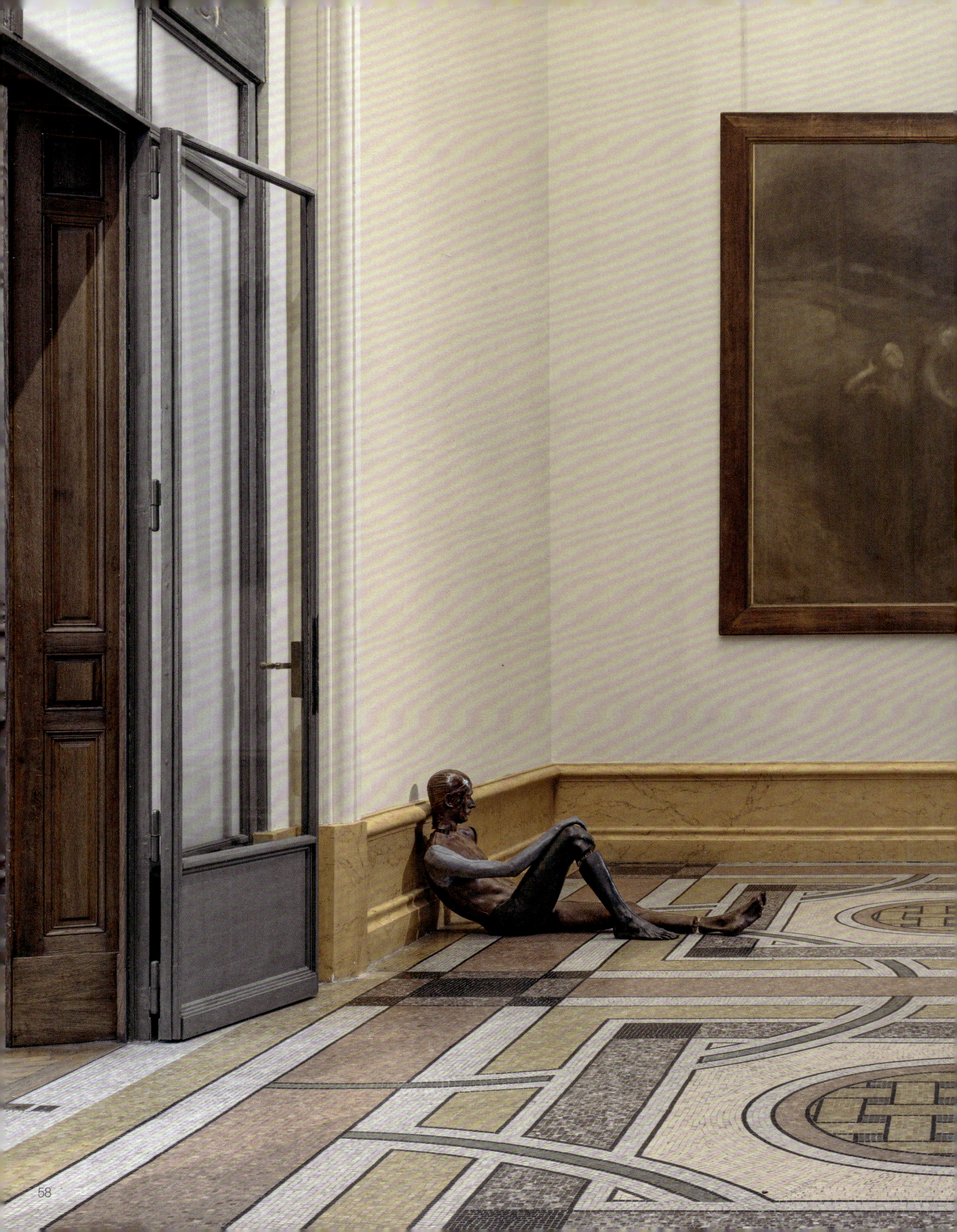

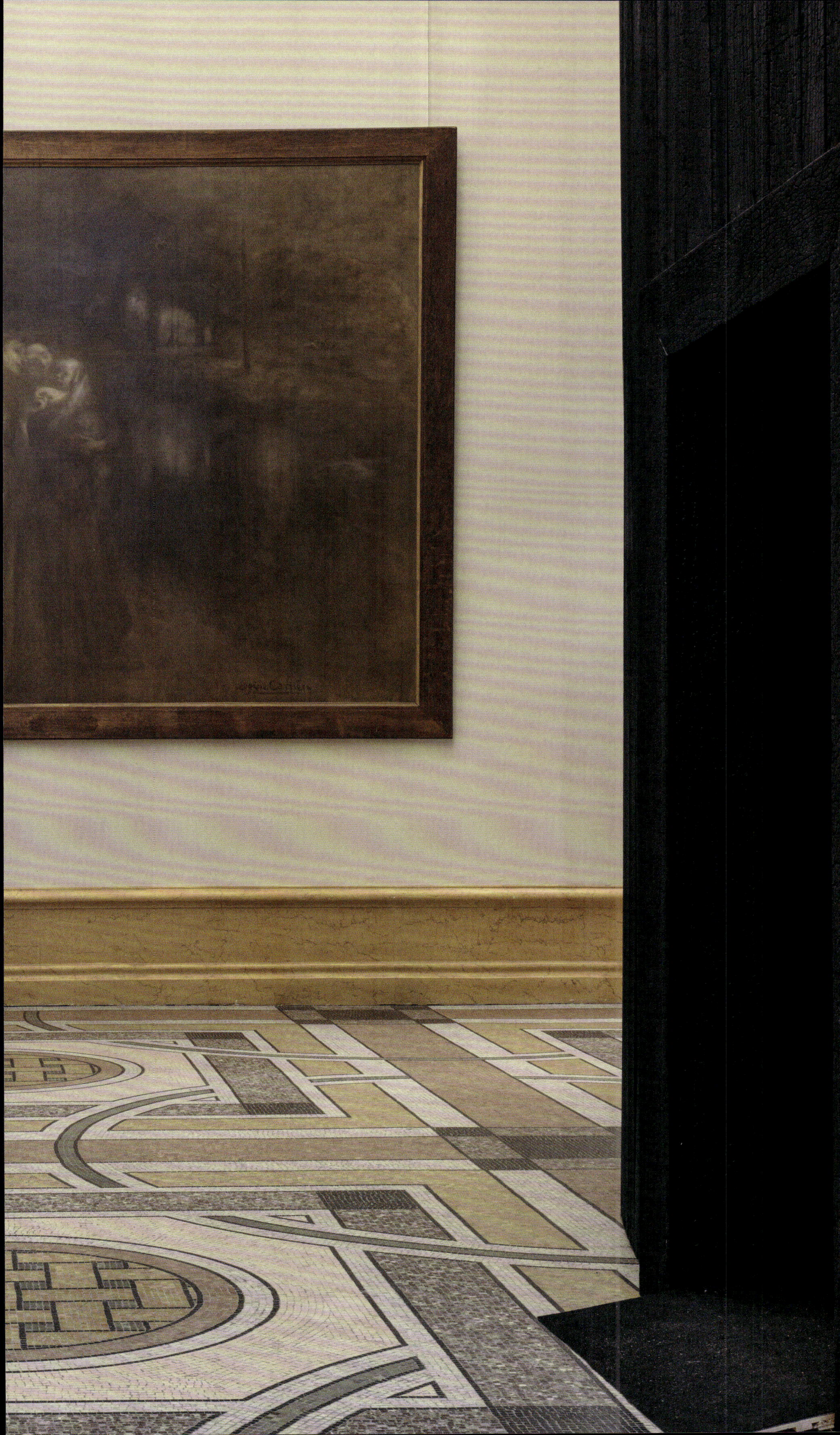

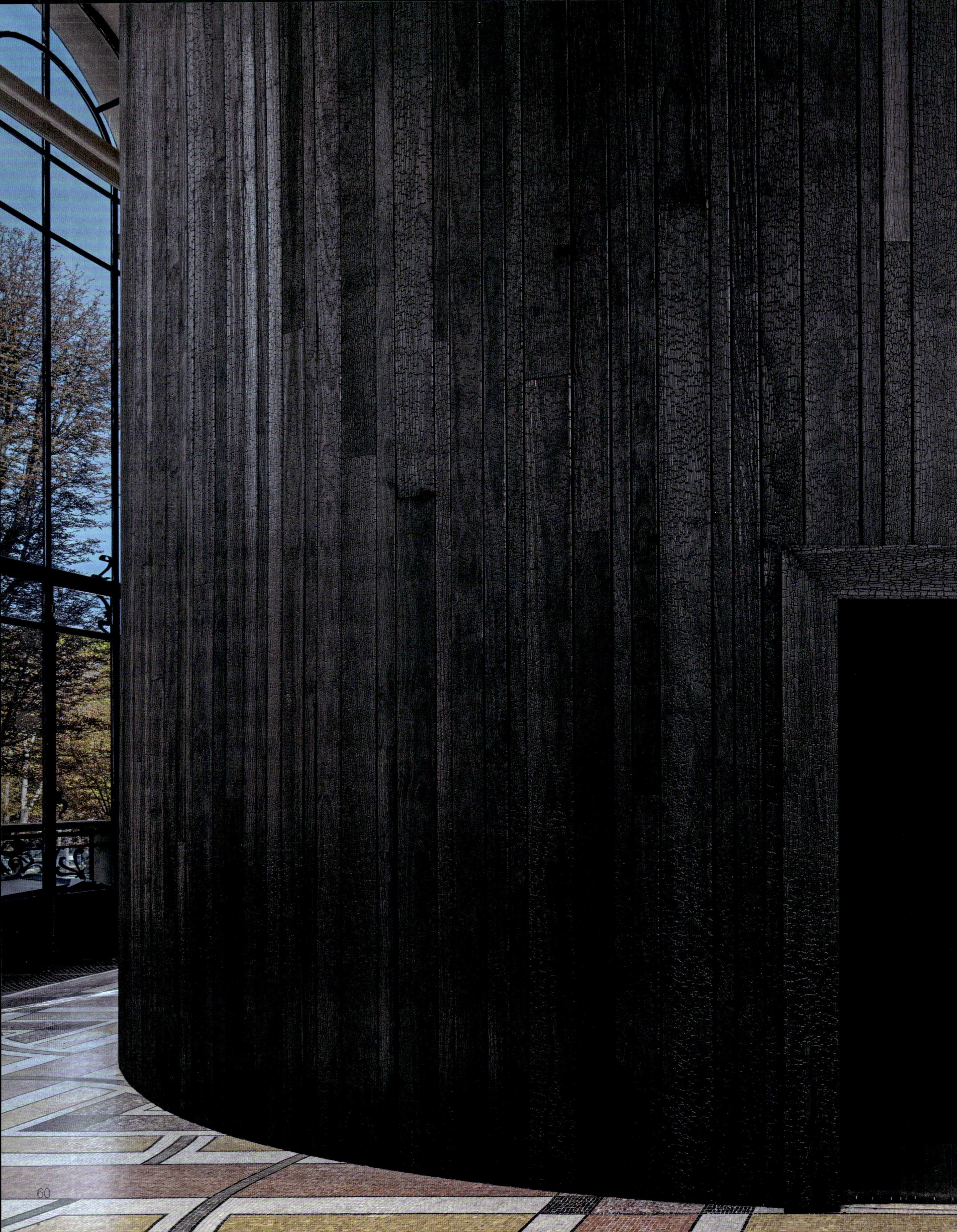

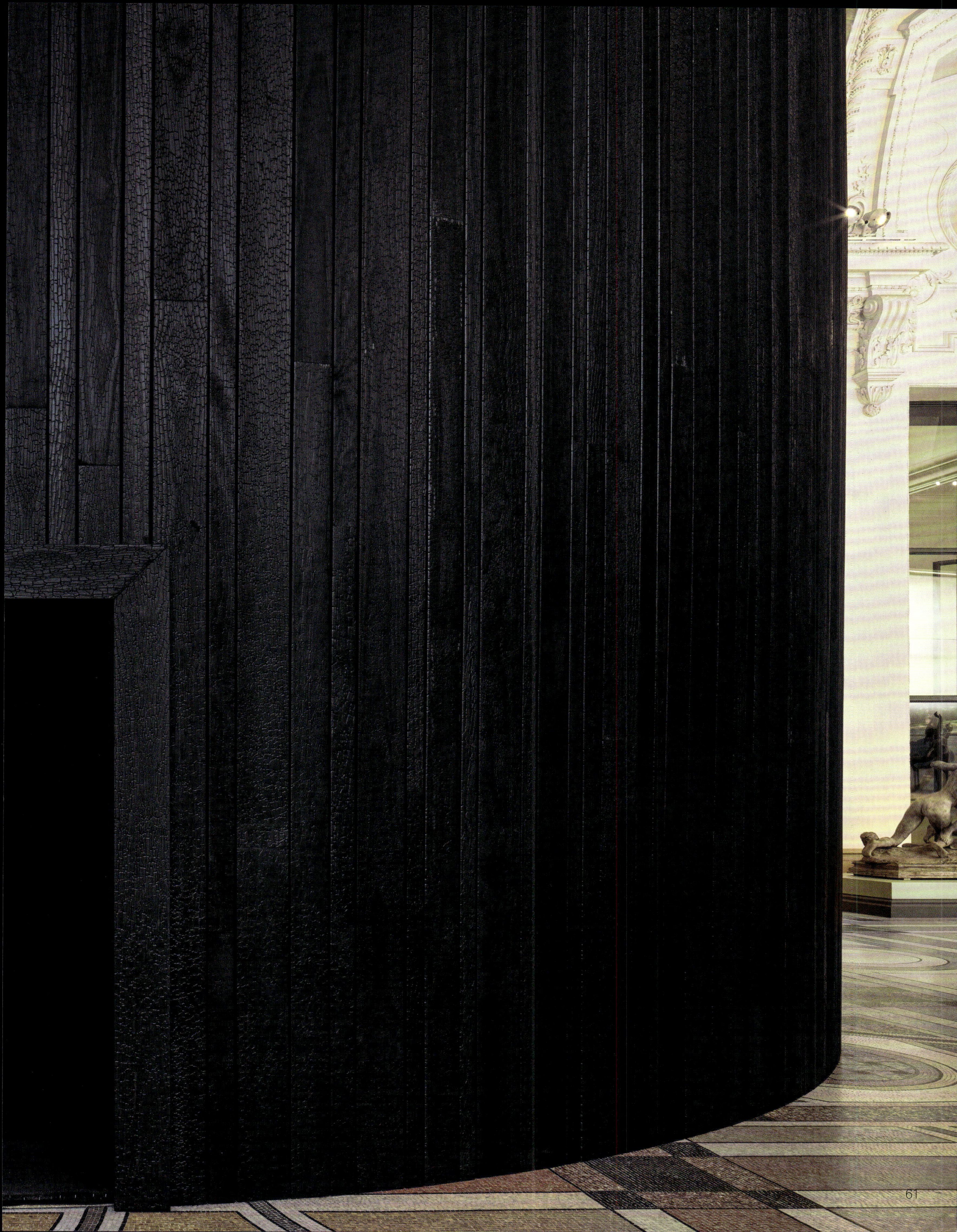

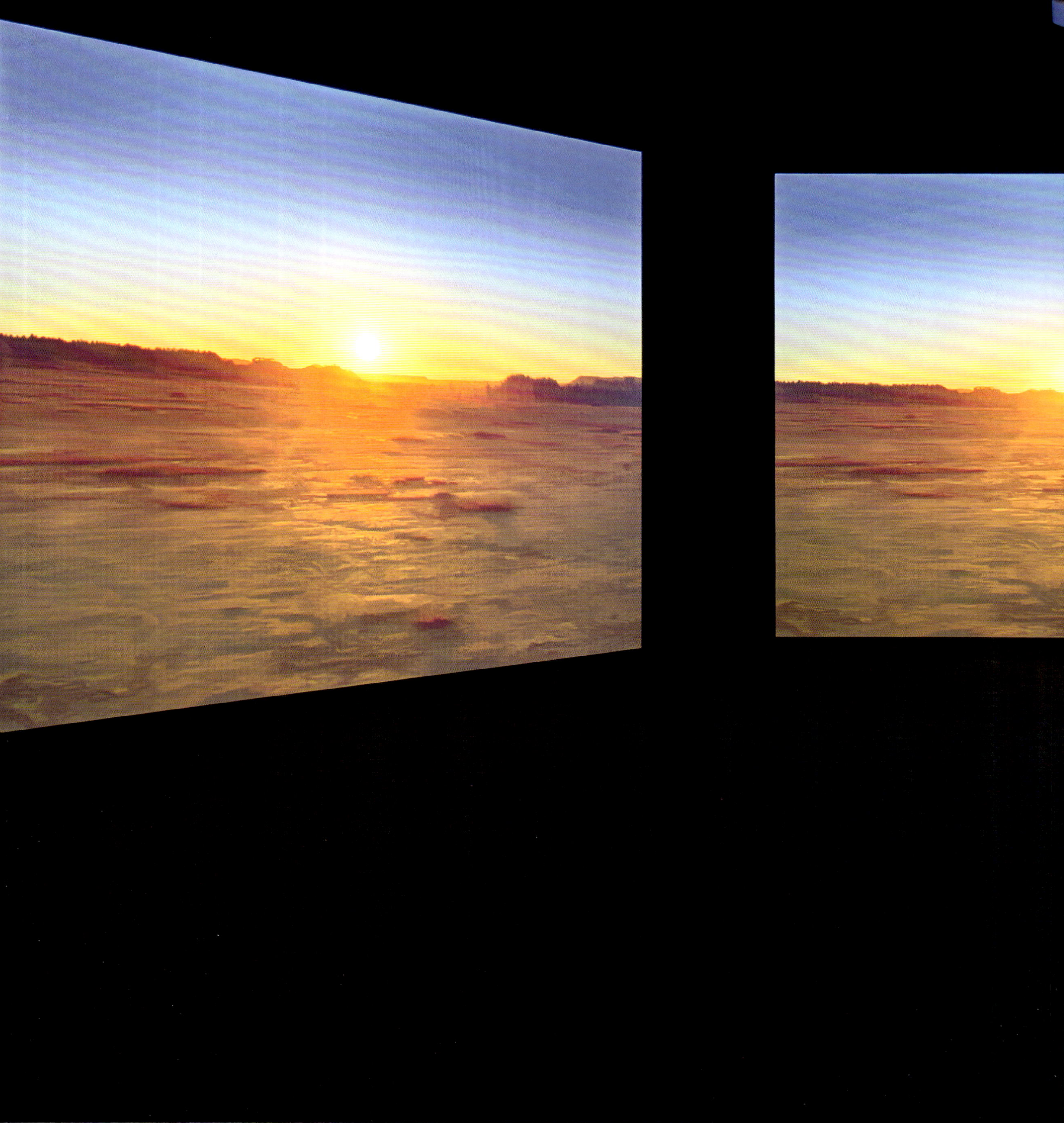

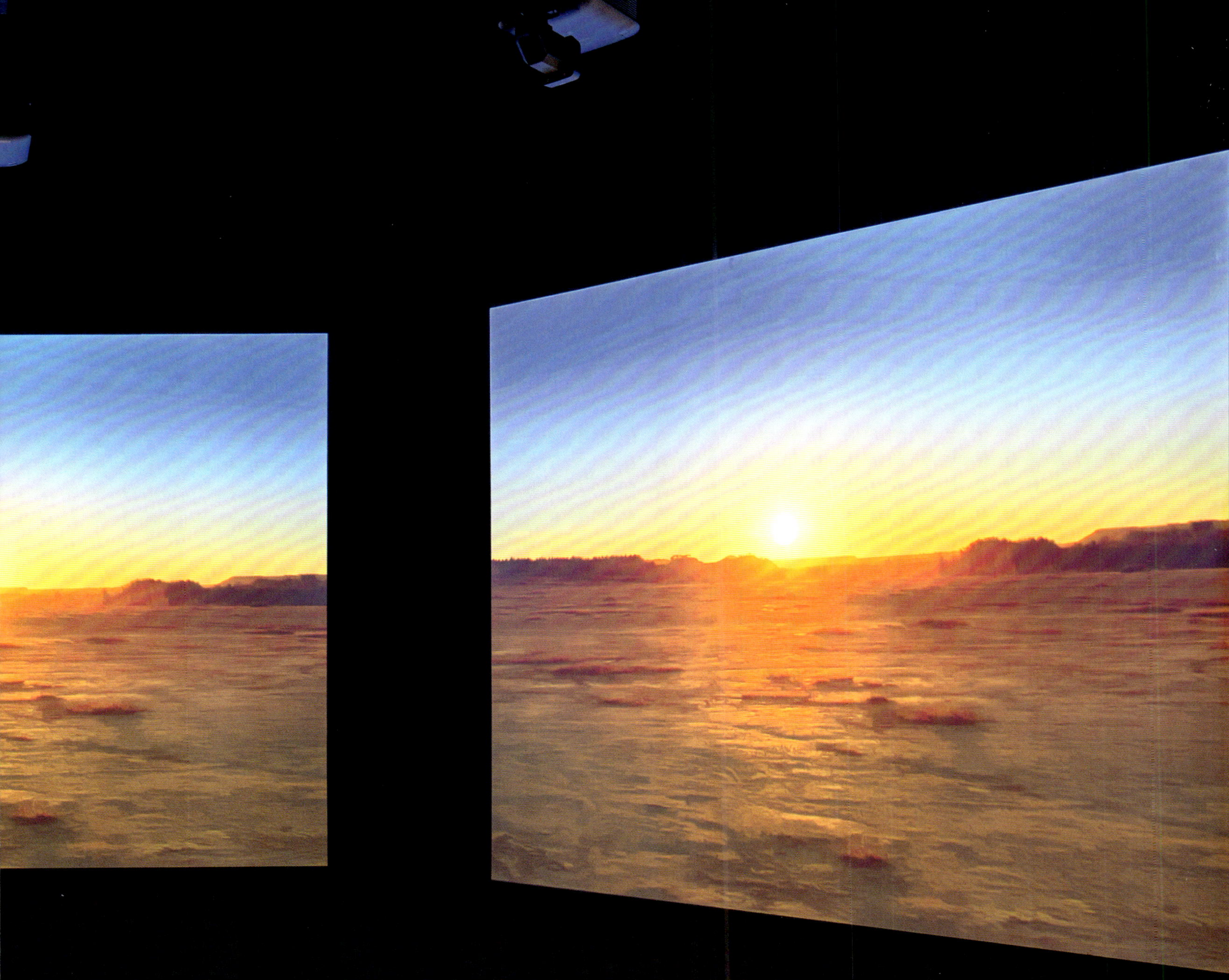

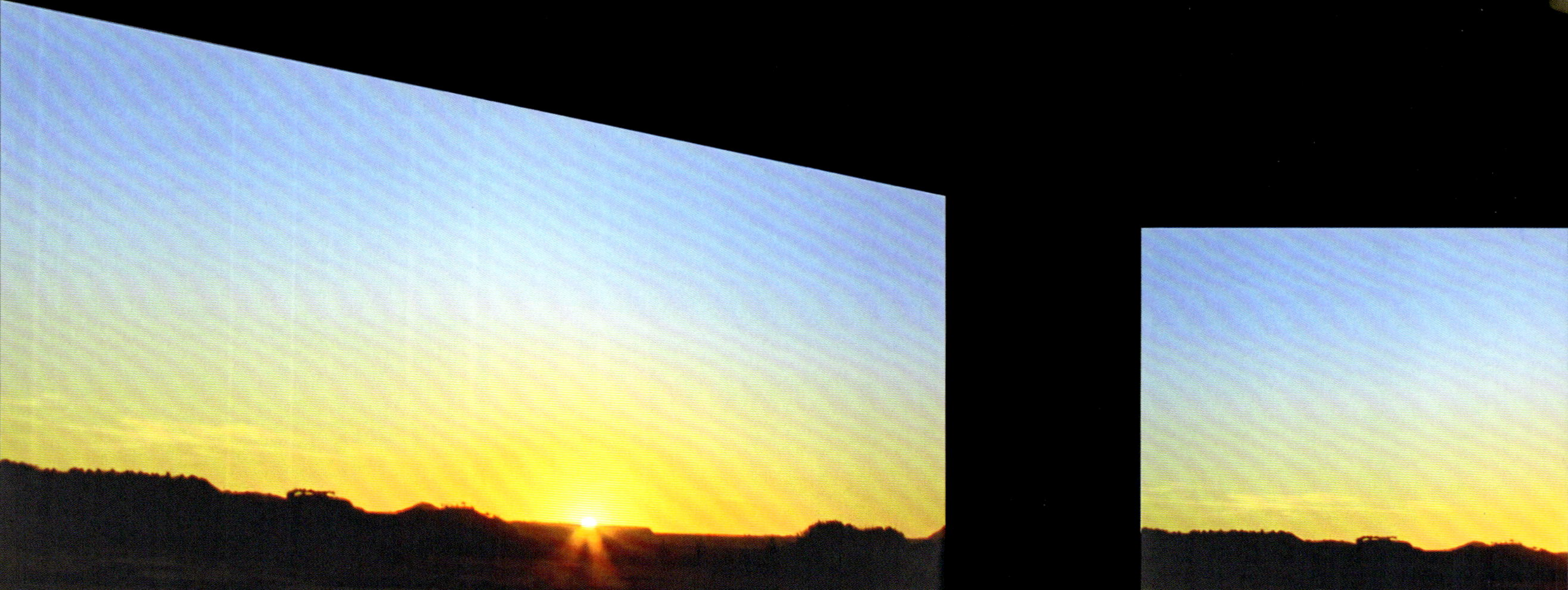

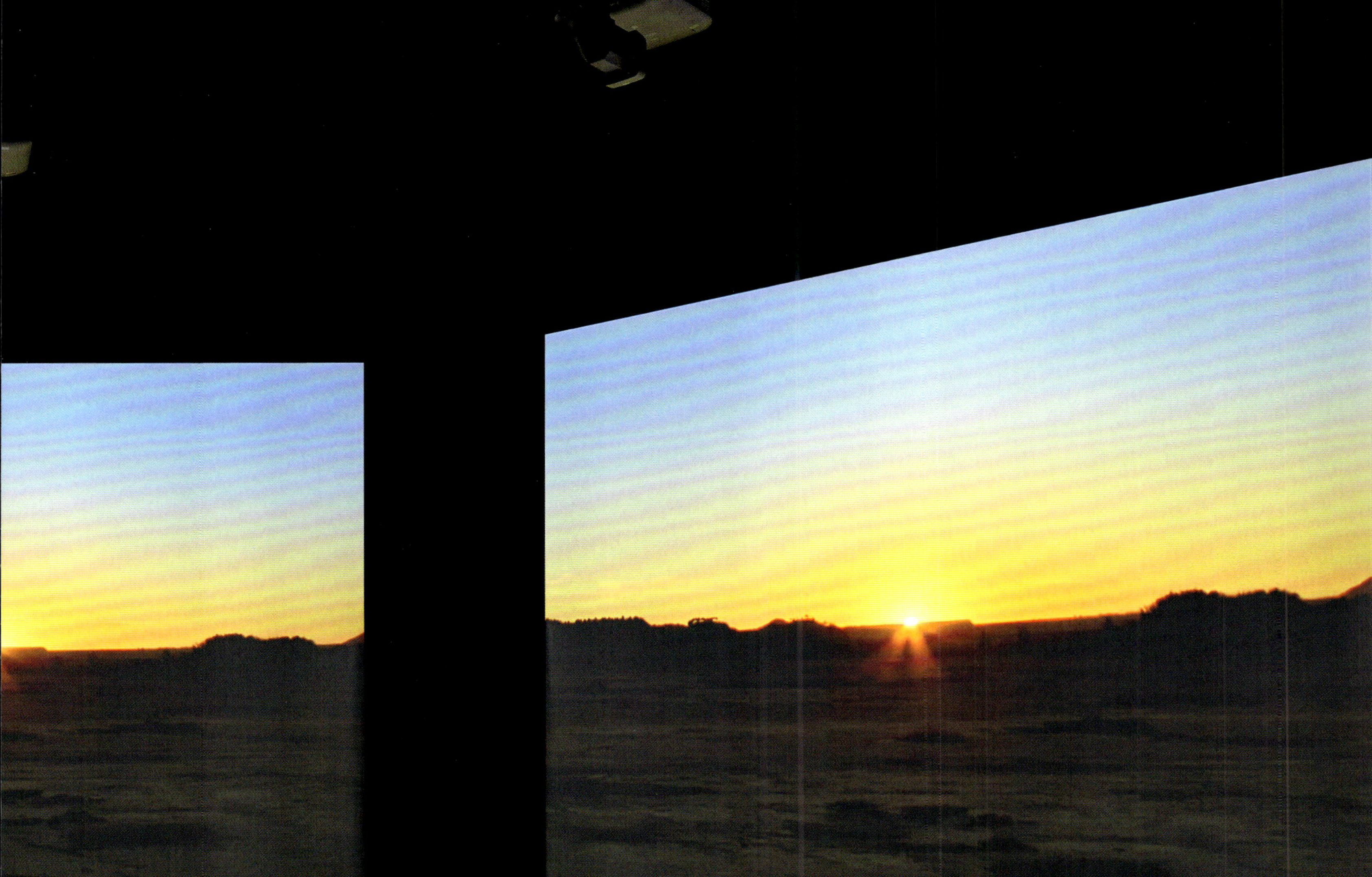

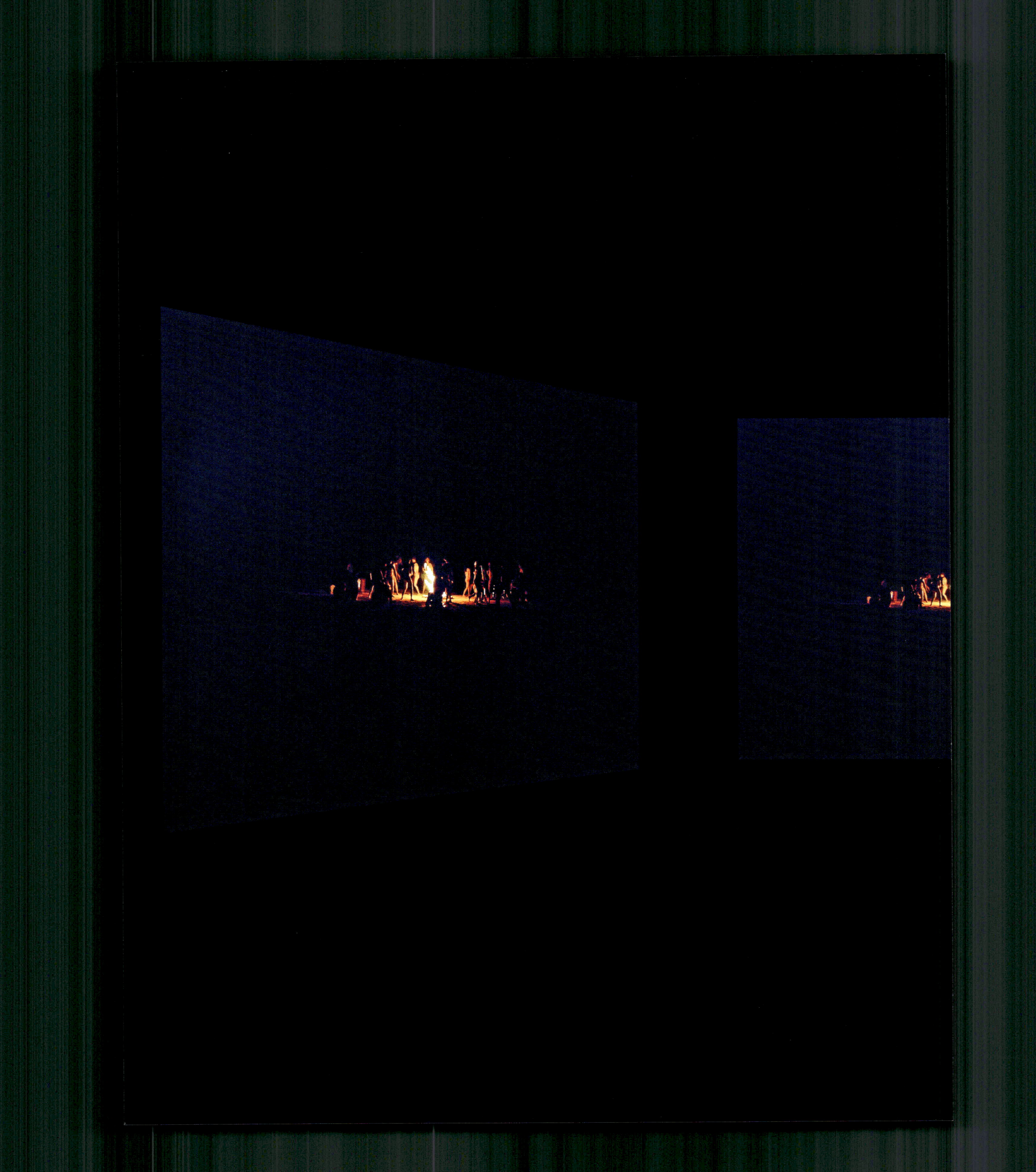

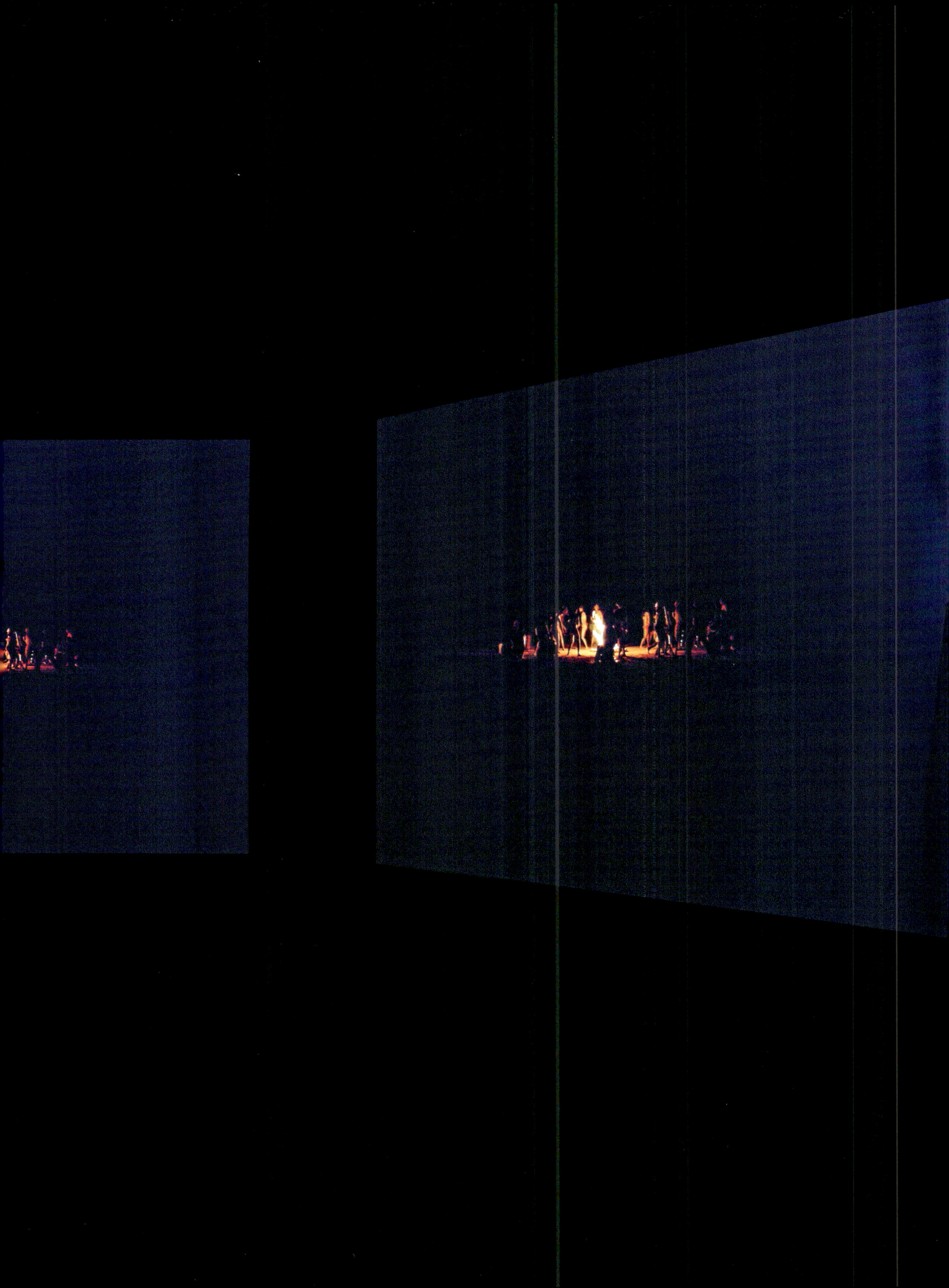

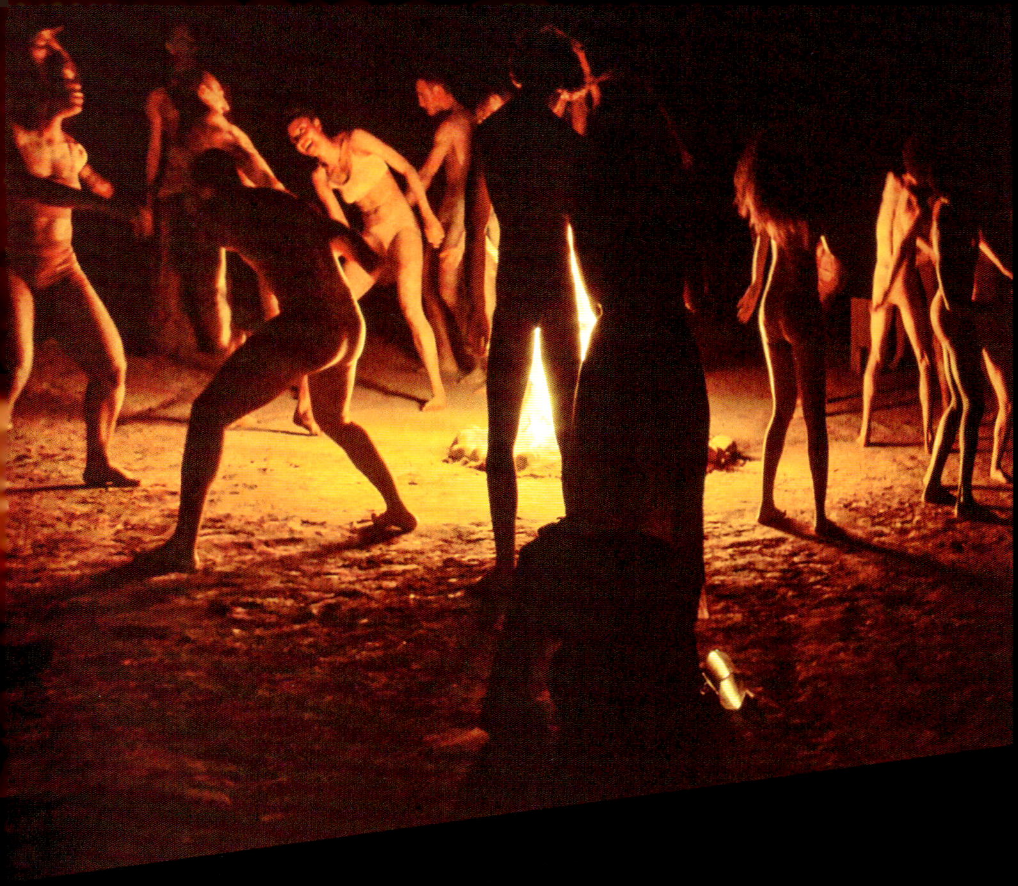

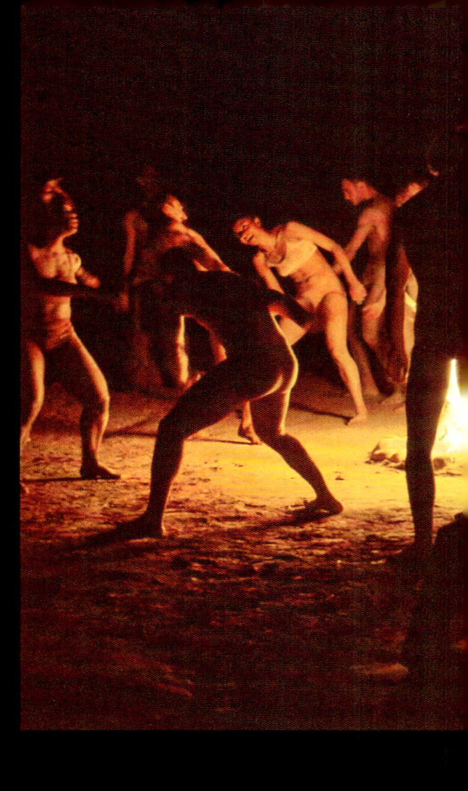

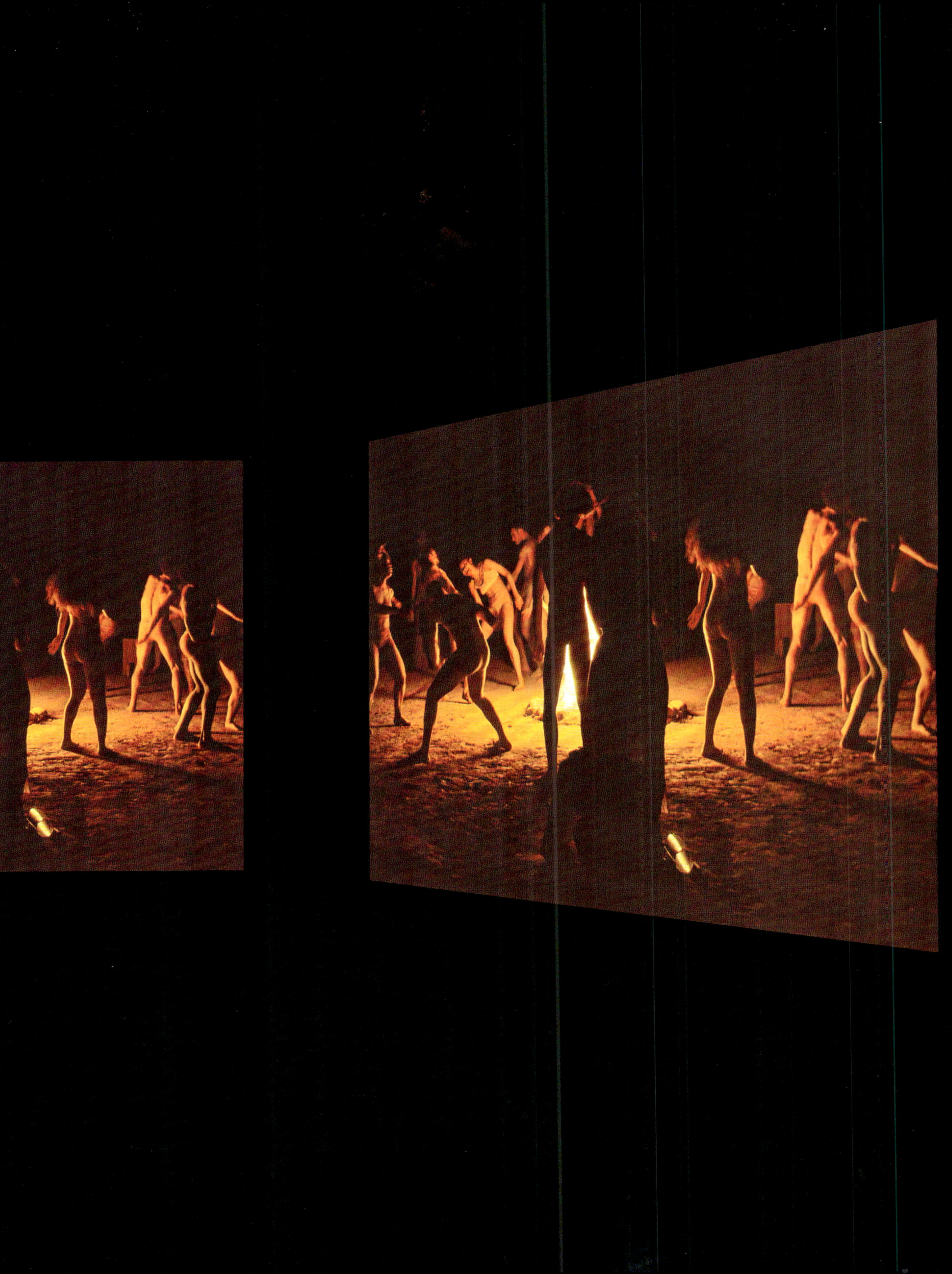

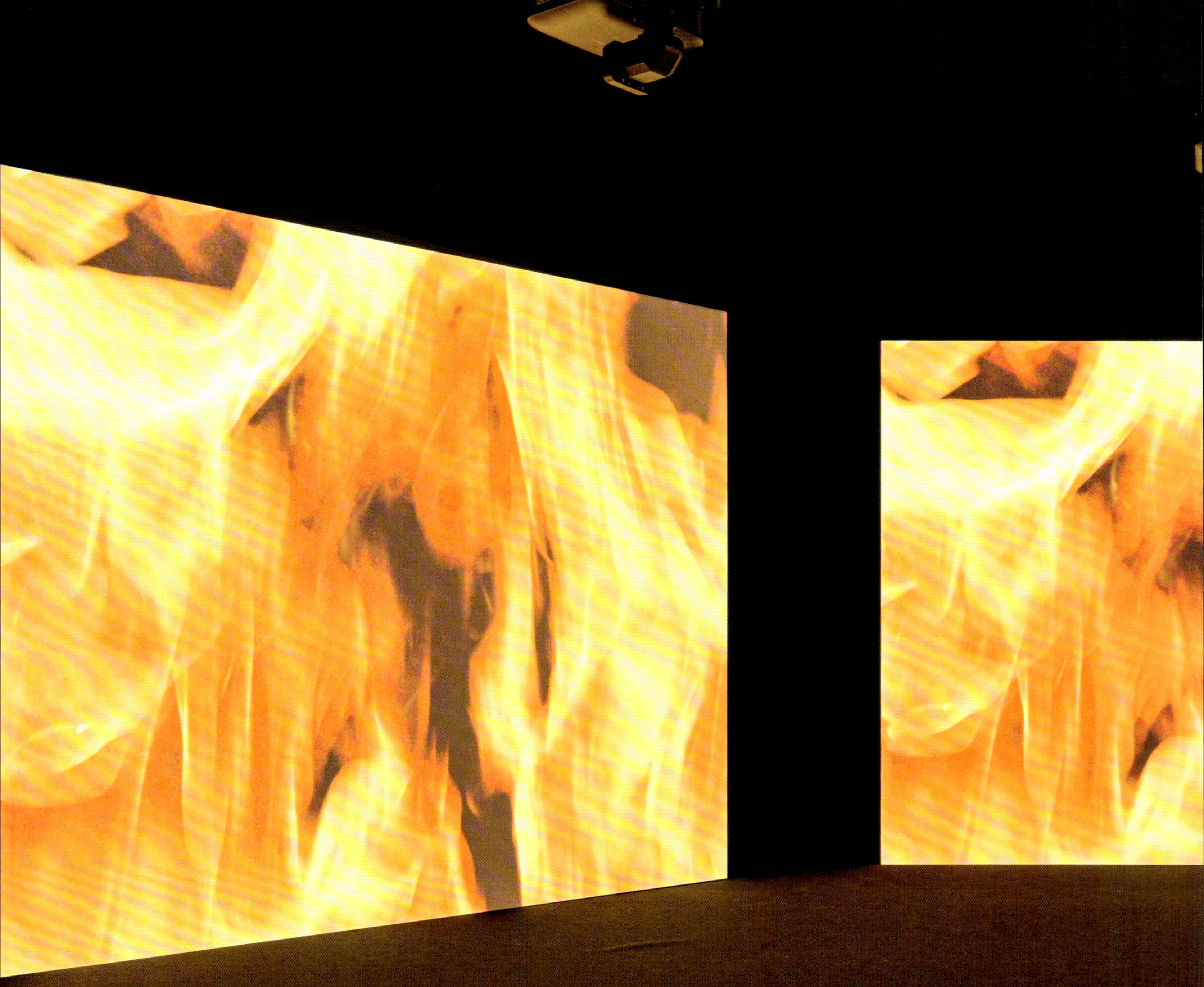

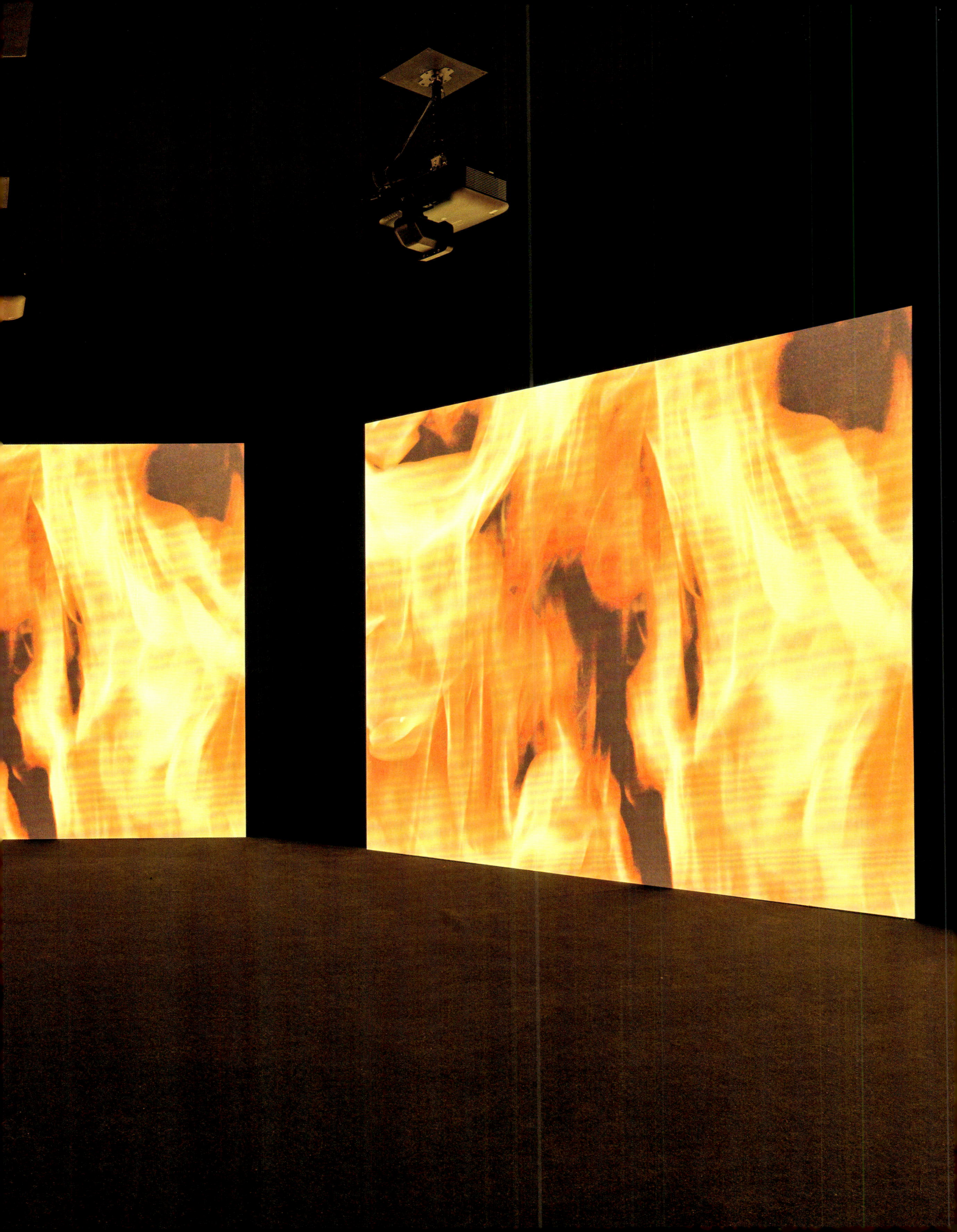

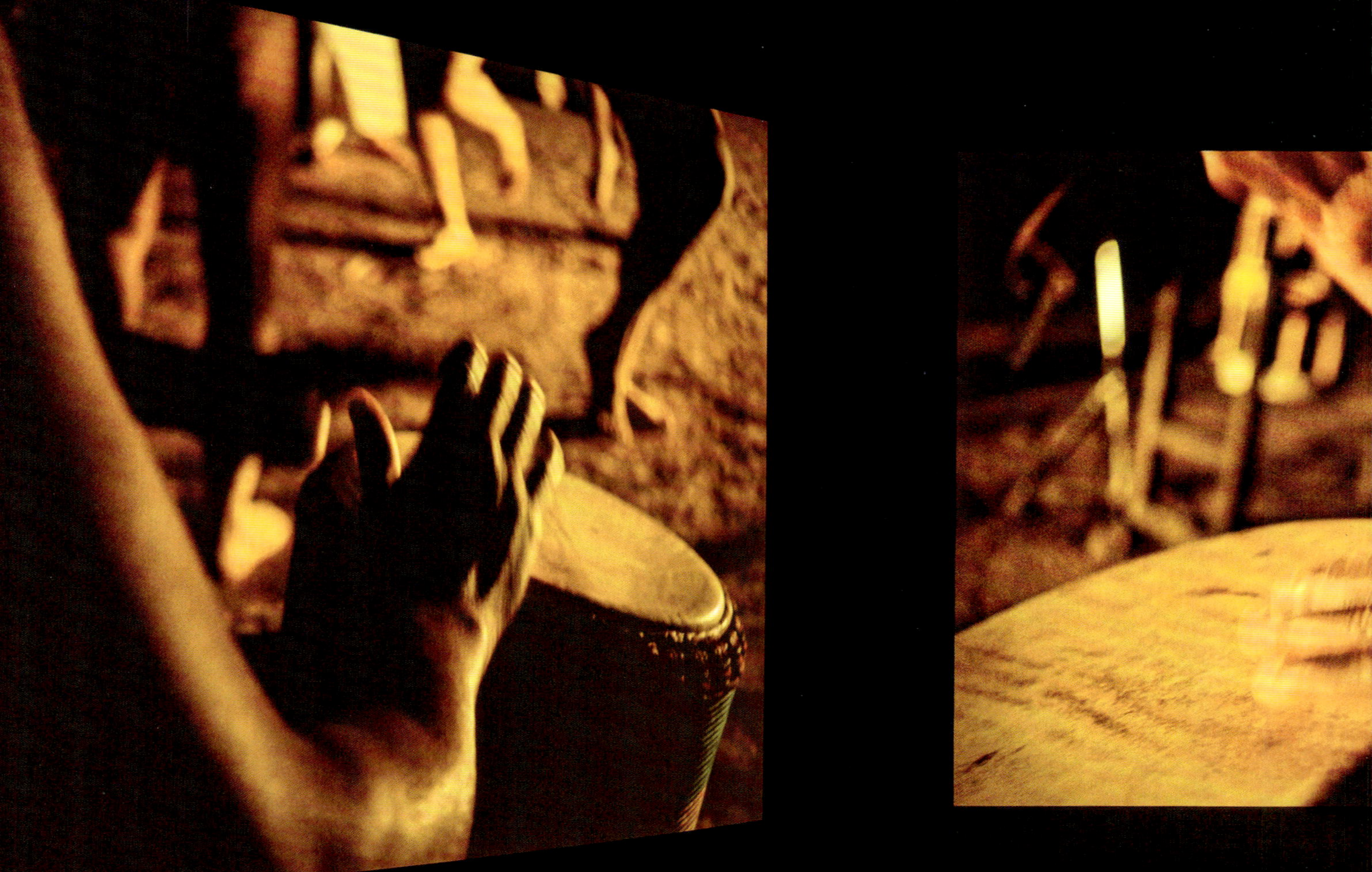

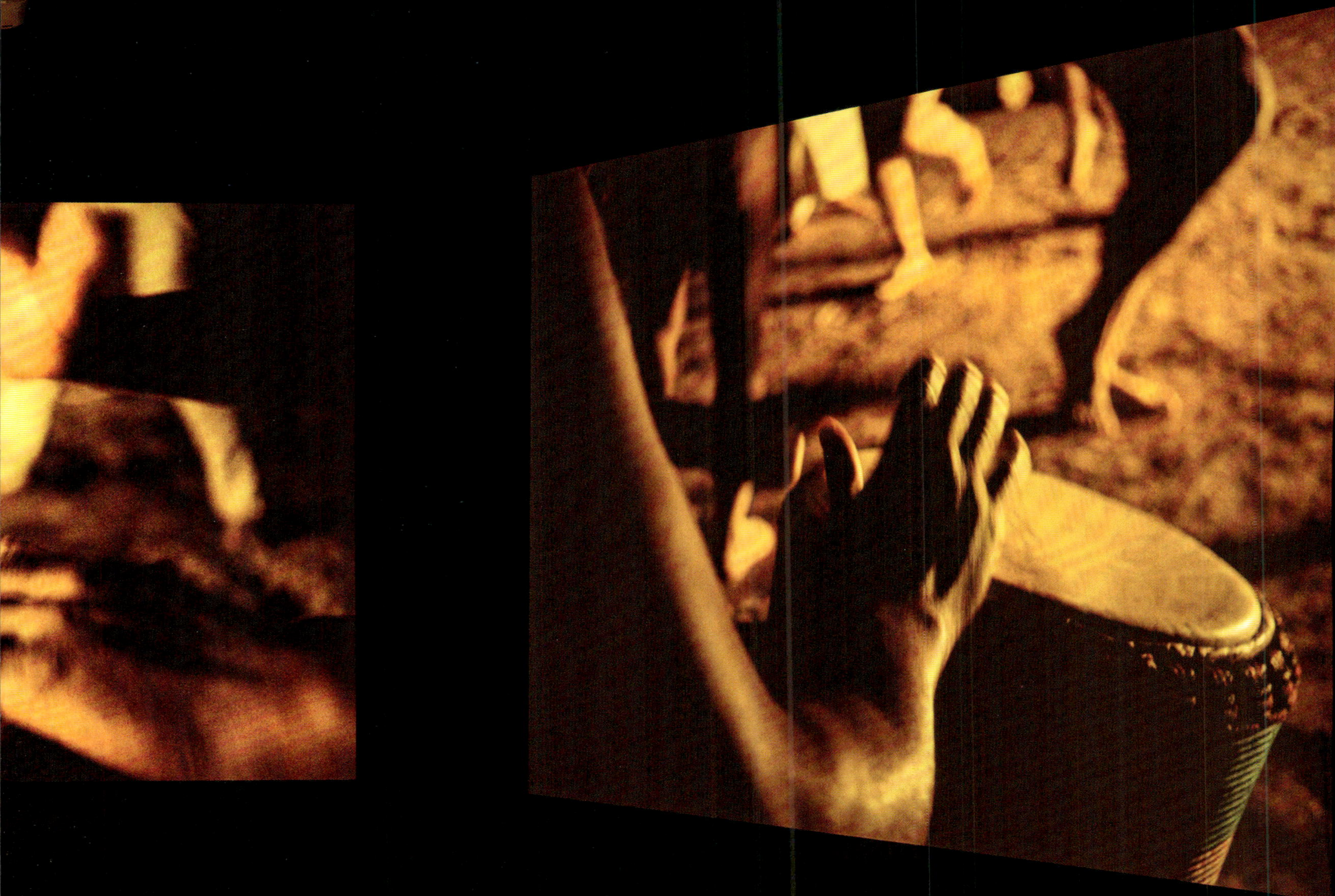

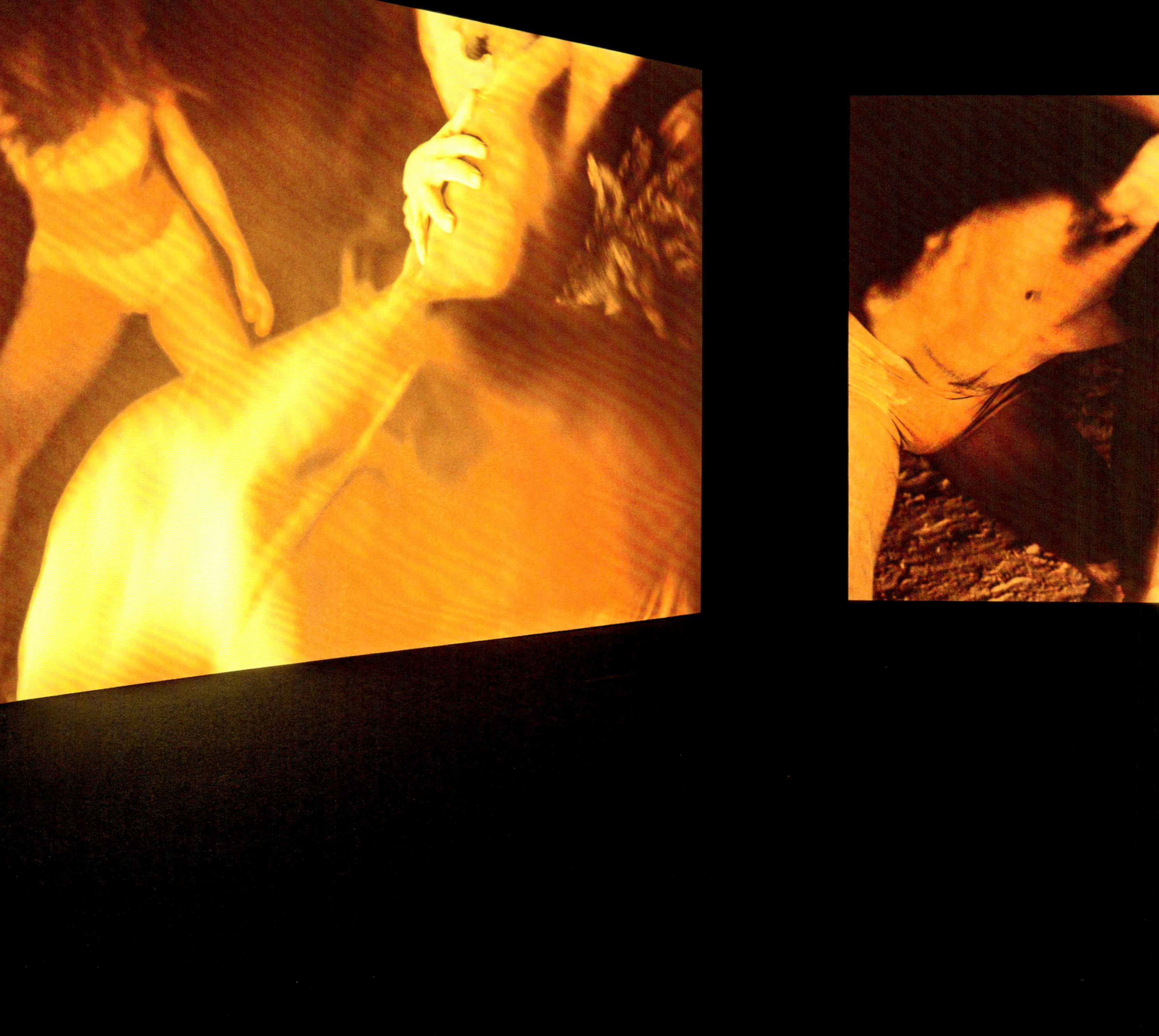

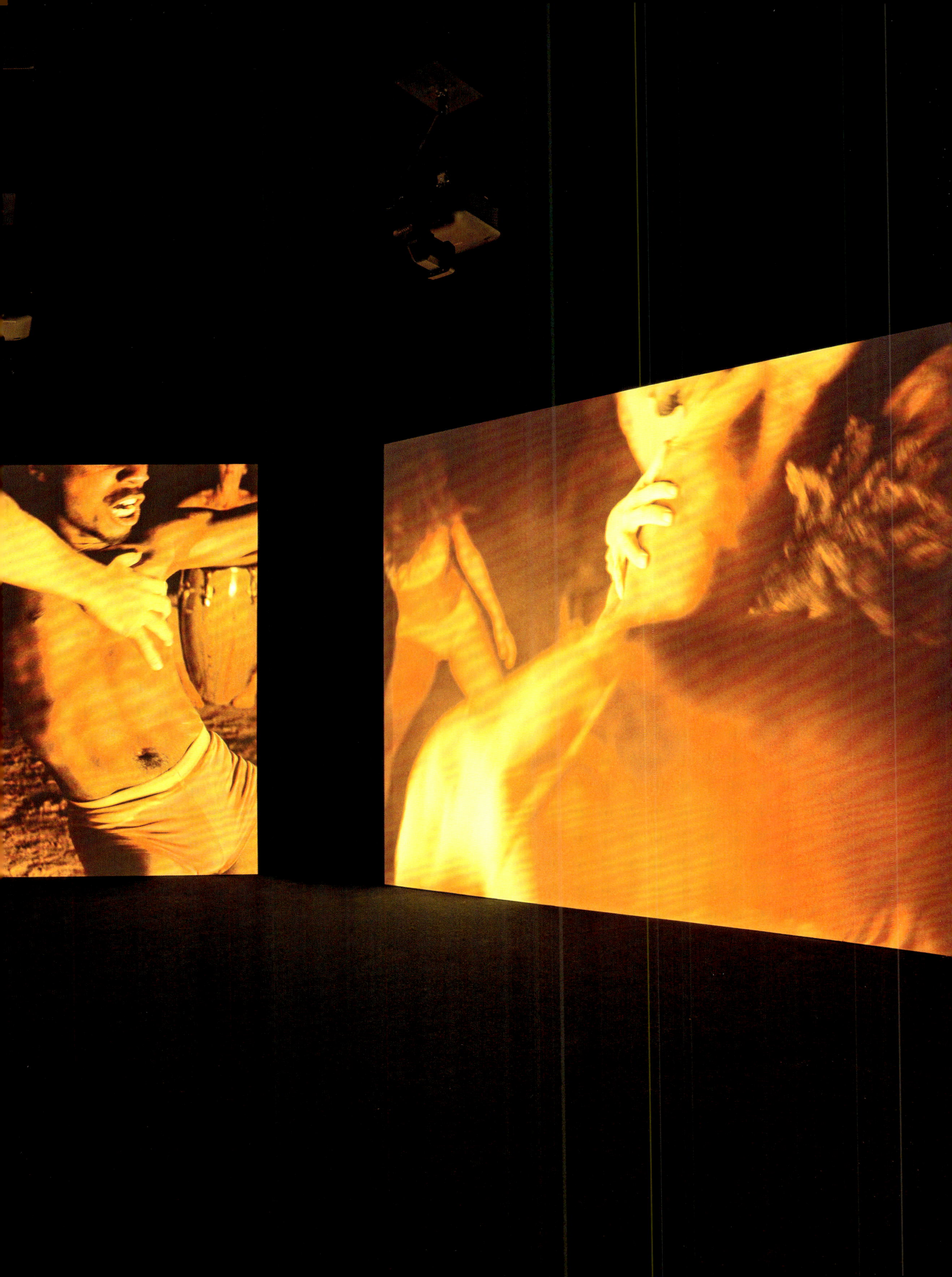

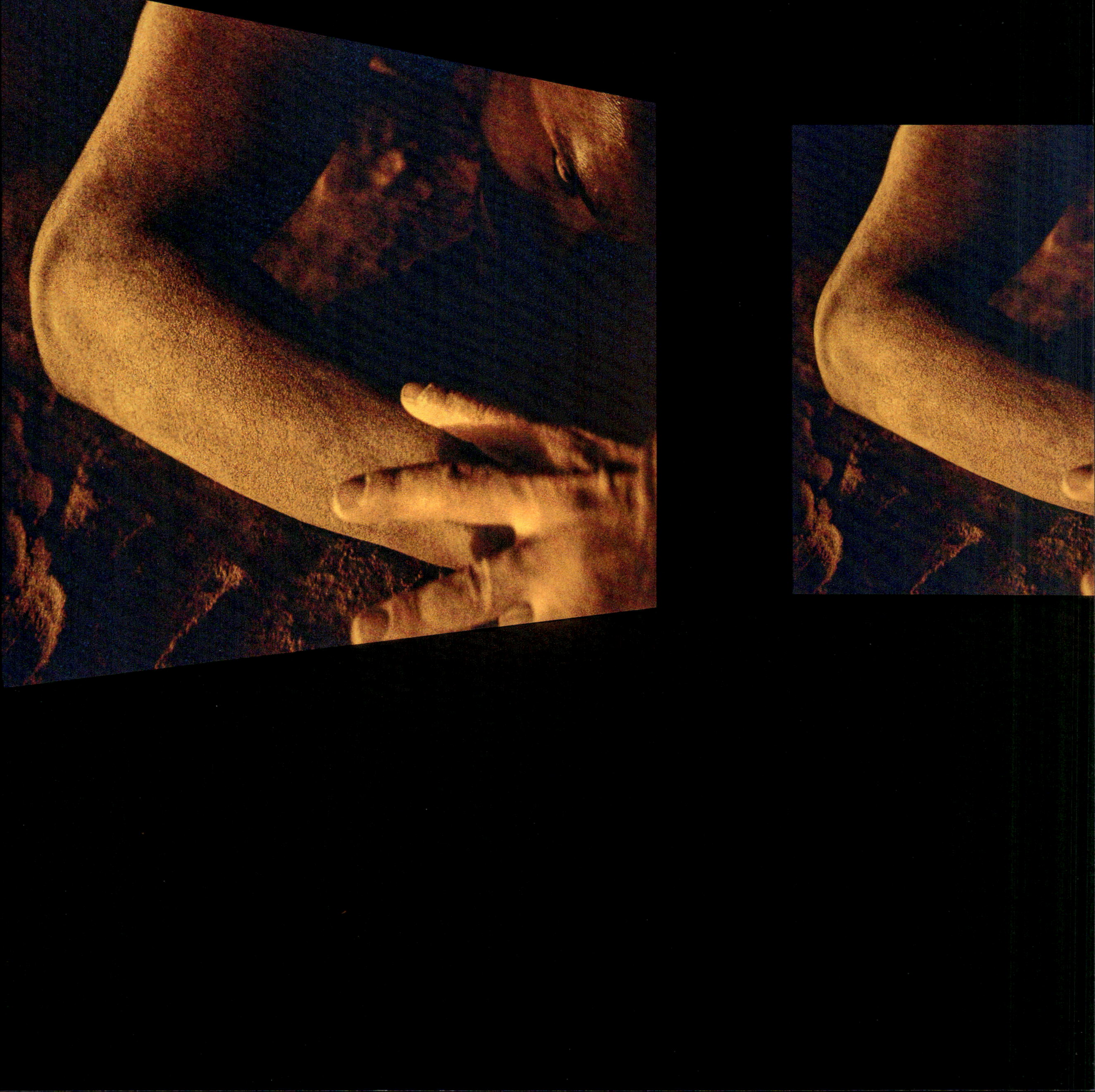

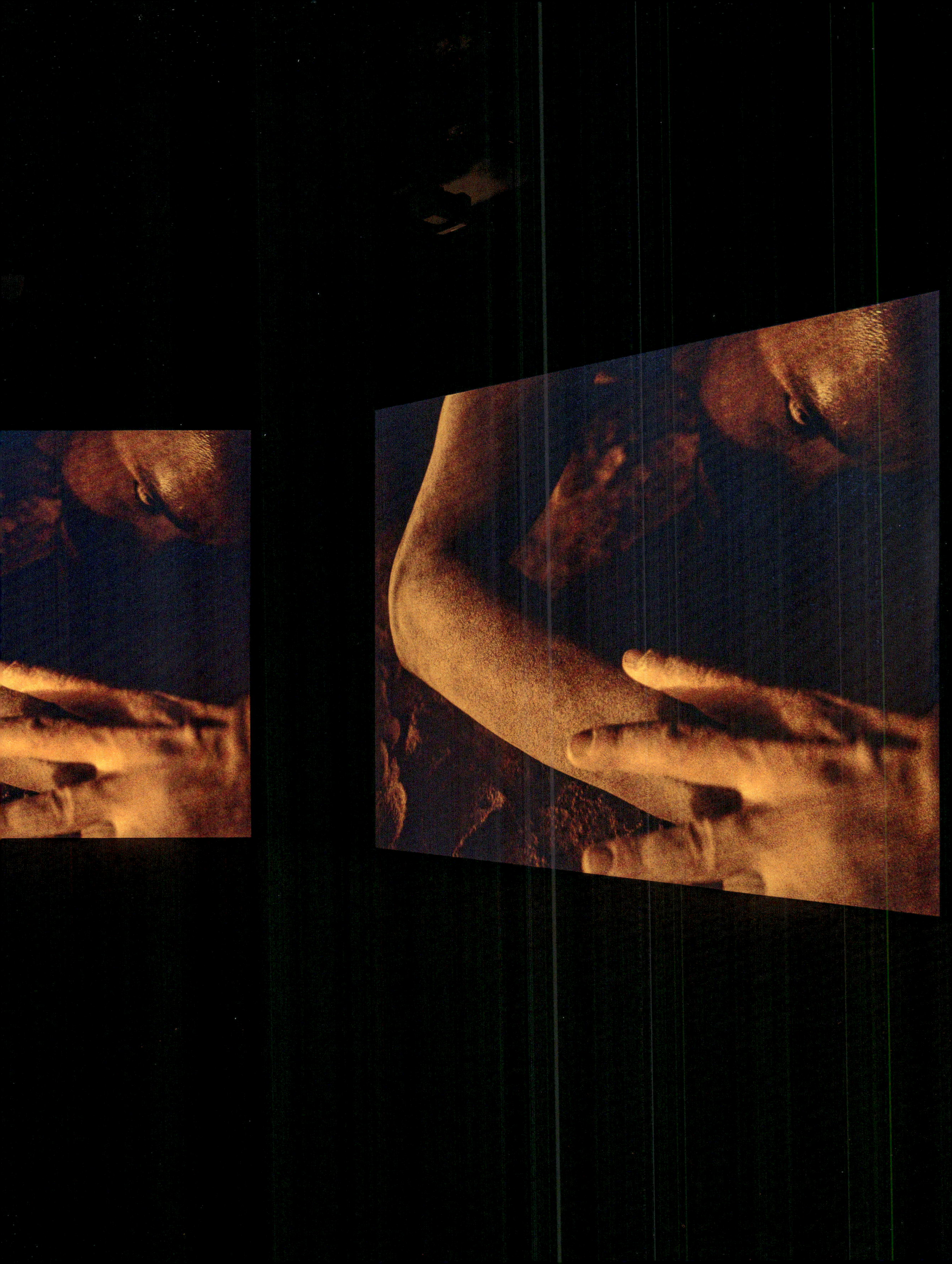

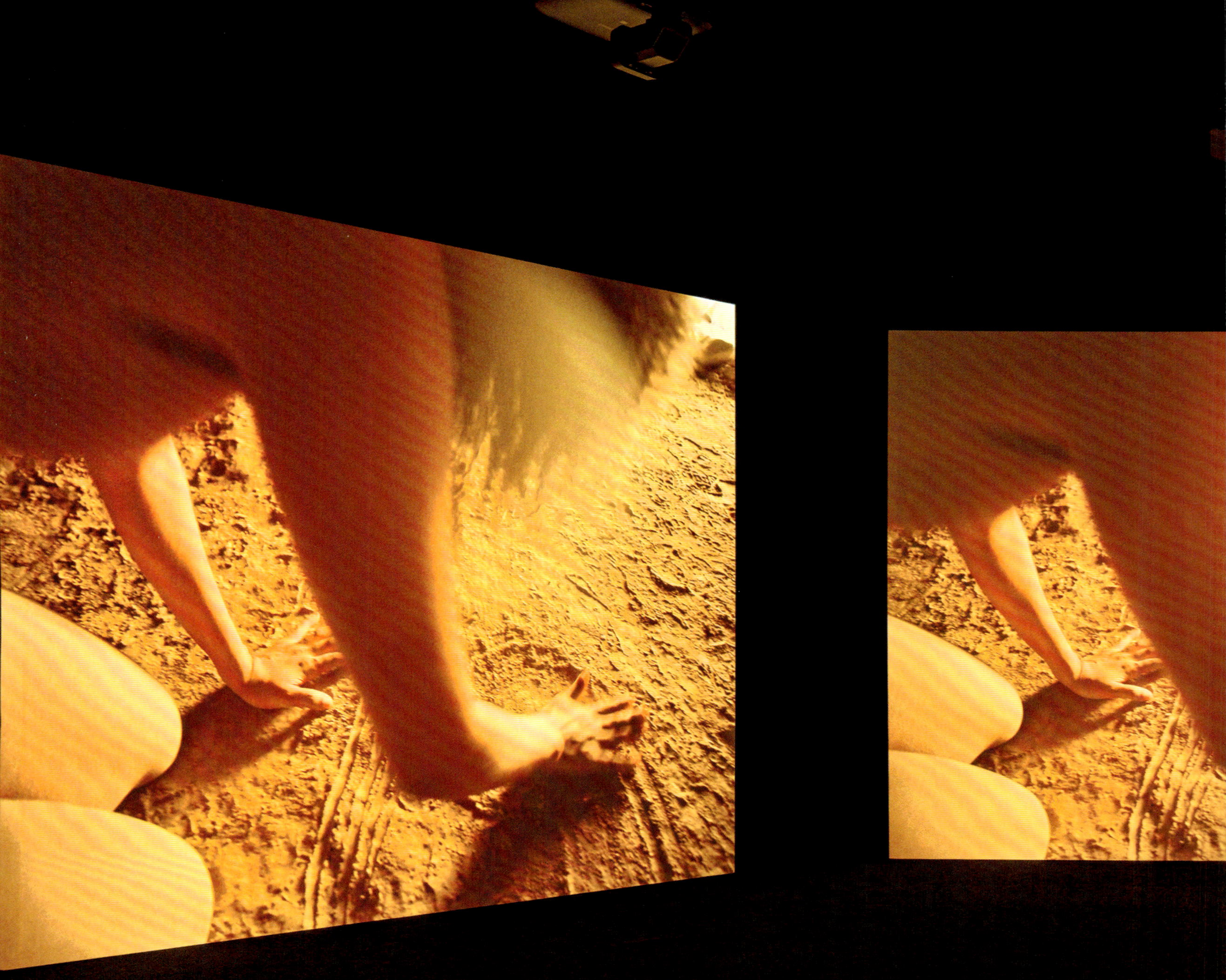

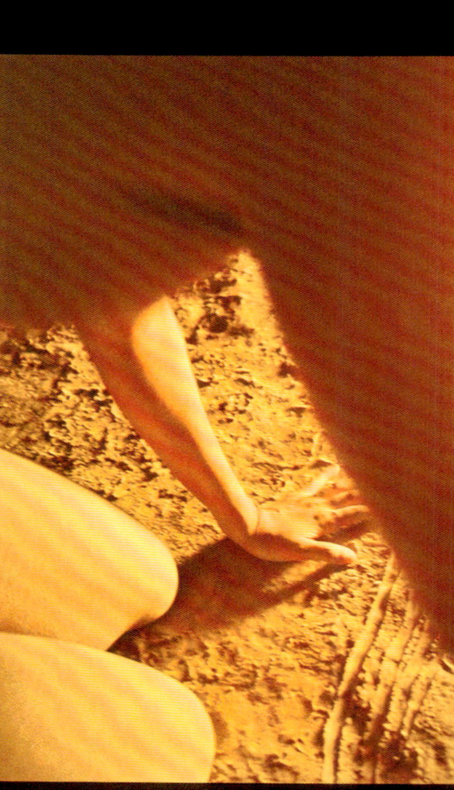

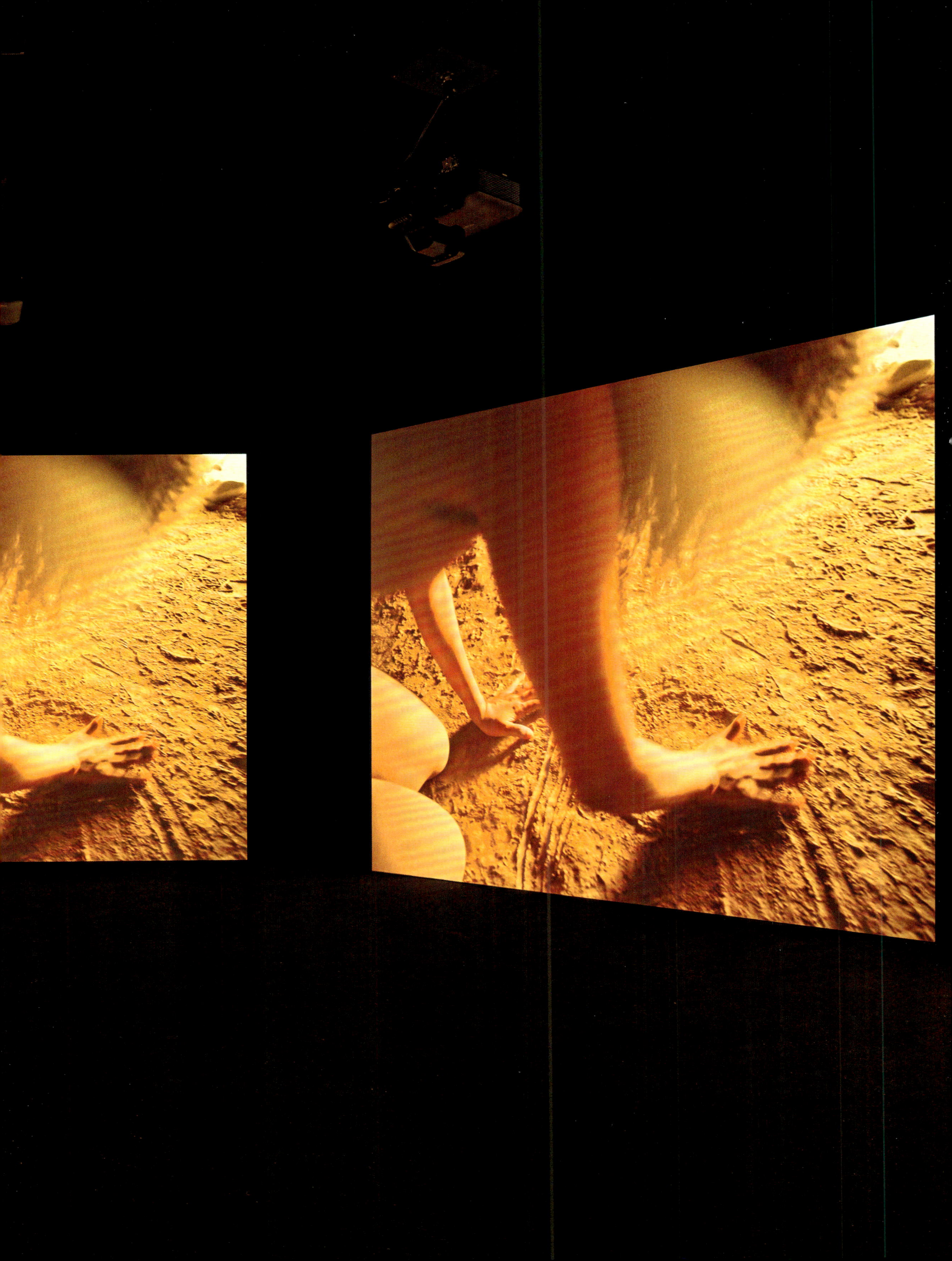

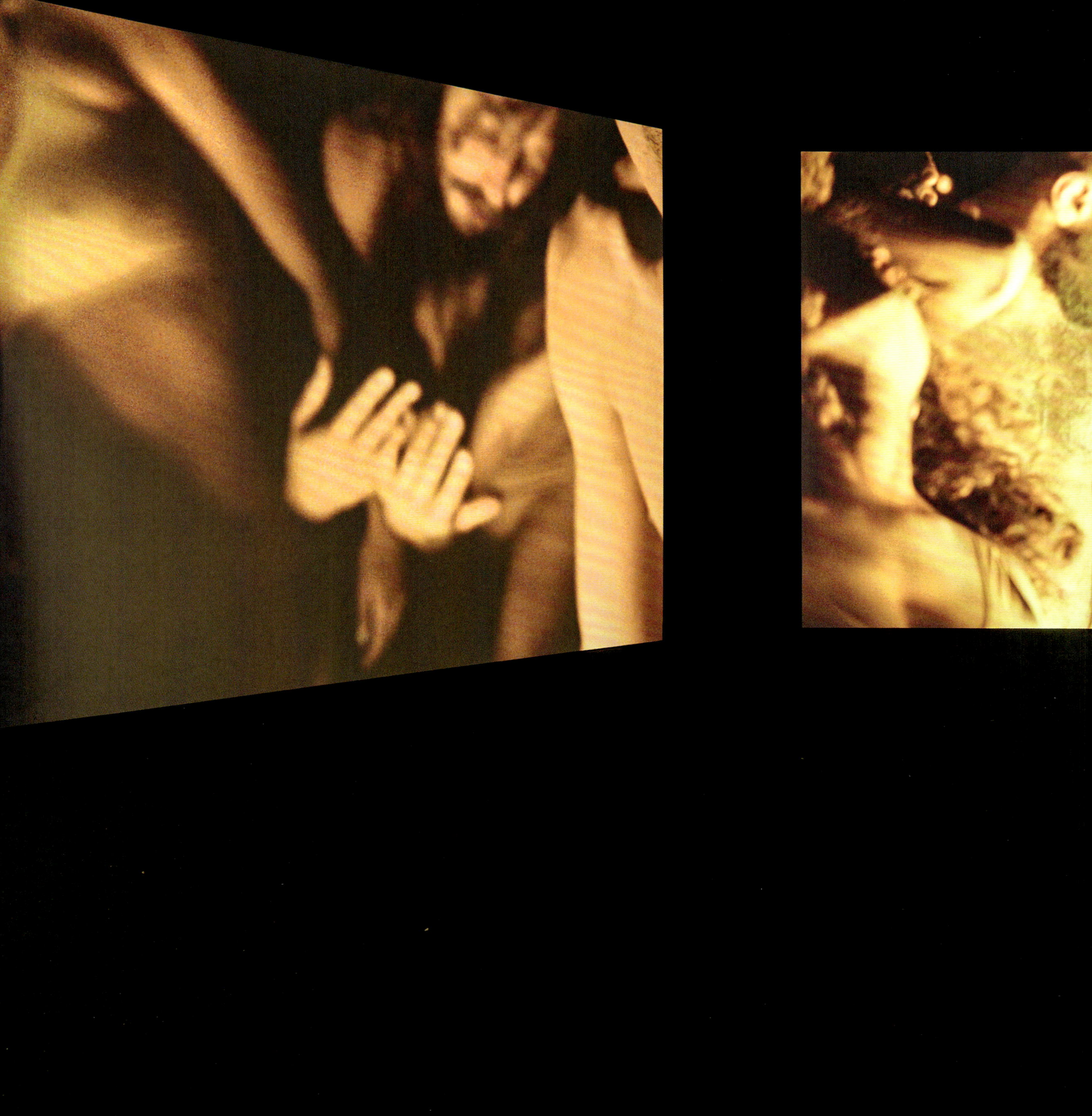

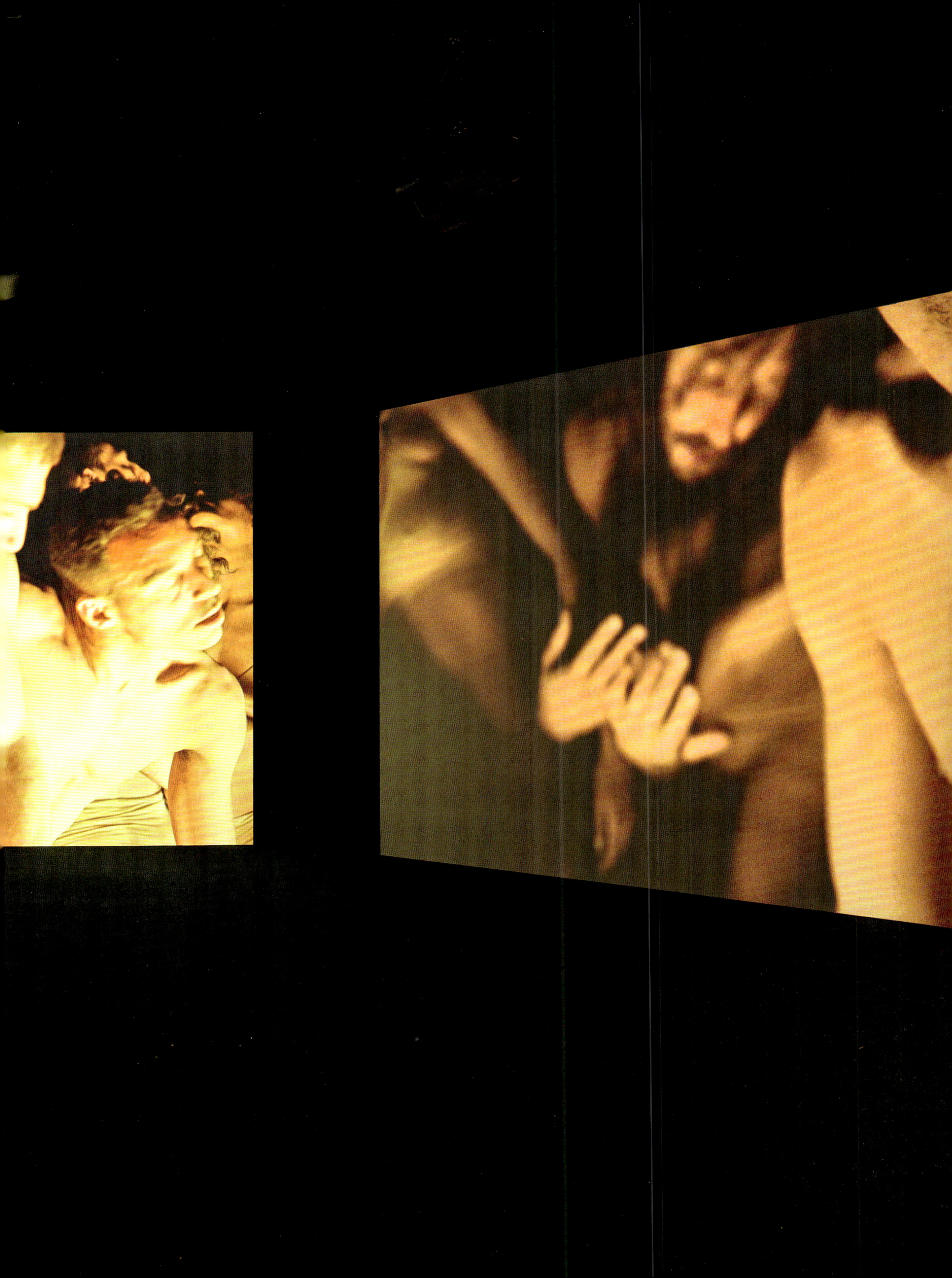

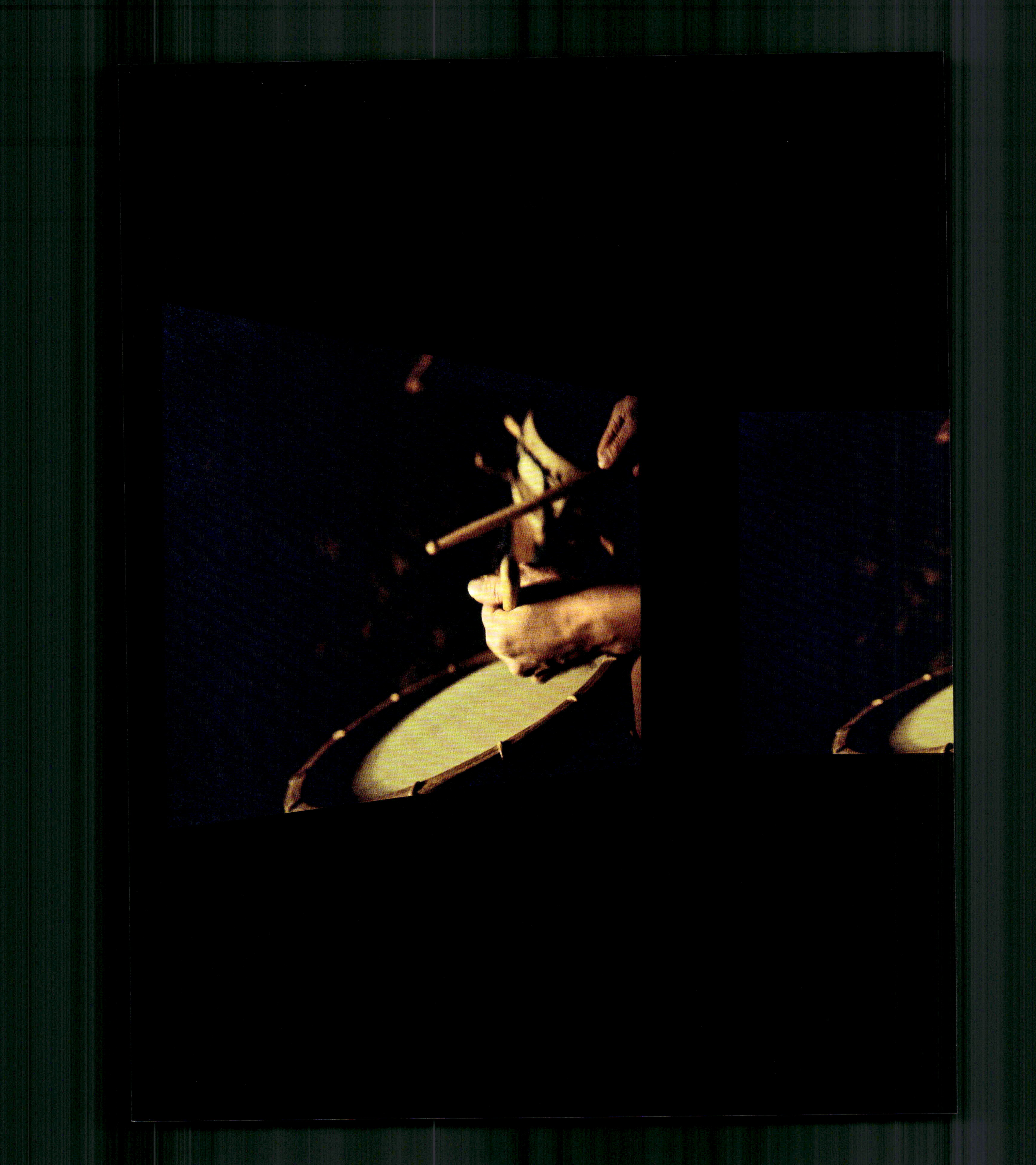

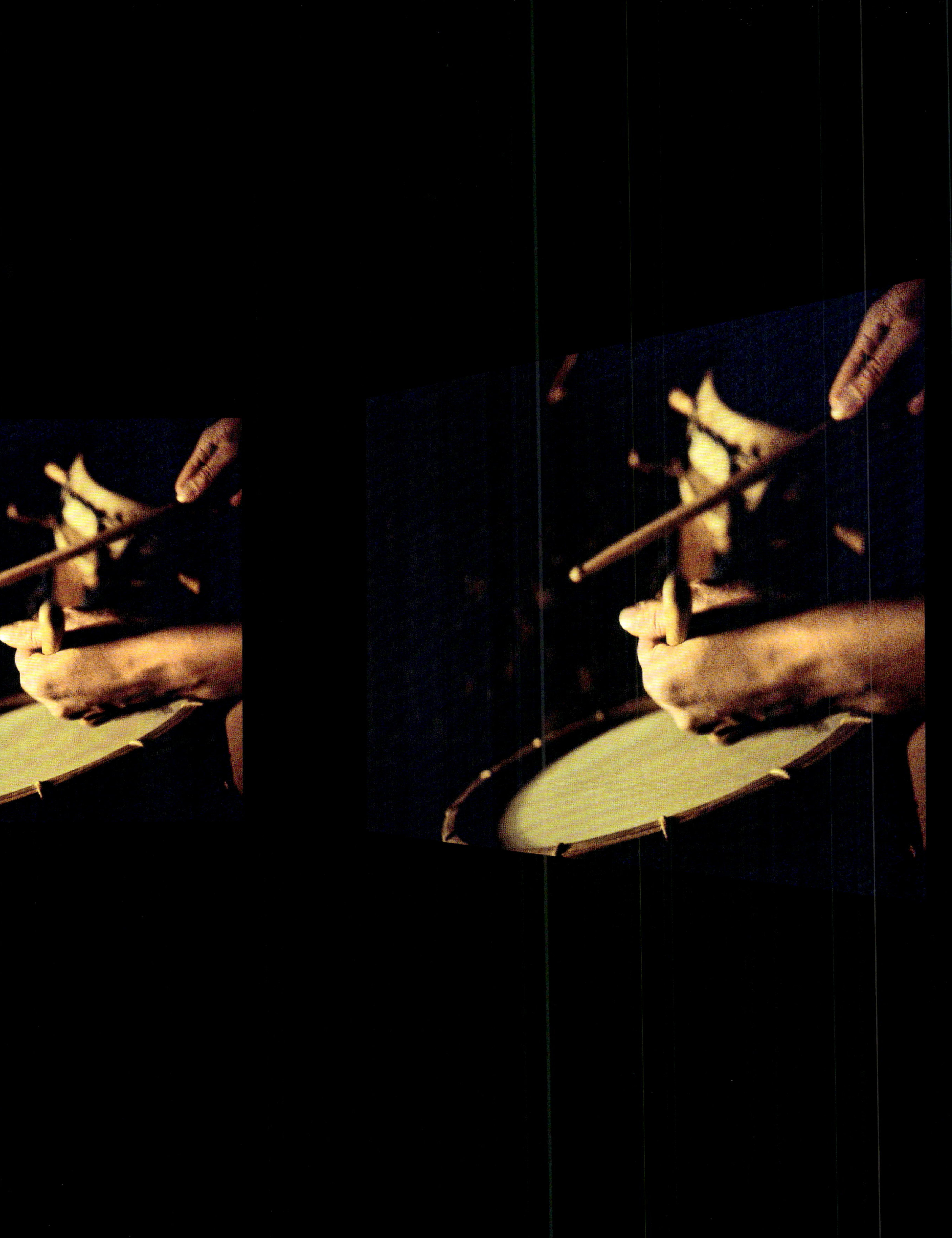

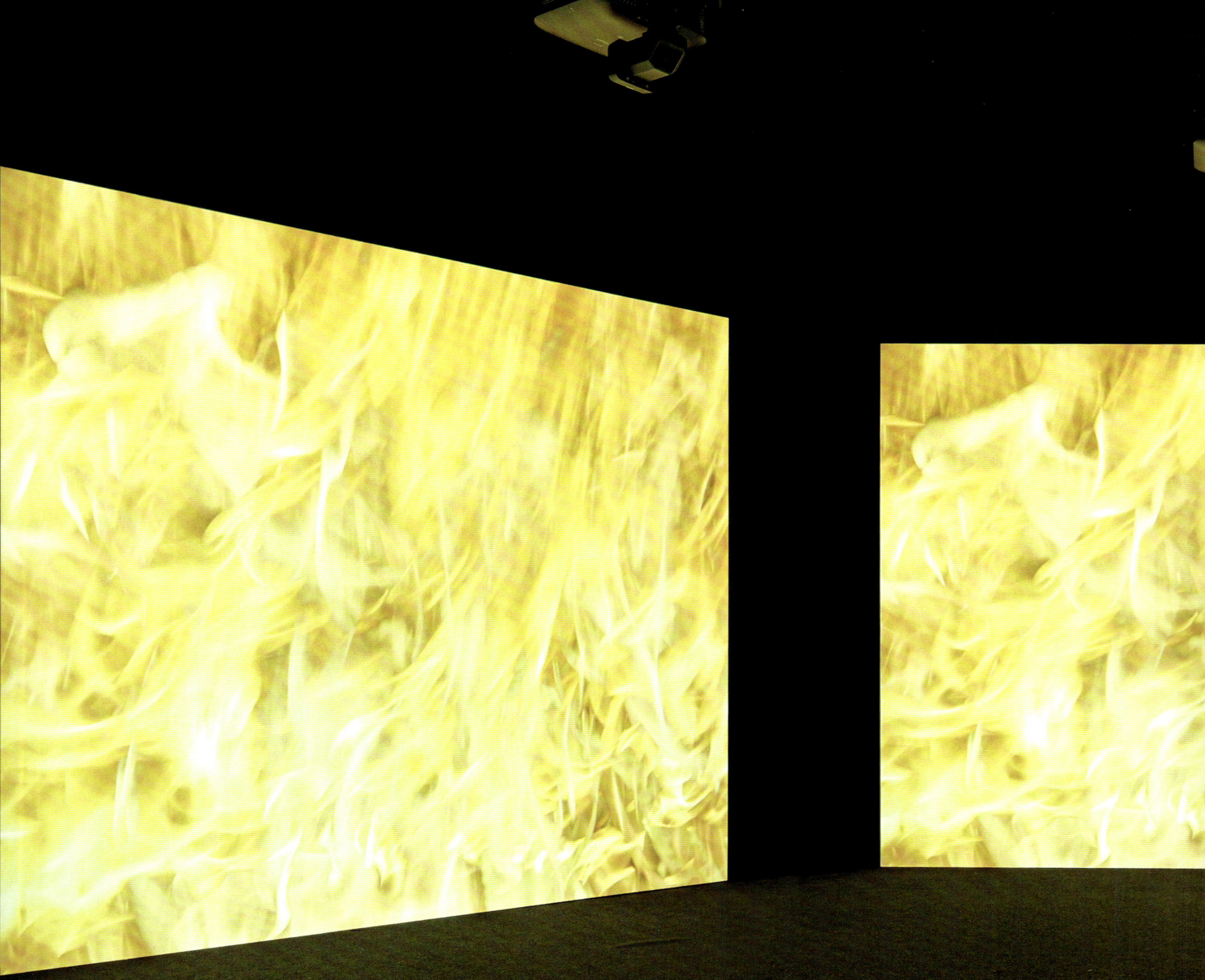

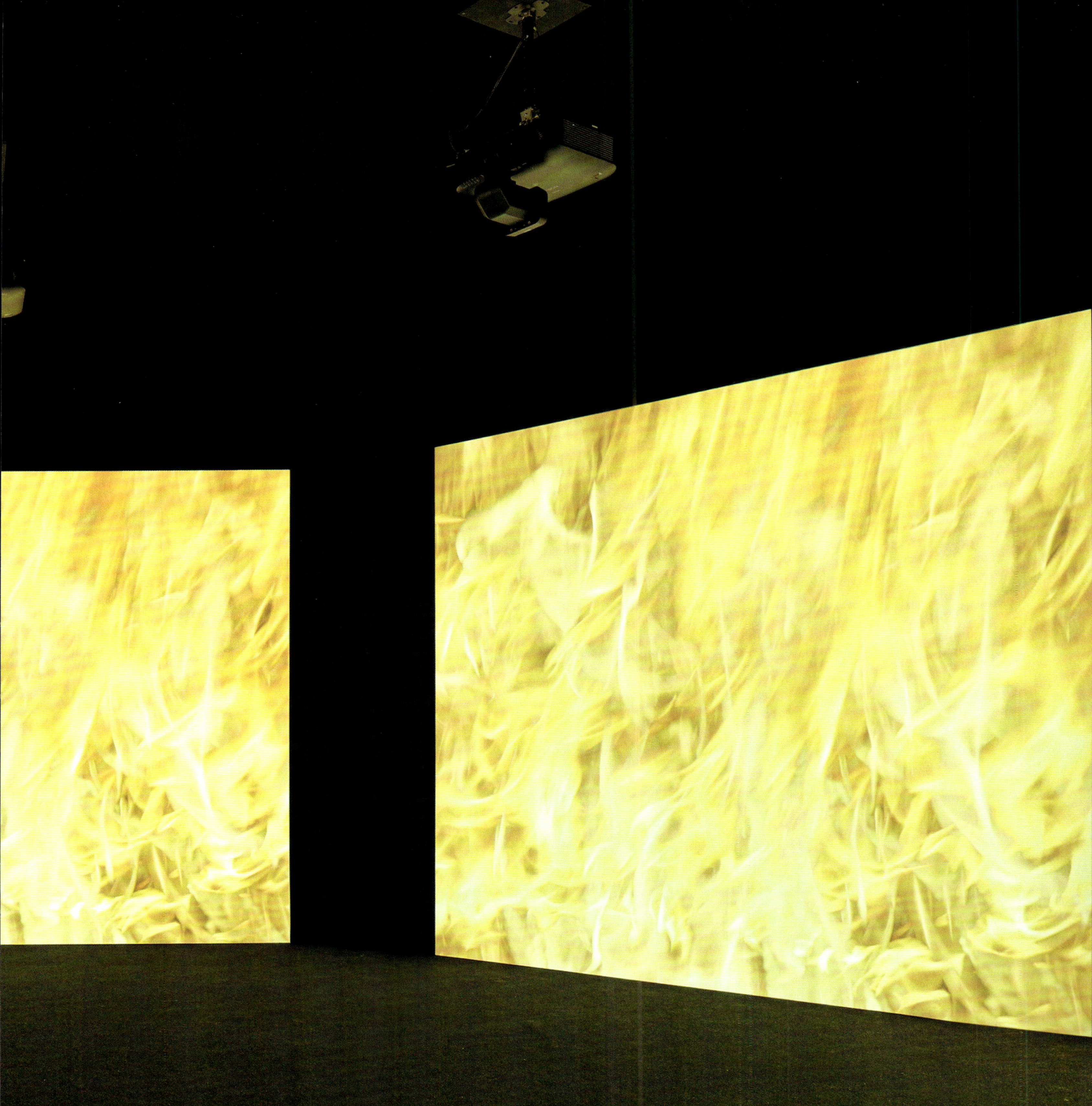

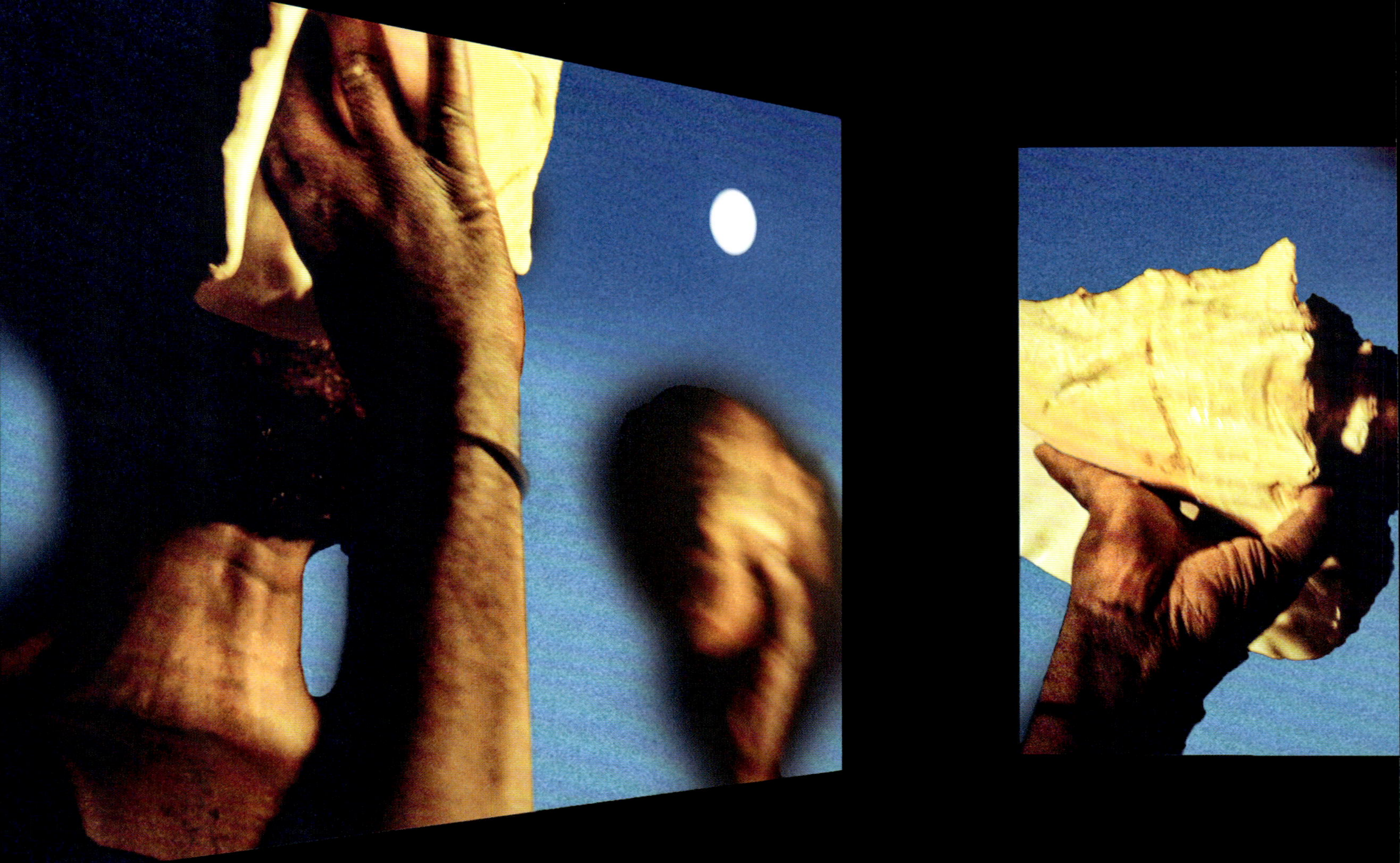

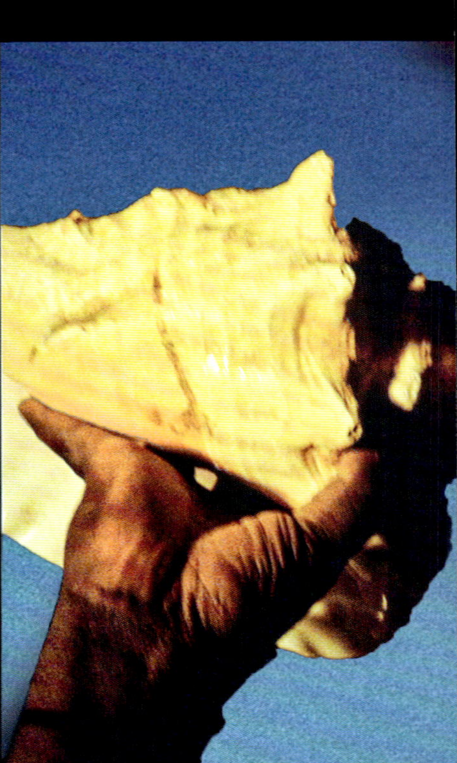

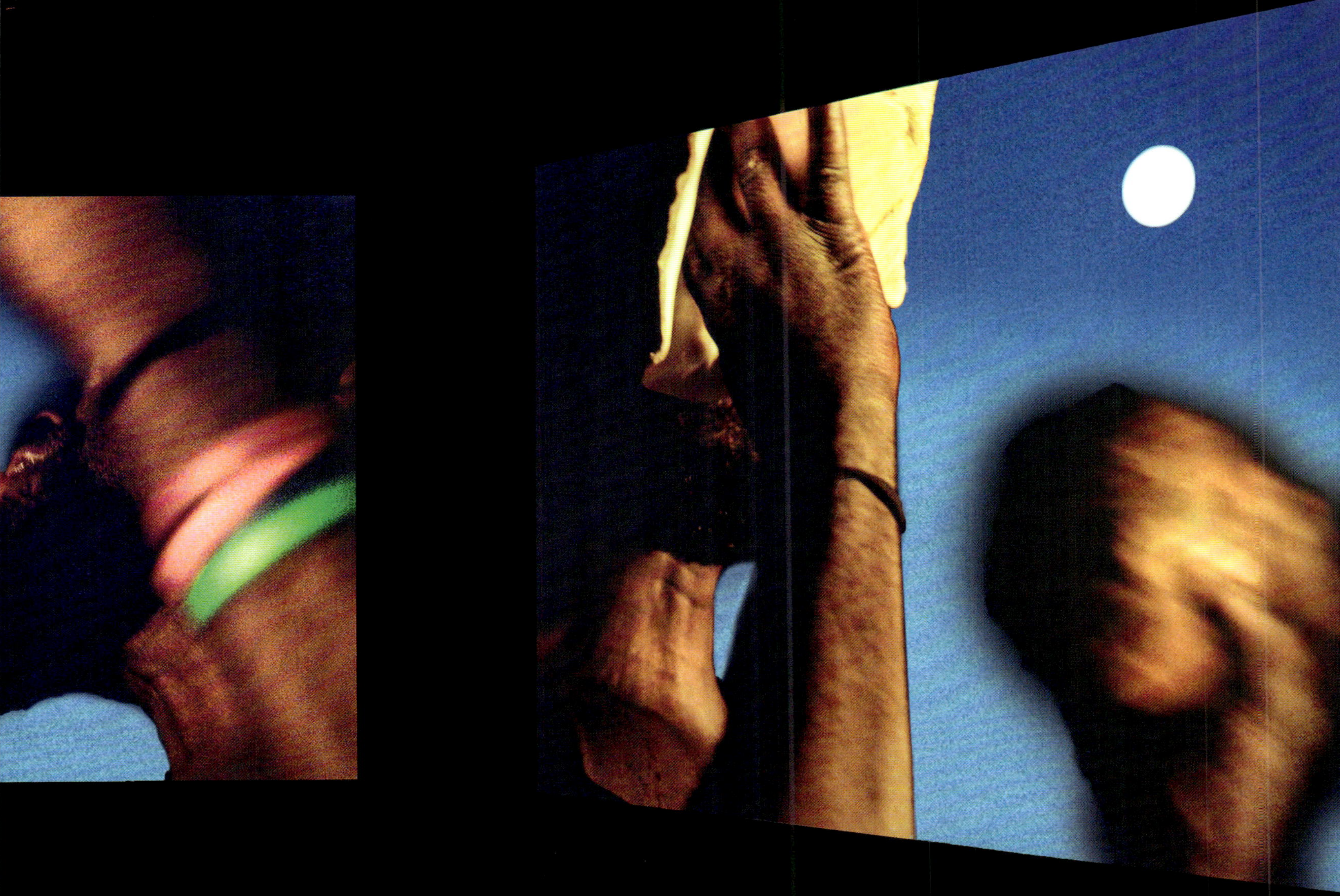

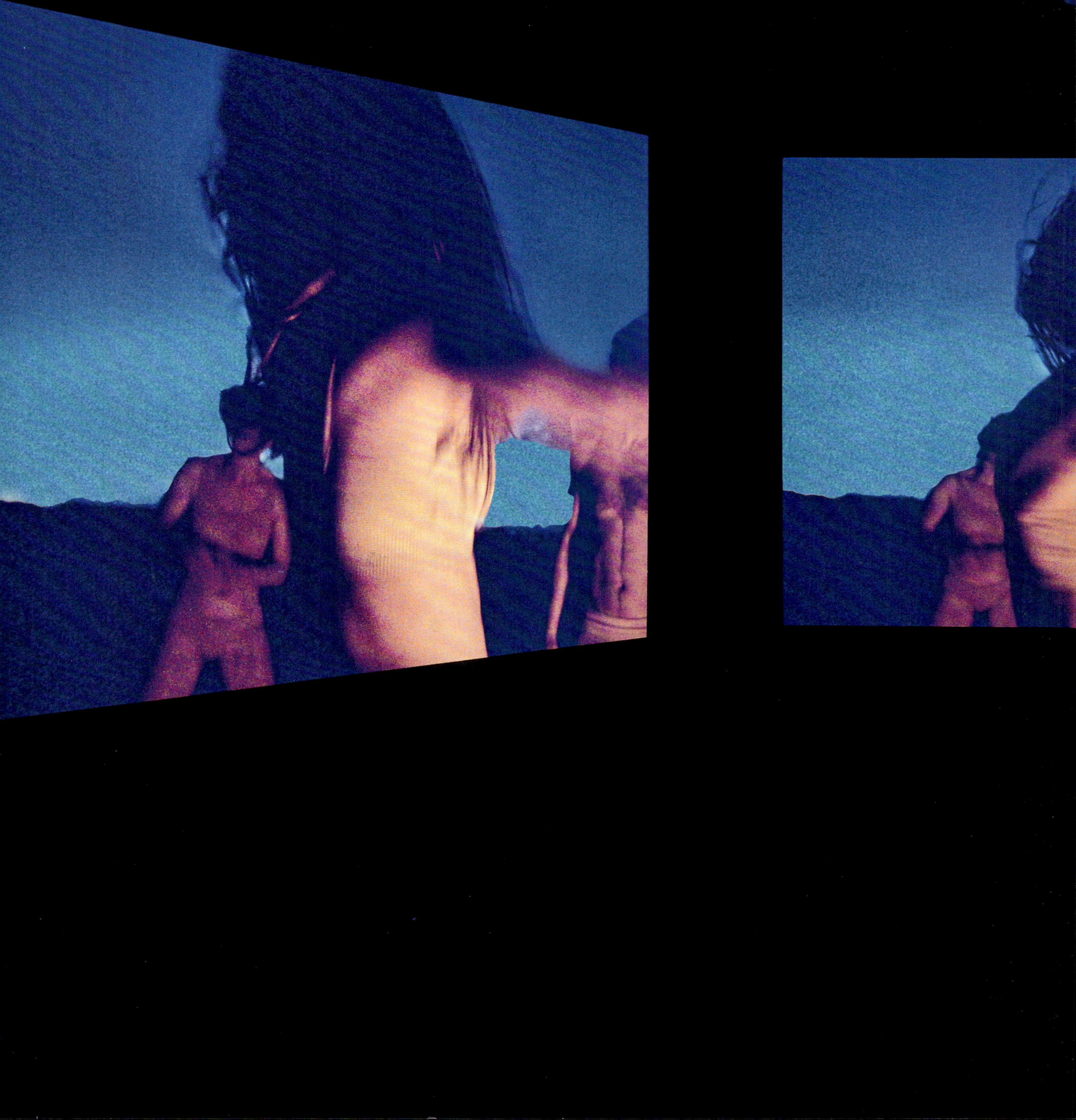

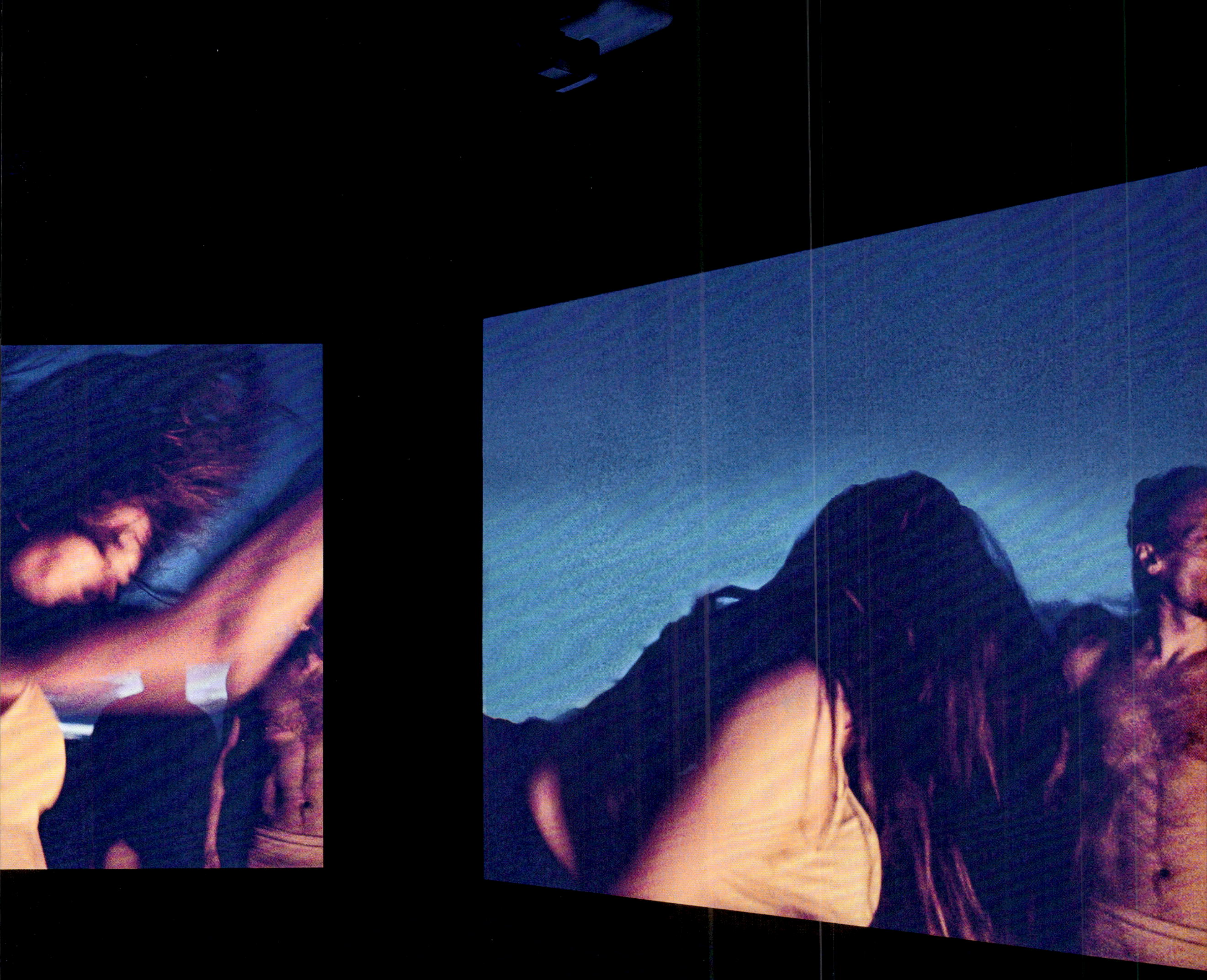

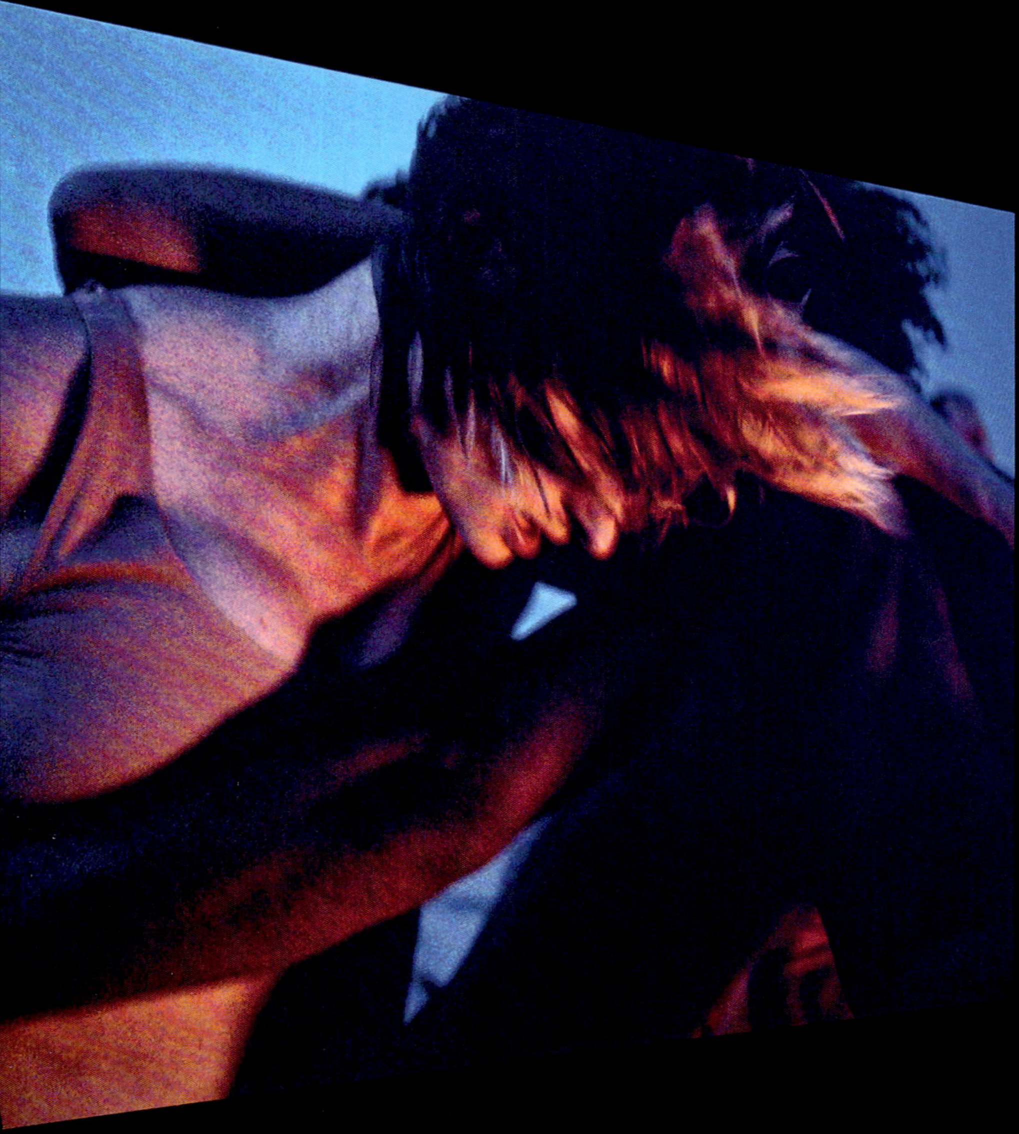

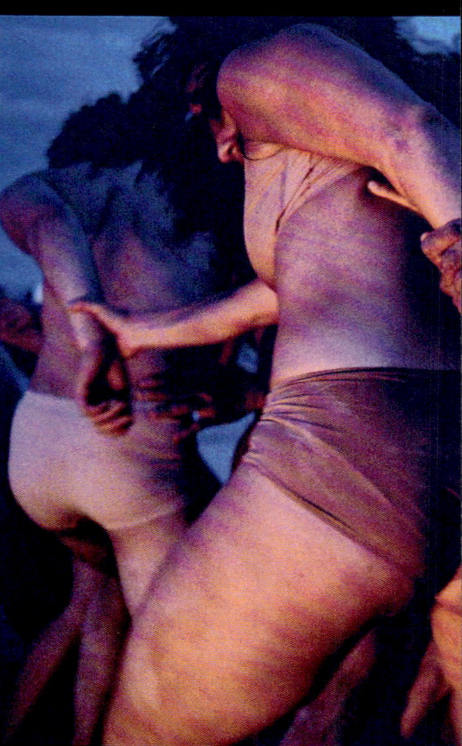

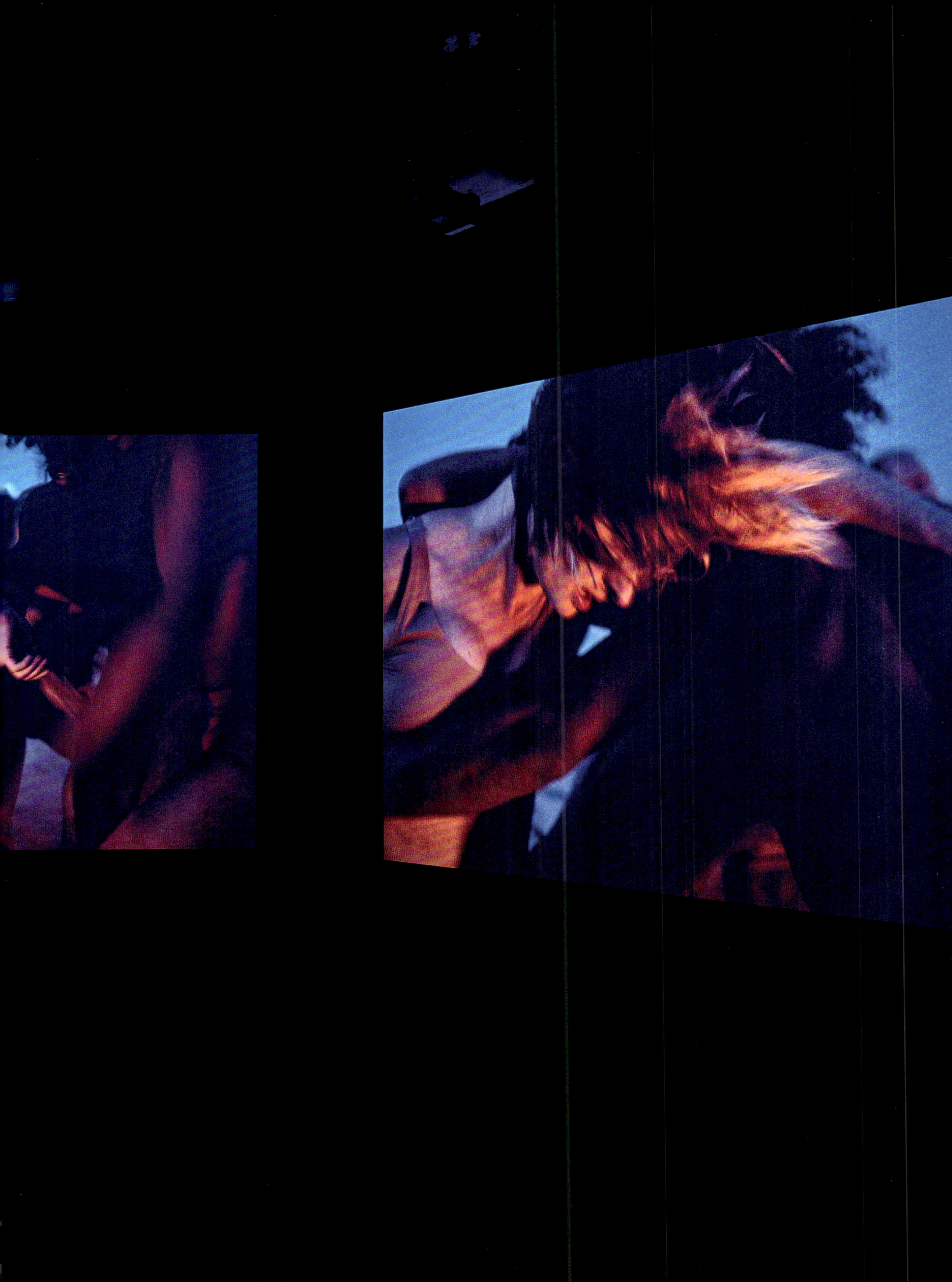

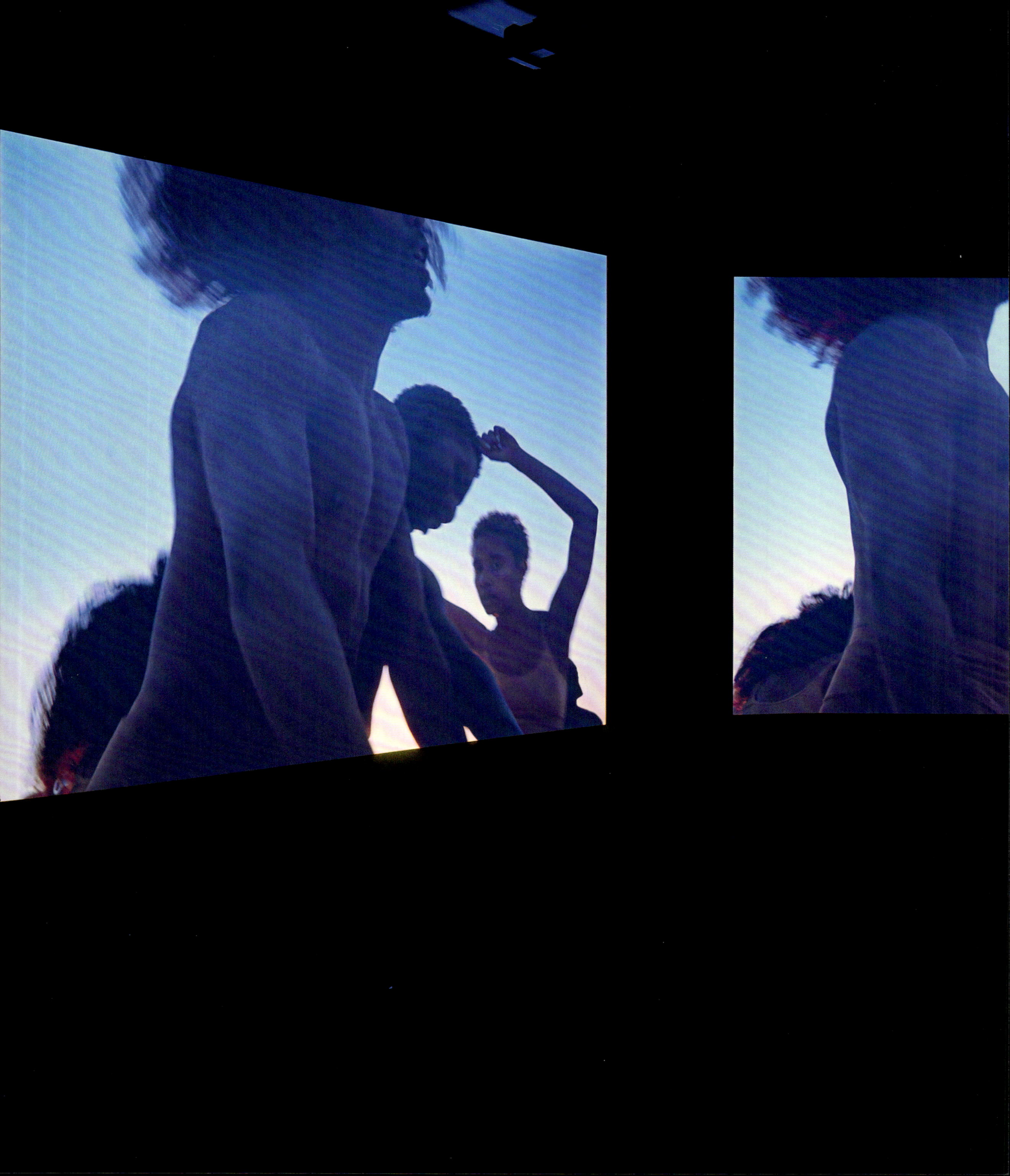

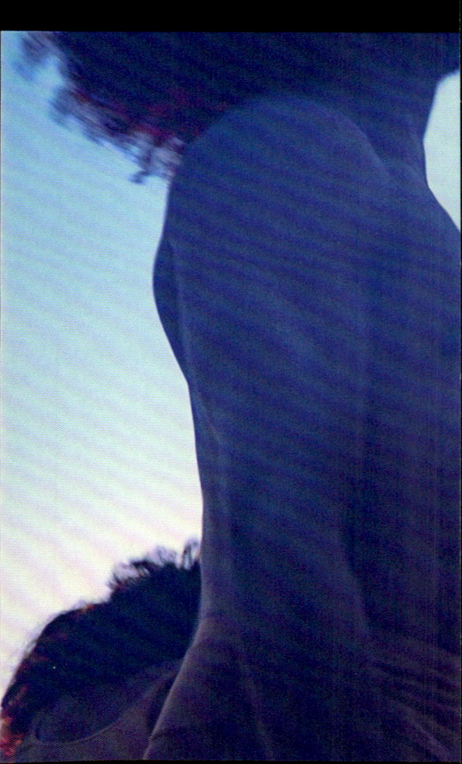

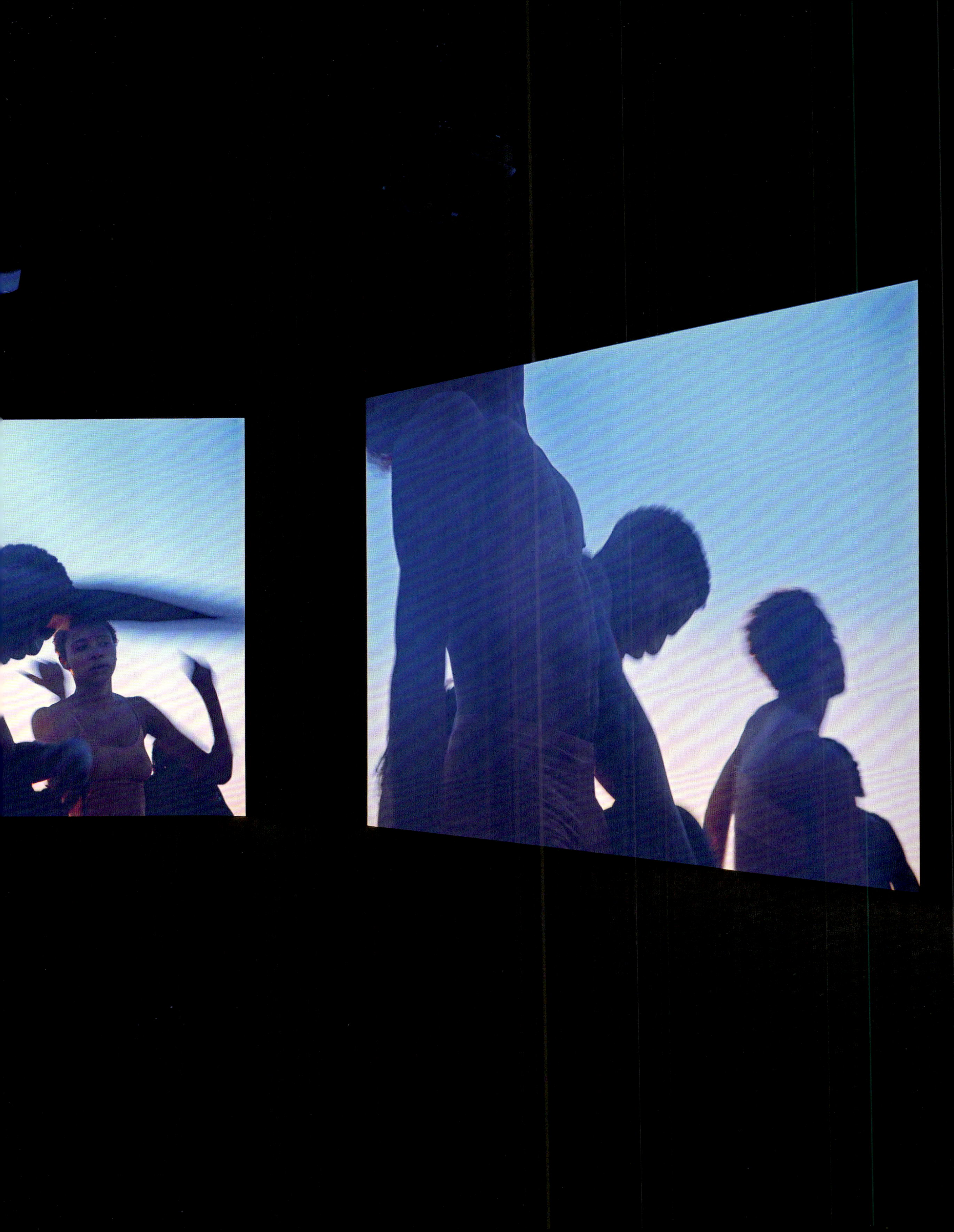

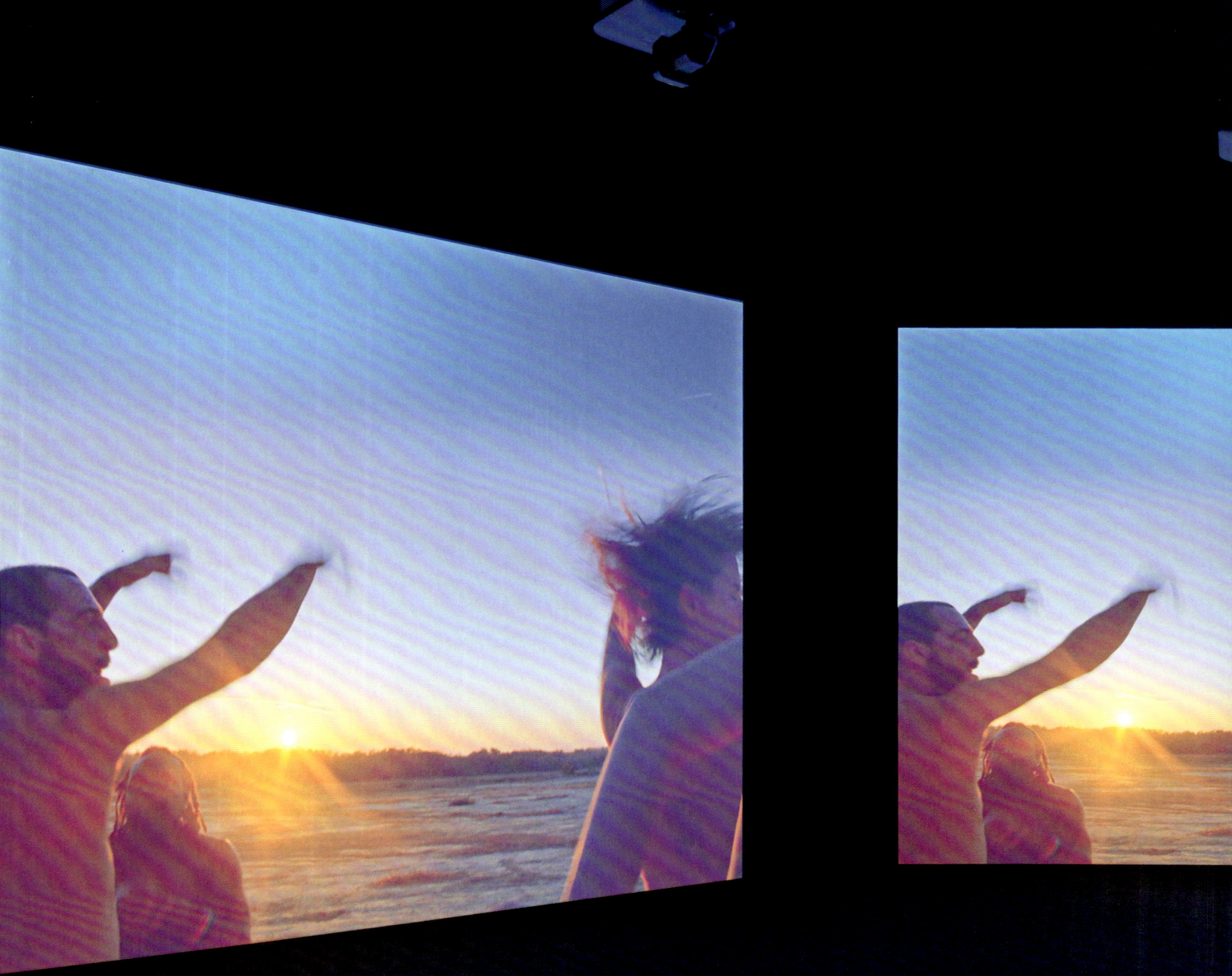

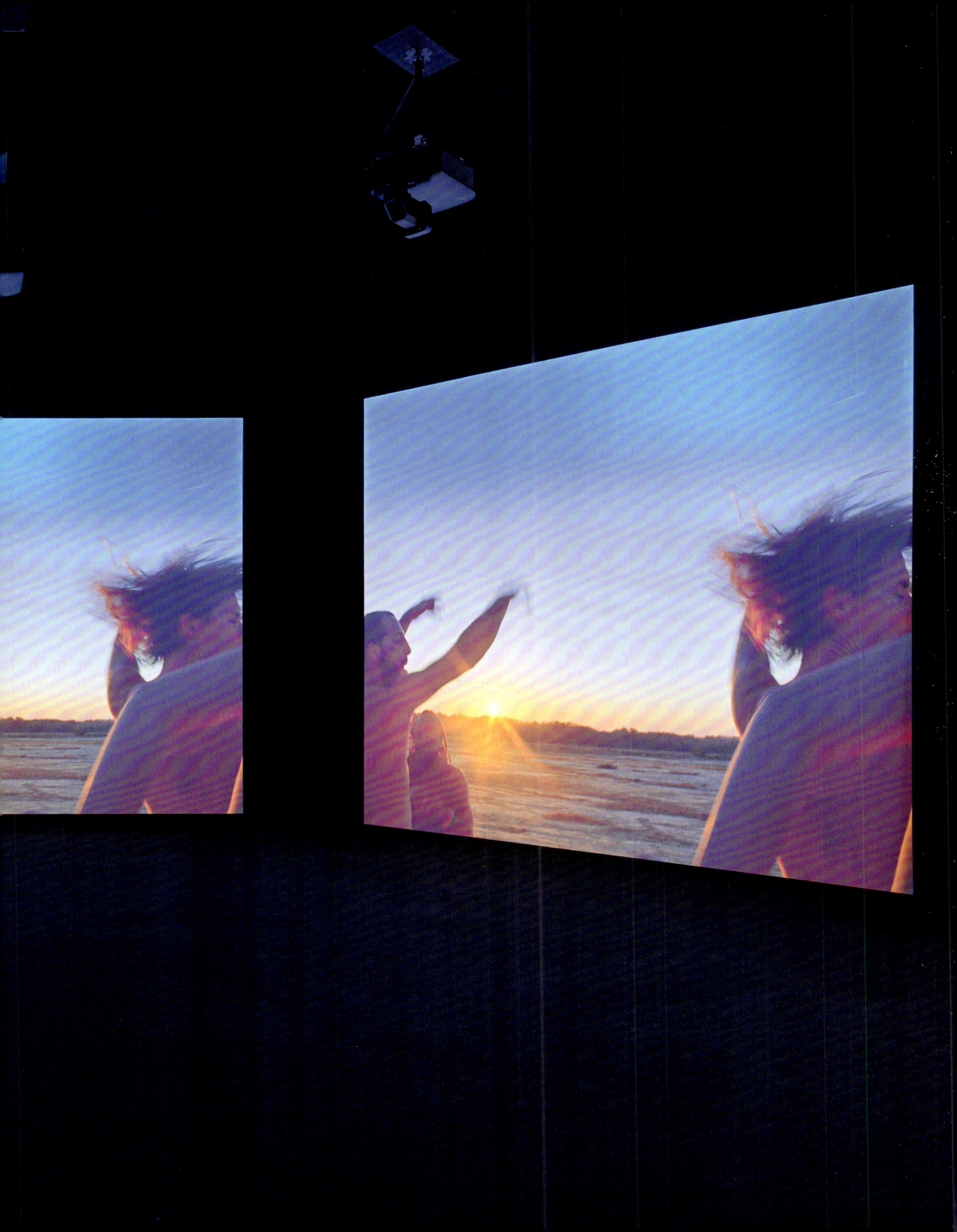

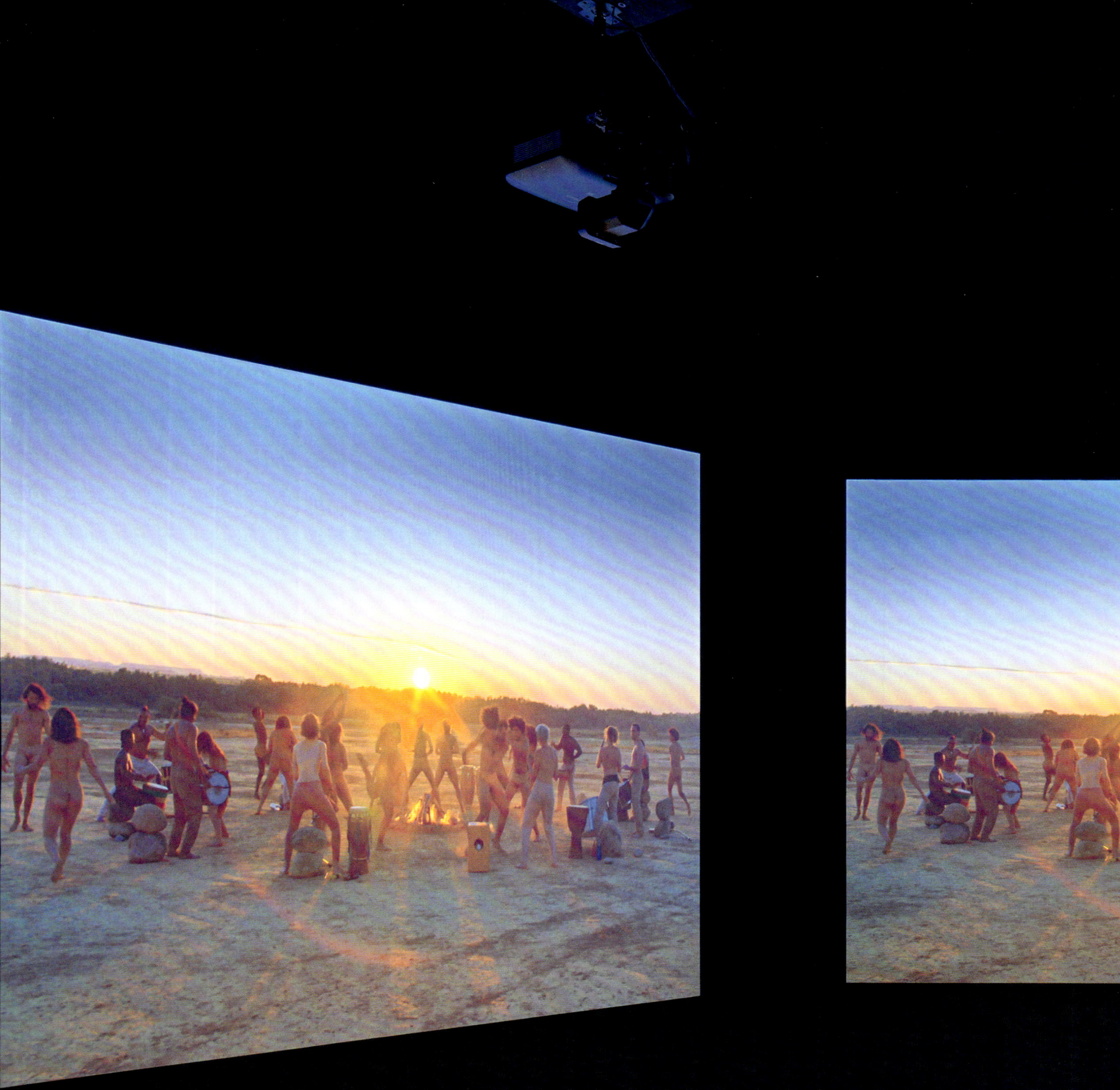

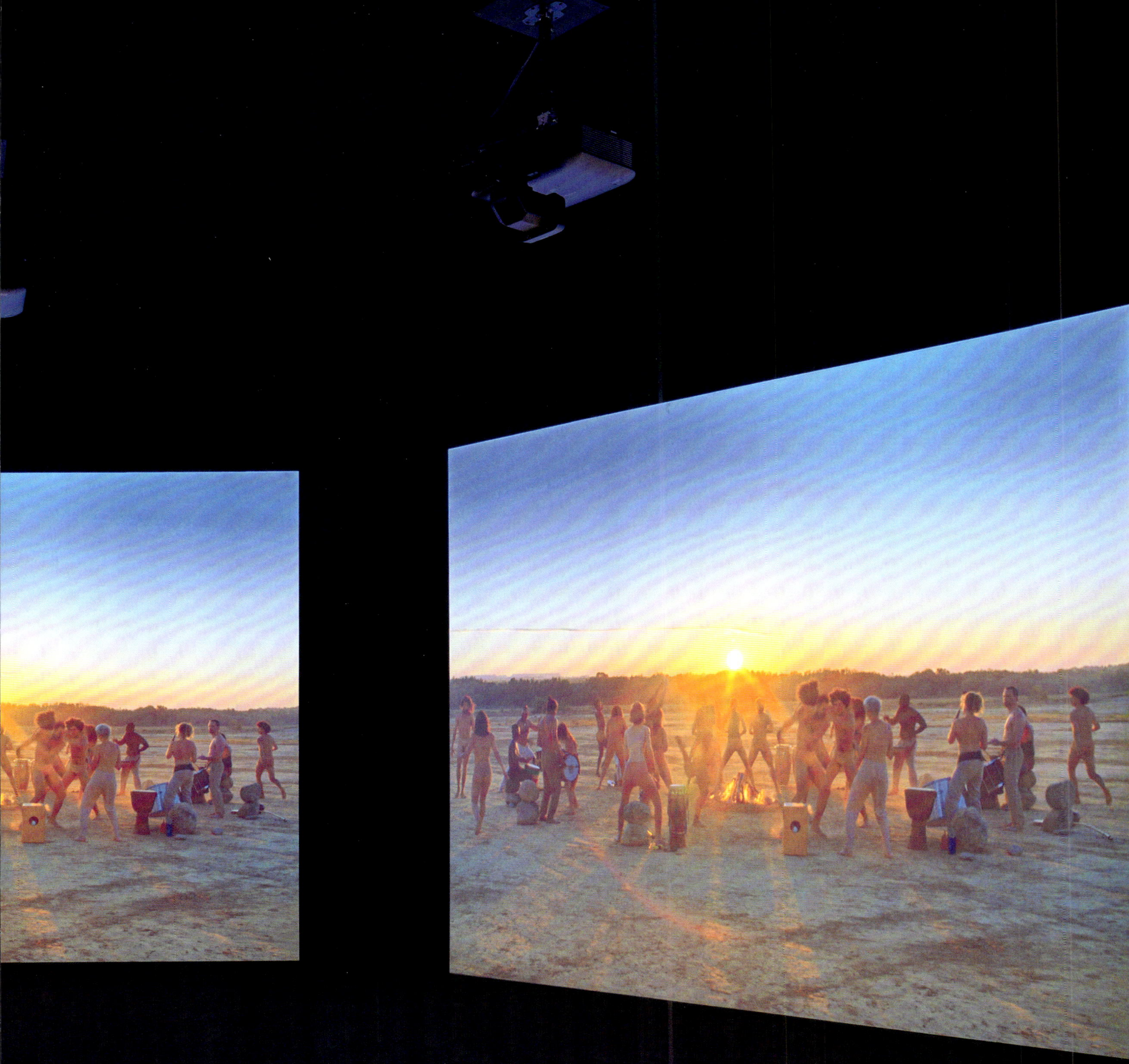

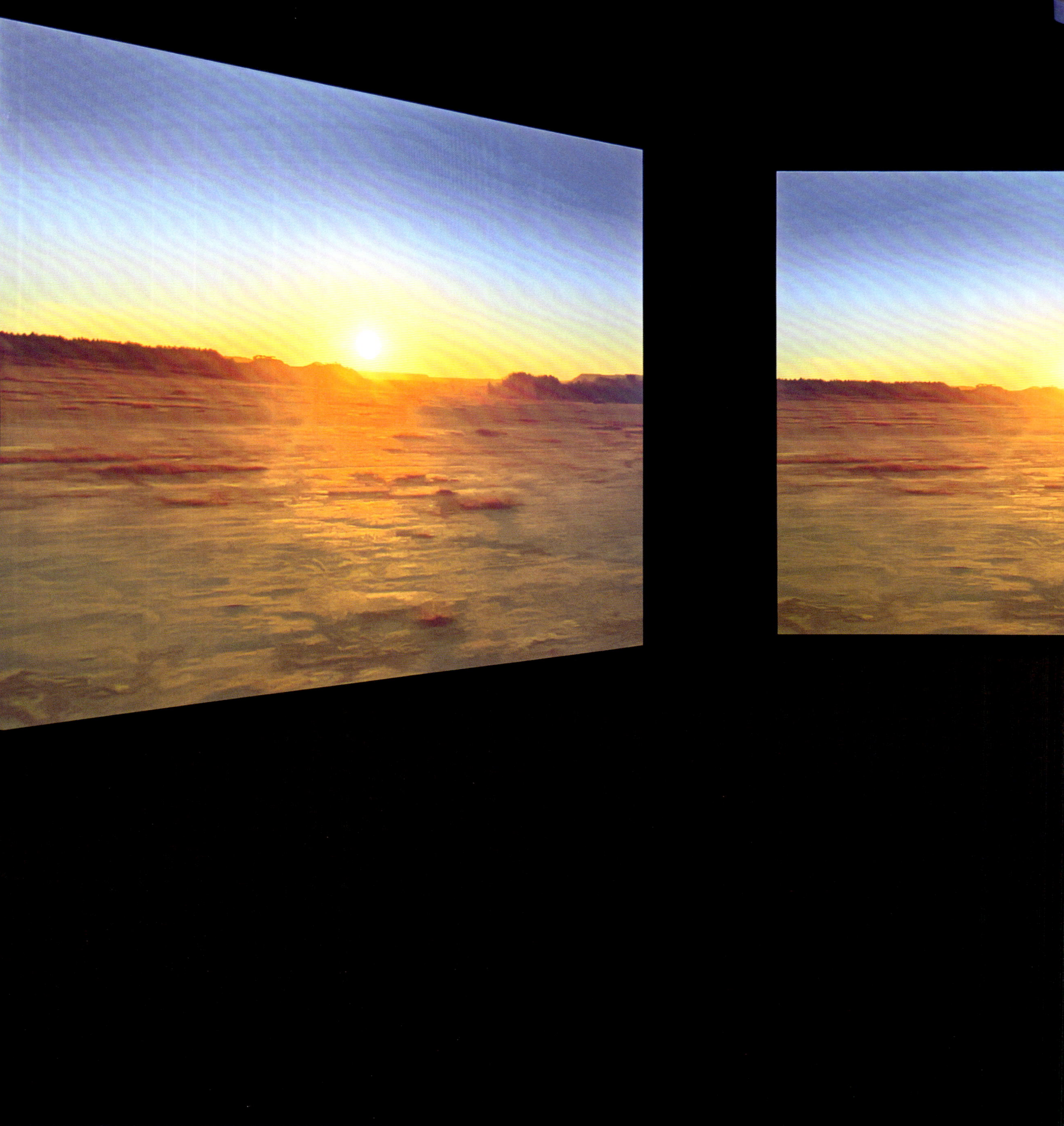

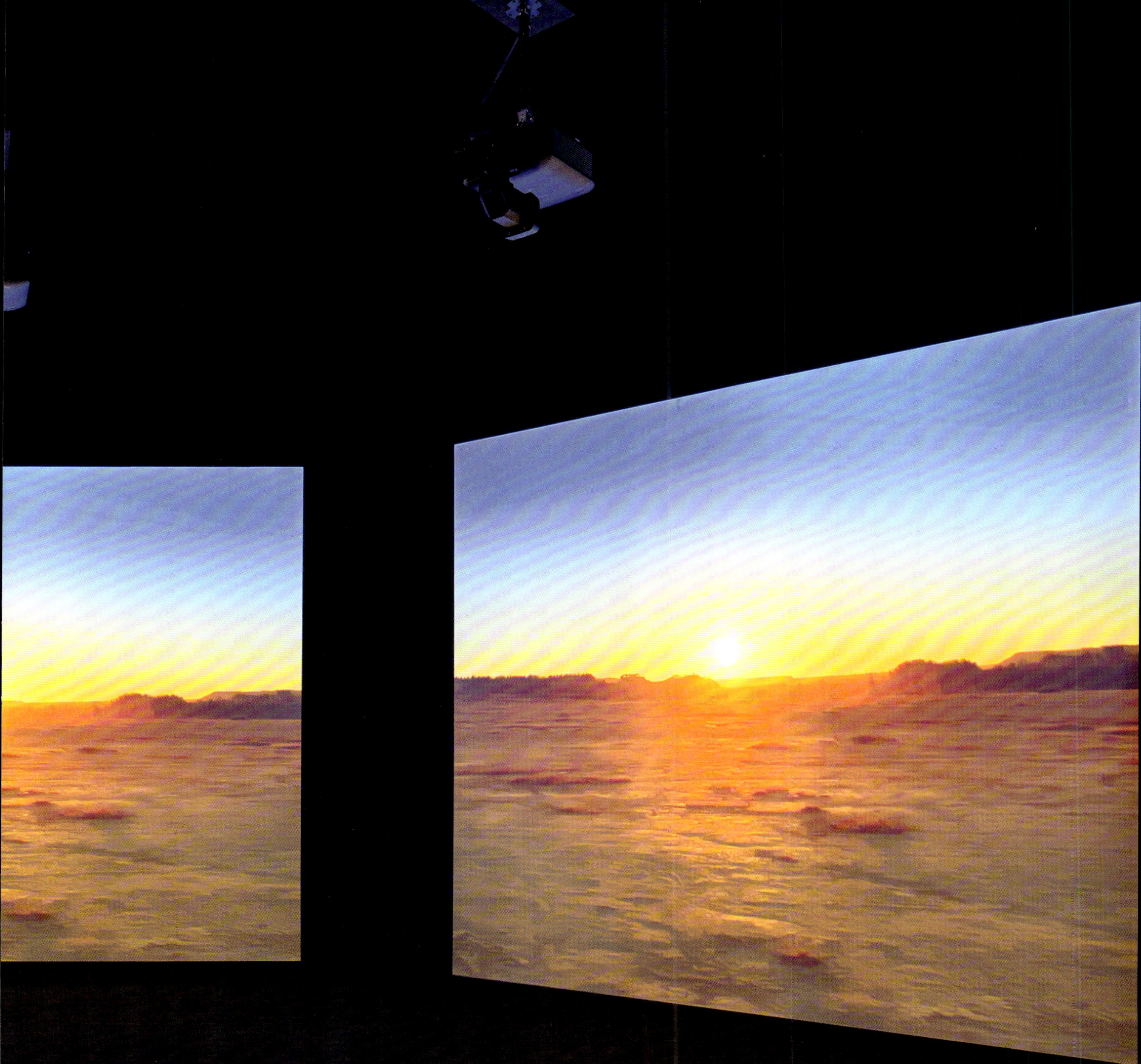

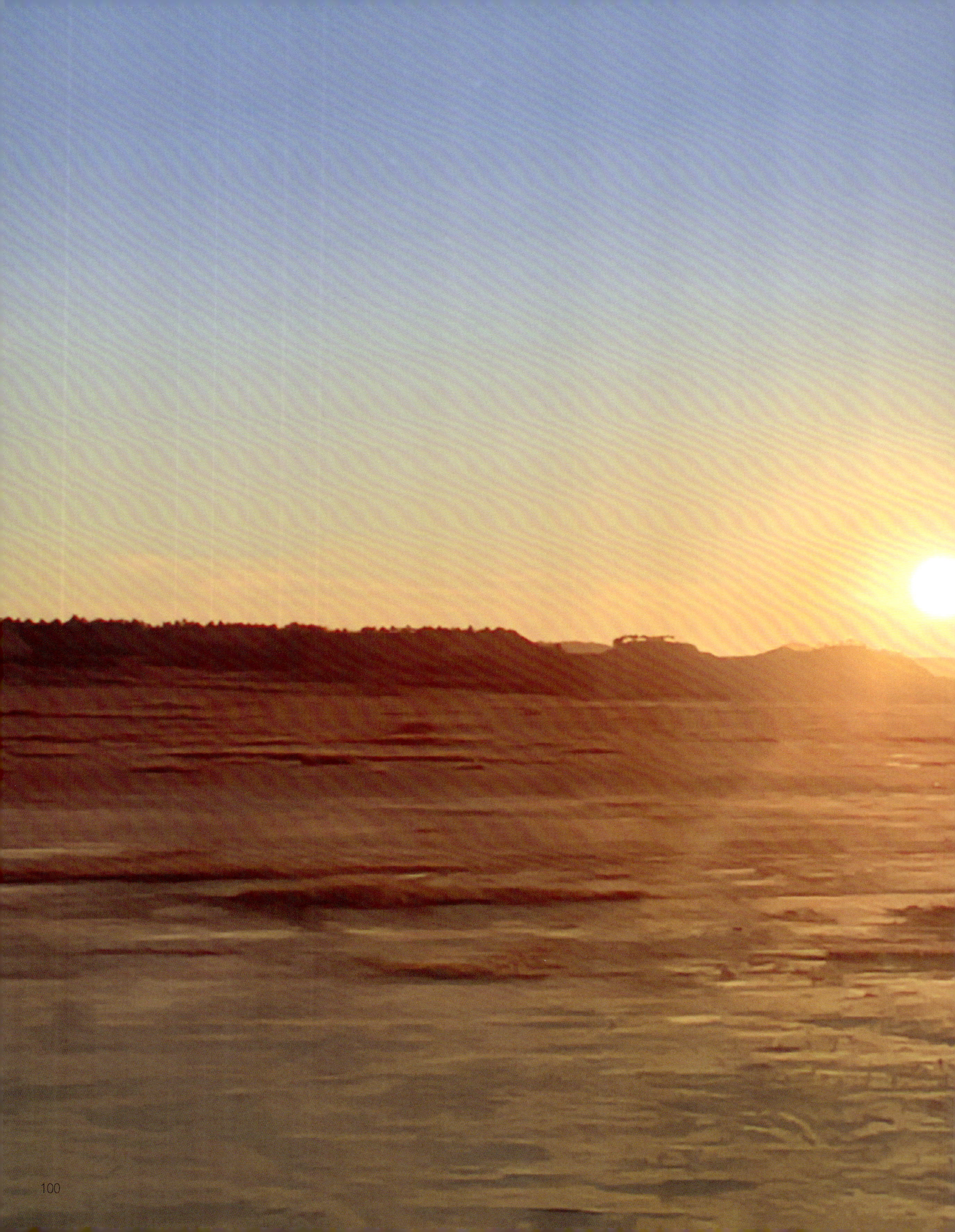

Every year the contemporary artists who exhibit their work at the Petit Palais renew the way visitors perceive the building and its collections. Ugo Rondinone's installation was masterfully integrated into the museum designed by architect Charles Girault for the 1900 Paris Exposition, and generated a fruitful dialogue with the collection's historic artworks.

To link his work with the city, Ugo Rondinone presented three colorful sculptures from his *nuns + monks* series at the bottom of the Petit Palais grand staircase. Their silhouettes evoked a crowd or a passageway between the profane and the sacred. Installed on the esplanade, the sculptures also acted as a beacon, inviting passersby to walk up the steps and enter the museum.

Inside, visitors discovered three bodies of work by Rondinone, each evoking different natural elements: air, water, earth, and fire. In the main rotunda, visitors were first greeted by *humansky*. The sculptures drew the eye up toward a graceful farandole illuminated by stained-glass windows made by the Champigneulle studio, and crowned by symbolist paintings by Albert Besnard. Rondinone's celestial beings gravitated around the *Gloria Victis* (1875), a winged glory figure which Antonin Mercié made in honor of France after the 1870 defeat. It was inspired by both the *Victory of Samothrace* and Raphael's *Saint Michel Terrassant le dragon*.

The artist applied filters on the sulpture hall windows to dim the light, thus distancing the Petit Palais's surroundings. With this intervention titled *when the sun goes down and the moon comes up*, Rondinone conveyed the impression of time slowing down, and altered the exhibition space perception.

The second ensemble was made up of wax sculptures realized from casts of dancers' bodies at rest, assembled to reveal caesuras and differences in hue. The artist placed his nudes on the floor and spread them throughout the museum's plaster sculptures, such as *La Défense de Paris* (1880) by Louis Ernest Barrias, *Monnaie de singe* (1882) by François-Laurent Rolard, or *La danseuse Sacha-Lyo* (1933, COARC deposit) by Serge Youriévitch. Also marked by irregularly hued seams and patinas, these plasters entered into a delicate dialogue with Ugo Rondinone's *nudes*.

A black cylinder stood out in the north rotunda, visible from the entrance. Monolithic, it reached up to the ceiling, assertively imposing its silhouette, and breaking the symmetry conceived by the architect between the north and south wings of the museum. This installation was framed by four paintings from Eugène Carrière's last unfinished great ensemble titled *Ages of Life* (1897–1900), which was commissioned for the city hall of the 8th district of Paris. The paintings' dark hues echoed both the earthy tones of four wax nudes seated beneath each of them, and the charcoal of the cylinder. Entering through a concealed door, visitors were immersed in semi-darkness in which they discovered Rondinone's latest film installation: *burn to shine*. Surrounded by images, visitors found themselves on the same level as a group of dancers caught up in a wild circle choreographed by Fouad Boussouf. Presented as a world premiere in the exhibition, *burn to shine* was reproduced on the poster on the museum's facade, extending the force of its vital and spiritual radiance over and beyond the entire museum.

Juliette Singer

Translated from French by Alix de La Chapelle

the water is a poem
unwritten by the air
no. the earth is a poem
unwritten by the fire

Ugo Rondinone's exhibition at the Petit Palais comprises two ensembles of works enhanced by a new video installation. Revolving around human bodies in contact with the elements and nature, these works are in keeping with the multiple families of works produced by the artist since the late 1980s. Earth, sky, air, water, and fire, associated with beings at rest or in movement, are invoked in the fullness of their spiritual dimension.

The first ensemble, *humansky*, welcomes visitors and immediately underlines the melding of being and the elements: seven molded, suspended bodies embellished with a blue cloud-dotted sky "camouflage" confronting visitors with water and air.

The second group, historically the source of this trilogy, consists of *nudes*. Made from a blend of transparent wax and earth collected from seven continents, these sculptures also have a "camouflaged" look stemming from the mixing of their non-homogeneous components. They depict the bodies of male and female dancers seated and at rest. Created on a human scale, these nudes seem realistic at first, until the visitor, coming closer, discovers their clearly artificial aspect, particularly visible at the junction of their limbs with their bodies. These sculptures are thus "paradoxical" in their compliance with the Rondinone aesthetic: he plays on the "opposition" between what is expected of a dancer, and the pose he makes each one assume. Banishing any choreographed gesture and any reference to the stage space, these motionless, withdrawn bodies seem to have become one with nature, intensely concentrated and lost in a meditative state.

From one ensemble to the next visitors witness a process of bodies in mutation: moving from the ethereal suspension of *humansky* to the quasi-lethargy of the *nudes*, the bodies are "reborn" in the film *burn to shine*, whose presentation at the Petit Palais is a world premiere. The film is projected onto six screens inside a cylindrical space made of charred wood and forming a circle, a recurring geometric figure for the artist.

The body is in movement here: 12 percussionists and 18 male and female dancers are gathered around a fire in the desert. Combining an ancestral trance from the Maghreb with the gestures of a contemporary dance conceived with the help of Franco-Moroccan choreographer Fouad Boussouf, they unite with nature from sunset until dawn, when the sun rises again.

The cylinder's wooden slats exclude any view of the outside; they indicate a path to follow. Since the beginning of his career, Ugo Rondinone has considered it necessary to create an enclosed "isolated" environment facilitating dialogue with nature. Hence the importance for him of presentation gambits attenuating the presence of the surrounding urban landscape. The filters placed on the windows—*when the sun goes down and the moon comes up*—are part of this quest and remind us above all that each of Rondinone's exhibitions is inherently a work of art in its own right.

According to the artist, the link between the first two groups and *burn to shine* is a desire for transformation: "The initial inspiration came from a poem by John Giorno titled *You Got To Burn To Shine*: a Buddhist proverb about the coexistence of life and death, reminiscent of the much older Greek myth of the phoenix, the immortal bird that regenerates cyclically or is reborn in a different way. Associated with the sun, the phoenix receives new life by resurrecting from the ashes of its predecessor."

Juliette Singer & Erik Verhagen

Translated from French by John Tittensor

The sculptures *nuns + monks* by Ugo Rondinone take their rightful place in the continuity of a narrative introduced by the artist thirty-two years ago. A narrative composed of chapters that would never cease to interact with one another throughout a trajectory made up of intertextual questions, back-and-forths, survivals, displacements, and reinventions of shapes and attitudes, or of interrogations that are constantly being renegotiated. This narrative originated in 1988 with the death of Manfred Kirchner, then Ugo Rondinone's partner, from an AIDS-related illness. "In the midst of the AIDS crisis, I turned away from my grief and found a spiritual guard rail in nature, a place for comfort, regeneration, and inspiration. In nature, you enter a space where the sacred and the profane, the mystical and the secular vibrate against one another."

The resulting works, landscapes with Romantic overtones painted in ink on paper, were first shown at the Kunstmuseum in Lucerne, then in several other exhibitions, including one at Galerie Walcheturm in Zurich, always with the same constraint: hung in confined spaces, their windows nailed shut with wooden boards, "cut off from the world," turned inward. From that point on, the opening up onto nature specific to the landscape found itself counterbalanced by a feeling of enclosure conducive to introspection.

And a *spiritual* turning inward that would find itself perpetuated in the artist's self-portrait (*Heyday*), inspired by Joris Karl Huysmans and his fictional character, the reclusive Jean des Esseintes, and shown in the framework of his exhibition *cry me a river*, also in Zurich, in 1995. Returned to its initial function, the window of Galerie Walcheturm was once again visible. In front of it was now a frame and double pane, which opened like an arched backdrop through which one could see the self-portrait of the artist, portrayed as a passive figure, from the outside. The relationship between content and container, artwork and receptacle therefore responded to an inverted antagonistic principle. But *in fine* a precarious, equivalent equilibrium had been achieved, from which the spirituality expressed by the artist via the different chapters of the narrative in progress would then unfold.

The *nuns + monks* sculptures express in turn this dialectic from within and without. From opening up onto the world and from turning inward on oneself. From an introspective gaze combined with an exteriority receptive to nature's elements of which these sculptures bear the traces. *The imprint*. Rondinone's works have never stopped oscillating between extremes, entangling, suspending them. *Aufheben*... The sculptures of *nuns + monks* possess a natural beauty. An archaic beauty that evokes other sculptural ensembles by the artist: *Human Nature* in Rockefeller Plaza in 2013 and *Seven Magic Mountains* in the Nevada desert in 2016. They manifest visibility yet at the same time seem to avoid the gaze of those to whom they are shown. Their features are indistinct. And in this era of multiple gender identities, they are divested of sexual characteristics, even though their titles allow us to differentiate them. It would certainly be extremely difficult to distinguish the nuns from the monks based on their mere appearance. Wrapped and protected in their cloaks, they seem, like his 1995 self-portrait and the ensuing clowns and nudes, absorbed, in the same way that Diderot characterized the figures depicted in certain paintings by Jean Siméon Chardin. Absorbed in what? In whom? In the spectators wandering around them? In the architectural space that serves as the backdrop for their paradoxically motionless choreography? Unless, as is extremely likely, the space in question is mental. Meditative. Transcending the matter that still seems to determine their heft. Or, more than transcended, one could say the matter in *nuns + monks* is *transfigured*, revealing a radiance reinforced by the chromatic contrasts, the harmony generated by the juxtaposition of different body parts — the head and the cloak — and by the sculptures, perfectly integrated from one to the next, the radiance evoking medieval statuary serving the same religious and spiritual purpose to which the artist is deeply committed. It should be explained that the creation of these works was nourished by Rondinone's assiduous frequentation of the medieval sculpture department at the Metropolitan Museum in New York, and in addition by a powerful confrontation with Giacomo Manzù's cardinals, whose own particular modernity, permeated by a classicism that defies time and categorization, inevitably corresponded to his interest. Between matter and its negation, these sculptures invest a polarized field. *Amphibological*. Made in bronze, they were conceived from limestone models, scans of which were "three-dimensionalized" with digital tools. In response to the friable limestone, the solidity of the bronze. In response to the stone's natural, ancient origins, the here and now contemporaneity of the polychrome castings. Of course, we must, as is often the case in Rondinone's work, seek the response, ineluctably unstable, inherent in his propositions in the interpenetration of the extremes and intervals they bring about. In a game of equivalences. Opening up onto the world, to nature, and turning inward on oneself. In matter that is as embodied as it is disembodied. And given its elevated spiritual coefficient, so remarkable these days and, in a manner of speaking, absent from contemporary art, in an anagogical principle that re-transcribes and accompanies the process of transfiguration underlying this group of sculptures.

Erik Verhagen

Translated from French by Laurie Hurwitz

L'intervention des artistes contemporains au sein du Petit Palais renouvelle chaque année le regard porté sur ses collections et son bâtiment. Ugo Rondinone a déployé un parcours magistral qui s'intégrait totalement à l'espace construit par l'architecte Charles Girault pour l'Exposition de Paris 1900, et a généré un dialogue fructueux avec les collections historiques du musée.

Afin de faire la jonction avec l'espace de la ville, Ugo Rondinone a disposé au pied du majestueux escalier d'honneur menant au musée, un ensemble de trois sculptures colorées appartenant à la série des *nuns + monks*. Ces silhouettes évoquent une foule, un passage entre l'espace profane et le sacré, ouvert sur une autre dimension. Sur l'esplanade, les sculptures agissaient aussi comme un signal d'appel, invitant les passants à gravir les marches pour pénétrer à l'intérieur du musée.

Le seuil franchi, le visiteur pouvait découvrir trois corpus d'œuvres d'Ugo Rondinone réunis pour la première fois, chacun évoquant différents éléments naturels : l'air, l'eau, la terre et le feu. Dans la rotonde d'honneur, les visiteurs étaient d'abord accueillis par un ensemble de sculptures suspendues : *humansky*. Ces voltigeurs obligeaient le regard à s'élever pour suivre une gracieuse farandole éclairée par les vitraux de l'atelier Champigneulle, et surmontée par les peintures symbolistes d'Albert Besnard. Moulés sur des danseurs et un athlète, les êtres célestes de Rondinone gravitaient autour de la *Gloria Victis* (1875), une figure ailée par laquelle Antonin Mercié rendit hommage à la France vaincue de 1870, inspirée à la fois de la *Victoire de Samothrace* et du *Saint Michel terrassant le dragon* de Raphaël.

Sur les fenêtres de la salle des sculptures, l'artiste avait appliqué des filtres qui atténuaient la lumière, mettant ainsi à distance l'environnement urbain du Petit Palais. Avec cette intervention intitulée *when the sun goes down and the moon comes up*, l'artiste imposait l'impression d'un temps ralenti, et modifiait la perception de l'espace muséal.

Le deuxième ensemble était composé de sculptures en cire réalisées à partir de moulages effectués sur les corps de danseurs au repos, assemblés en laissant apparaître des césures, et des différences de teintes. L'artiste avait disposé ces *nudes* au sol, parmi les sculptures en plâtre du musée, telles que *La Défense de Paris* (1880) de Louis-Ernest Barrias, *Monnaie de singe* (1882) de François-Laurent Rolard, ou *La danseuse Sacha-Lyo* (1933, dépôt de la COARC) de Serge Youriévitch. Également marqués par des coutures et des patines aux teintes irrégulières, les plâtres entraient dans un dialogue délicat avec les nus de l'artiste.

Visible depuis l'entrée, un cylindre monolithique noir dressé dans la rotonde nord s'élevait jusqu'au plafond, imposant sa silhouette de manière affirmée et brisant la symétrie conçue par l'architecte entre l'aile nord et l'aile sud du musée. Au mur, l'installation était encadrée par le dernier grand ensemble d'Eugène Carrière intitulé *Les âges de la vie*

(1897-1900), commandé pour la salle des fêtes de la mairie du 8e arrondissement et resté inachevé. Ses teintes sombres faisaient écho, dans un double élan, aux nuances charbon du cylindre ainsi qu'aux tons chauds de quatre nus en cire assis sous chaque tableau. En entrant par une porte dérobée, les visiteurs se trouvaient soudain plongés dans une semi-obscurité, face à la nouvelle œuvre vidéo de Rondinone : *burn to shine*. Cerné d'images, le visiteur se trouvait soudain au même niveau qu'un groupe de danseurs pris dans un cercle endiablé chorégraphié avec le concours de Fouad Boussouf. Présenté en première mondiale au sein de l'exposition, *burn to shine* était reproduit sur l'affiche de la façade du musée, déployant ainsi sa force vitale et spirituelle sur l'ensemble du musée.

Juliette Singer

the water is a poem
unwritten by the air
no. the earth is a poem
unwritten by the fire

L'intervention d'Ugo Rondinone au sein du Petit Palais réside en deux ensembles de travaux, prolongés par une installation vidéo inédite. S'articulant autour de corps humains en prise avec les éléments et la nature, ceux-ci s'inscrivent dans la continuité des multiples familles d'œuvres produites par l'artiste depuis la fin des années 1980. La terre, le ciel, l'air, l'eau et le feu associés à des êtres au repos ou en mouvement sont ici convoqués, dans toute leur dimension spirituelle.

Le premier ensemble de travaux qui accueille les visiteurs, *humansky*, souligne d'emblée cette confusion entre l'être et les éléments. Sept corps moulés, agrémentés d'un « camouflage » évoquant un ciel bleu constellé de nuages, sont suspendus. Ils confrontent le visiteur à l'eau et à l'air.

Le deuxième ensemble, d'où historiquement, est née cette trilogie, est constitué des *nus*. À base de cire transparente mélangée avec de la terre, prélevée sur sept continents, ces sculptures présentent aussi un aspect « camouflé », produit par l'assemblage de ces matières non homogènes. Elles mettent en scène des corps de danseurs et danseuses assis et au repos. Réalisés à échelle humaine, ces *nus* semblent d'abord réalistes, avant que le visiteur, en s'approchant, ne découvre leur aspect clairement artificiel, particulièrement visible au niveau de la jonction de leurs membres avec leur corps.

Ces sculptures sont ainsi « paradoxales » et conformes en cela à l'esthétique d'Ugo Rondinone : il joue sur « l'opposition » entre ce qui est attendu d'un danseur ou d'une danseuse, et la pose qu'il leur fait prendre. Ces corps immobiles, repliés sur eux-mêmes, évacuent tout geste chorégraphié et toute référence à l'espace scénique : ils semblent se fondre avec la nature, l'esprit concentré, perdus dans un état méditatif.

D'un ensemble à l'autre, les visiteurs assistent à un processus de mutation des corps : d'une suspension éthérée avec *humansky*, à une quasi léthargie avec les nus, les corps « renaissent » dans le film *burn to shine*, dont la présentation au Petit Palais constitue une première mondiale. Le film est projeté sur six écrans, à l'intérieur d'un écrin cylindrique en bois calciné qui forme un cercle, figure géométrique récurrente chez l'artiste.

Le corps est ici en mouvement : 12 percussionnistes, 18 danseurs et danseuses sont réunis dans le désert, autour d'un feu. S'adonnant à une transe ancestrale héritée du Maghreb, conjuguée aux gestes d'une danse contemporaine pensée avec le concours du chorégraphe franco-marocain Fouad Boussouf, ils s'unissent à la nature, du coucher du soleil jusqu'à l'aube, au moment où le soleil se lève de nouveau.

Les lattes en bois du cylindre obstruent toute vue extérieure : elles indiquent un passage. Depuis ses débuts, Ugo Rondinone considère en effet nécessaire de créer un environnement clos, « isolé », pour pouvoir engager un dialogue avec la nature, au sein d'un espace fermé. Pour lui, il est important d'imaginer des dispositifs visant à atténuer la présence du paysage urbain environnant. Les filtres posés sur les fenêtres – *when the sun goes down and the moon comes up* – participent de cette volonté et nous rappellent surtout que toute exposition de l'artiste est, en soi, une œuvre à part entière.

Selon Ugo Rondinone, ce qui relierait les deux premiers groupes à *burn to shine* est un désir de transformation : « L'inspiration initiale est venue d'un poème de John Giorno intitulé "Tu dois brûler pour briller". Un proverbe bouddhiste sur la coexistence de la vie et de la mort, semblable à la mythologie grecque bien plus ancienne du phénix, l'oiseau immortel qui se régénère de manière cyclique ou renaît d'une autre manière. Associé au soleil, un phénix reçoit une nouvelle vie en renaissant des cendres de son prédécesseur ».

Juliette Singer & Erik Verhagen

La série de sculptures *nuns + monks* (nonnes et moines) d'Ugo Rondinone s'inscrit dans la continuité d'un récit amorcé par l'artiste il y a trente-deux ans. Un récit composé de chapitres qui ne cesseront de se répondre tout au long d'une trajectoire placée sous le signe d'enjeux intertextuels, de va-et-vient, de survivances, déplacements et réinventions de formes et d'attitudes ou interrogations continuellement renégociées. Ce récit débute en 1988 avec la mort de Manfred Kirchner, alors partenaire d'Ugo Rondinone, d'une maladie liée au sida. « En pleine crise du sida, je me suis détourné de mon chagrin et j'ai trouvé un garde-fou spirituel dans la nature, un lieu de réconfort, de régénération et d'inspiration. Dans la nature, on entre dans un espace où le sacré et le profane, le mystique et le séculaire vibrent l'un contre l'autre. »

Les œuvres qui en ont résulté, des paysages aux accents romantiques peints à l'encre sur papier, ont été présentées dans un premier temps à Lucerne, puis à l'occasion de plusieurs expositions, notamment à la galerie Walcheturm de Zurich, avec la même contrainte : un accrochage dans des espaces clos aux fenêtres obstruées par des planches de bois clouées, « coupées du monde », tournées vers l'intérieur. L'ouverture sur la nature propre aux paysages se voyait dès lors contrebalancée par un sentiment d'enferment propice à l'introspection.

Un repli spirituel qui trouvera son prolongement dans l'autoportrait de l'artiste intitulé *Heyday*, inspiré par Huysmans et son personnage Jean des Esseintes, dévoilé dans le cadre de l'exposition « Cry me a river », toujours à Zurich, en 1995. Rendue à sa fonction première, la fenêtre de la galerie Walcheturm y était à nouveau visible et ouverte. Un cadre peint en brun et un double vitrage ouvraient sur une image semblable à une toile de fond. De l'extérieur, la fenêtre composait le cadre à travers lequel observer l'autoportrait de l'artiste, représenté en figure abandonnée et passive. La relation entre le contenu et le contenant, l'œuvre d'art et le réceptacle, répondait donc à un principe antagoniste inversé. Mais *in fine*, un équilibre précaire et équivalent était atteint, à partir duquel la spiritualité exprimée par l'artiste à travers les différents chapitres de la narration en cours allait se déployer.

Les *nuns + monks* expriment à leur tour cette dialectique de l'intérieur et de l'extérieur. De l'ouverture sur le monde et du repli sur soi. D'un regard introspectif conjugué à une extériorité perméable aux éléments de la nature dont ces sculptures conservent par ailleurs la trace. *L'empreinte*. Les œuvres d'Ugo Rondinone oscillent continuellement entre les extrêmes, elles les emmêlent, les suspendent. *Aufheben...* Les sculptures de moines et de nonnes possèdent une beauté naturelle. Une beauté « archaïque » qui évoque d'autres ensembles sculpturaux de l'artiste : *Human Nature* sur la Rockefeller Plaza en 2013 et *Seven Magic Mountains* dans le désert du Nevada en 2016. Dans le même temps, elles s'offrent et se dérobent au regard de ceux à qui elles sont montrées. Leurs traits sont indistincts. À l'ère des identités de genre multiples, ces personnages sont dépourvus de caractéristiques sexuelles. Seuls leurs titres nous permettent de les différencier. Il serait assurément difficile de distinguer les nonnes des moines à leur simple apparence. Enveloppés et protégés dans leurs étoffes, ils semblent, à l'image de l'autoportrait de 1995 et des clowns qui suivront, comme absorbés au sens où avait pu l'entendre Diderot à propos des personnes représentées dans certains tableaux de Jean-Siméon Chardin. Absorbés par quoi ? Par qui ? Par les spectateurs déambulant autour d'eux ? Par l'espace architectural qui sert de décor à une chorégraphie paradoxalement figée ? À moins, c'est fort probable, que l'espace en question soit mental. *Méditatif*. Transcendant la matière qui semble pourtant déterminer leur pesanteur. Plus que transcendée, on pourrait dire que la matière des *nuns + monks* est *transfigurée*, laissant transparaître un éclat renforcé par les contrastes chromatiques, l'harmonie générée par la juxtaposition des différentes parties des corps – la tête et l'étoffe – et par les sculptures accordées les unes aux autres, ledit éclat n'étant pas sans évoquer une statuaire du Moyen-Âge au service d'un même propos religieux et spirituel auquel l'artiste est très attaché. On précisera à ce titre que la réalisation de ces œuvres a été nourrie par une fréquentation assidue de Rondinone des départements de sculpture médiévale du Metropolitan Museum de New York et par ailleurs d'une confrontation intense avec les travaux de Giacomo Manzù et Marino Marini dont la modernité « décalée » et empreinte d'un classicisme défiant le temps et les catégorisations ne pouvait que rencontrer l'intérêt de l'artiste.

Entre la matière et sa négation, ces sculptures investissent un champ polarisé. *Amphibologique*. En bronze, elles ont cependant été conçues à partir de modèles en calcaire scannés et « tridimensionnalisés » à l'aide d'outils numériques. Au calcaire, friable, répond la solidité du bronze. À l'origine naturelle et plurimillénaire des pierres, la présence *ici et maintenant* des moulages polychromes. Sans doute faut-il, comme souvent chez Rondinone, chercher la réponse, forcément instable, inhérente à ses propositions dans l'interpénétration des extrêmes et des intervalles qu'ils autorisent. Dans un jeu d'équivalences. Une ouverture sur le monde, la nature et un repli sur soi. Dans une matière aussi incarnée que désincarnée. Et compte tenu de son haut coefficient spirituel, si exceptionnel de nos jours et pour ainsi dire absent de l'art contemporain, dans un principe *anagogique* qui retraduit et accompagne le processus de transfiguration sous-tendant ce groupe de sculptures.

Erik Verhagen

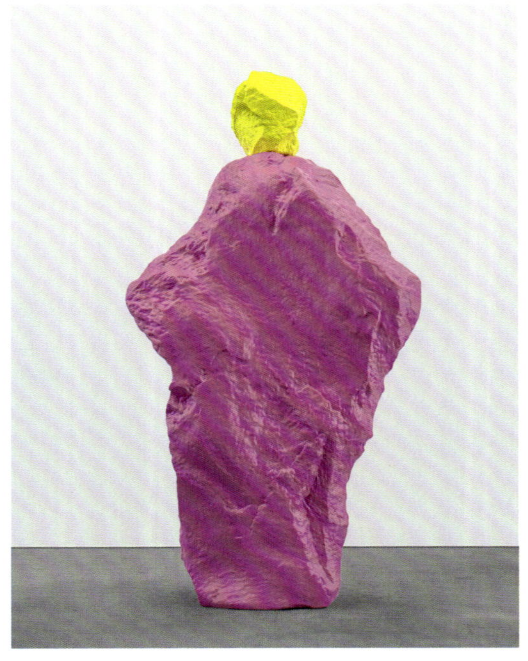

yellow pink monk, 2020
painted bronze
293 × 156.8 × 80 cm

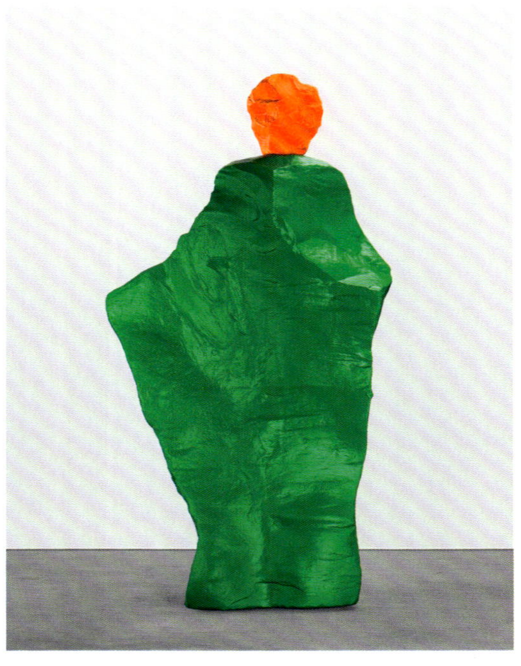

orange green nun, 2022
painted bronze
292 × 158 × 105 cm

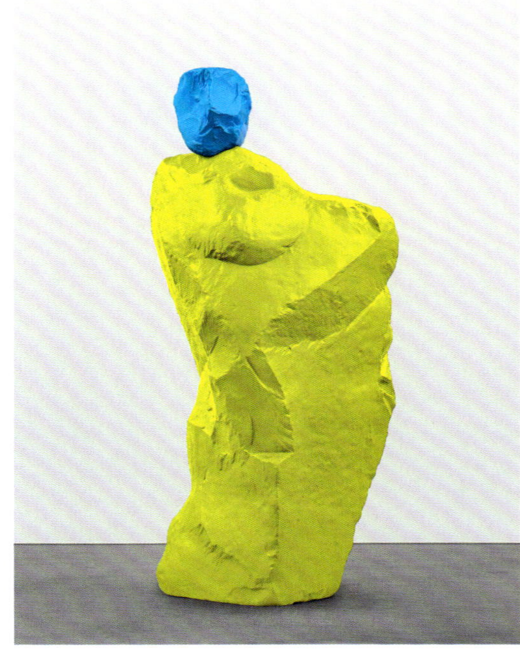

blue yellow nun, 2020
painted bronze
292 × 134.5 × 90.4 cm

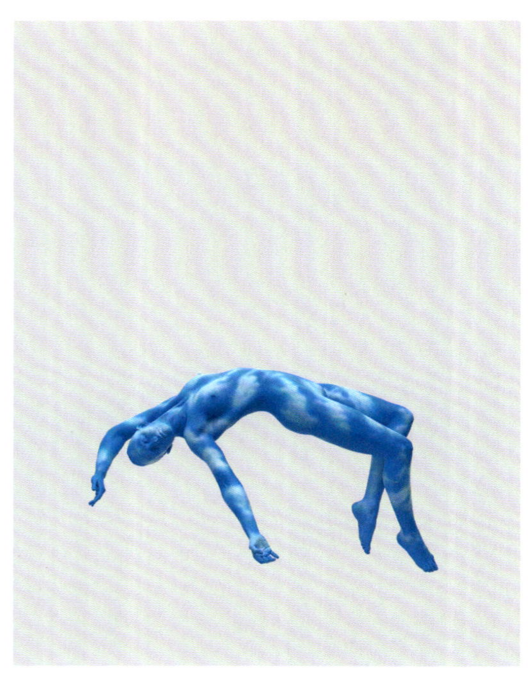

humansky four, 2022
polyurethane, paint
147 × 89 × 64 cm

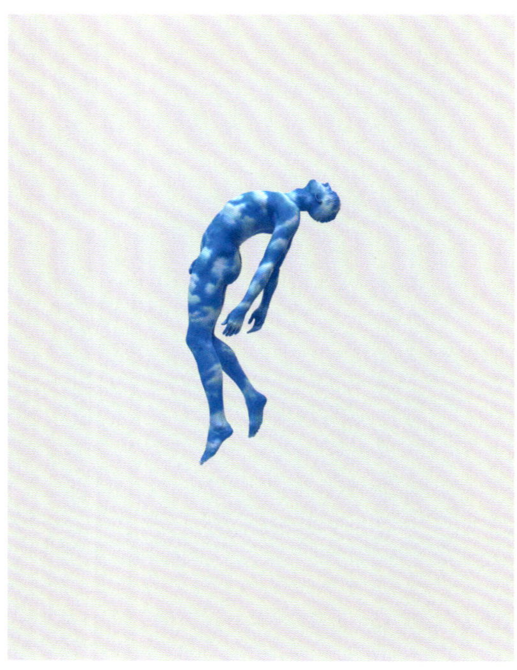

humansky five, 2022
polyurethane, paint
164 × 89 × 75 cm

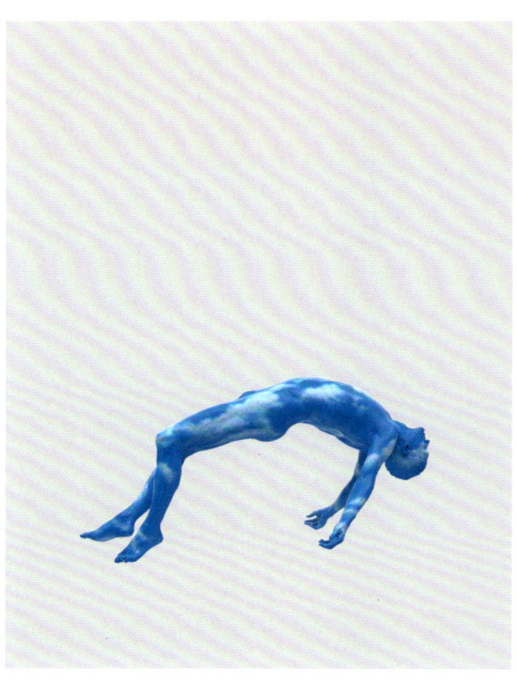

humansky six, 2022
polyurethane, paint
83 × 179 × 119 cm

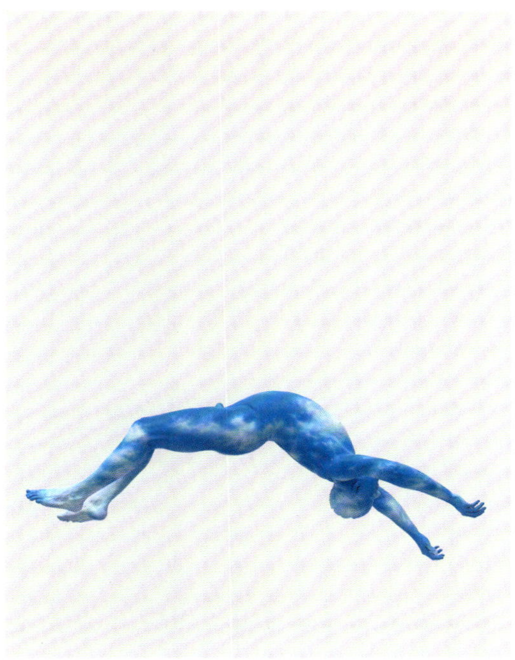

humansky one, 2022
polyurethane, paint
87 × 217 × 66 cm

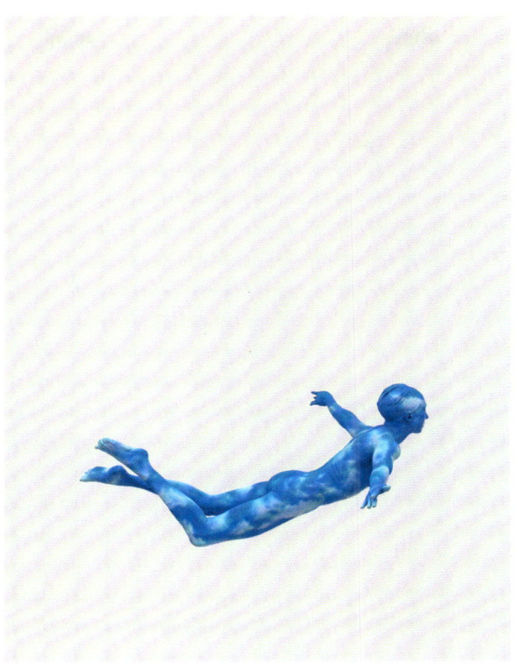

humansky two, 2022
polyurethane, paint
73 × 166 × 173 cm

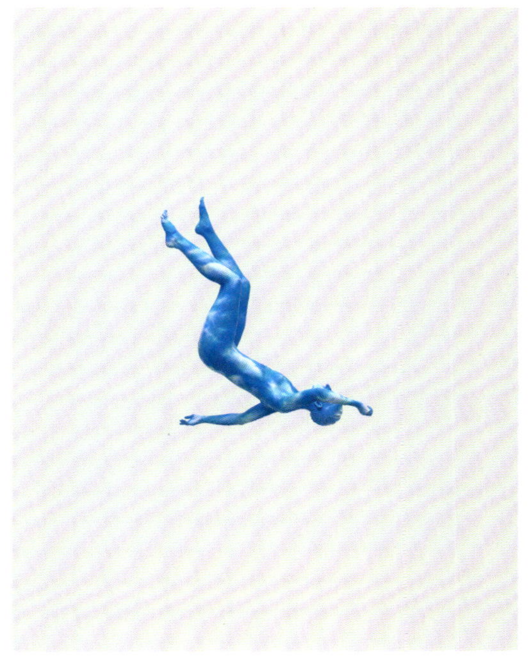

humansky three, 2022
polyurethane, paint
138 × 114 × 59 cm

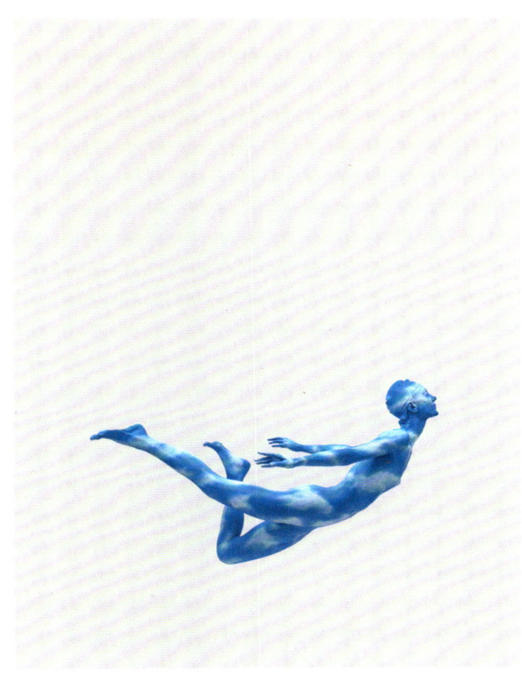

humansky seven, 2022
polyurethane, paint
86 × 162 × 95 cm

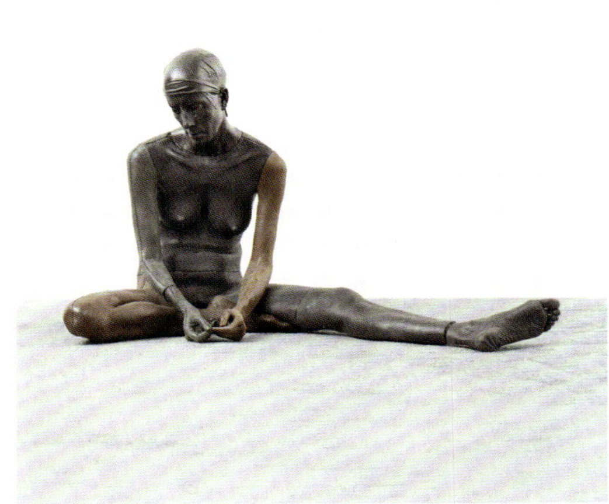

nude (x), 2010
wax, earth pigments
77.5 × 123 × 70.5 cm

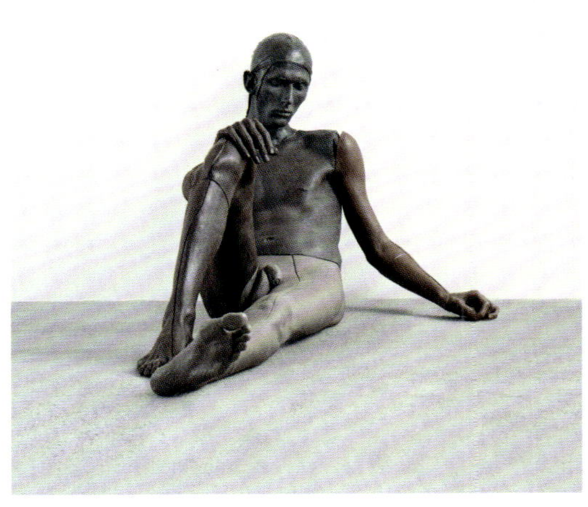

nude (xx), 2010
wax, earth pigments
74 × 151 × 90 cm

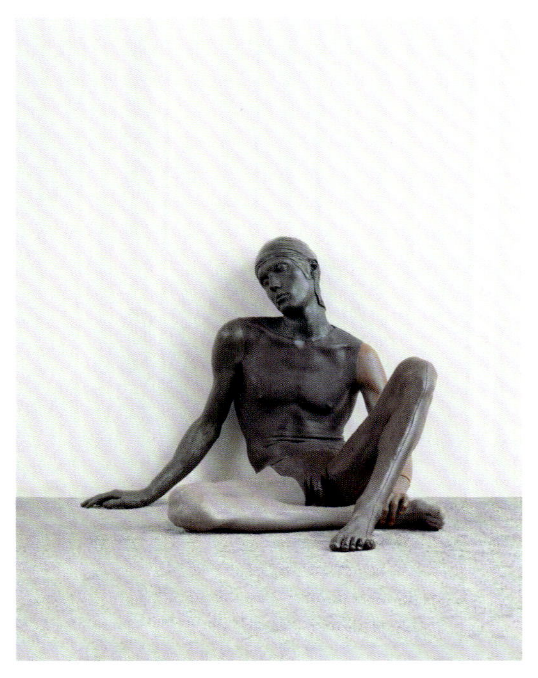

nude (xxxx), 2010
wax, earth pigments
77 × 87 × 85.5 cm

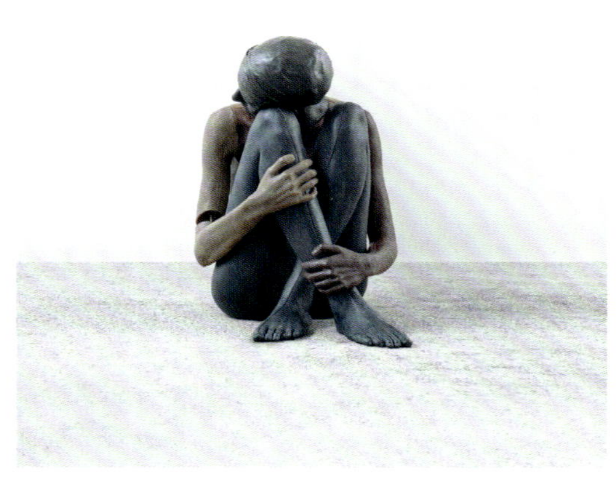

nude (xxxxxx), 2010
wax, earth pigments
65 × 63.5 × 54 cm

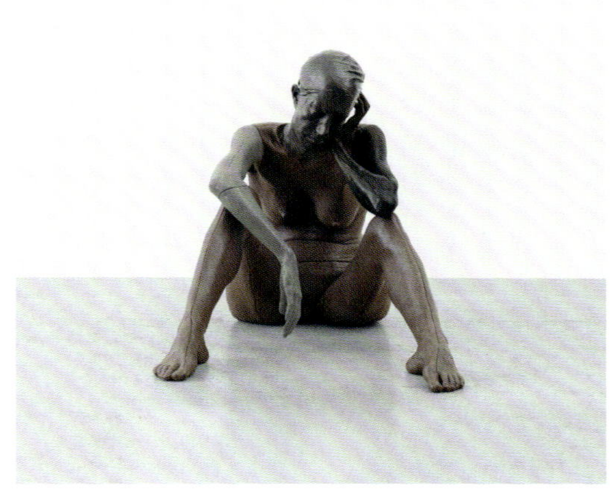

nude (xxxxxxx), 2010
wax, earth pigments
72 × 100 × 62 cm

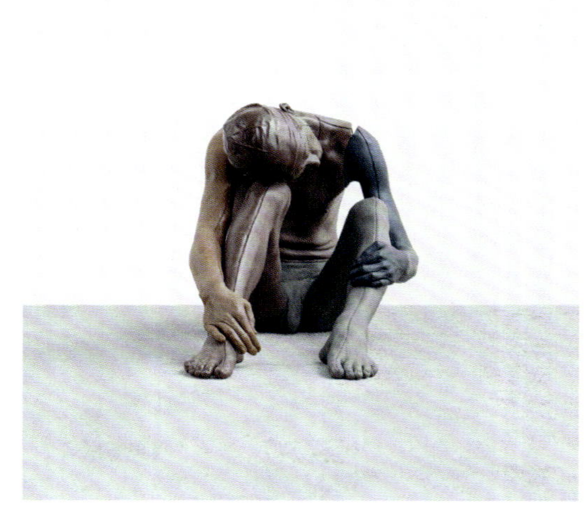

nude (xxxxxxxx), 2011
wax, earth pigments
59 × 101 × 54 cm

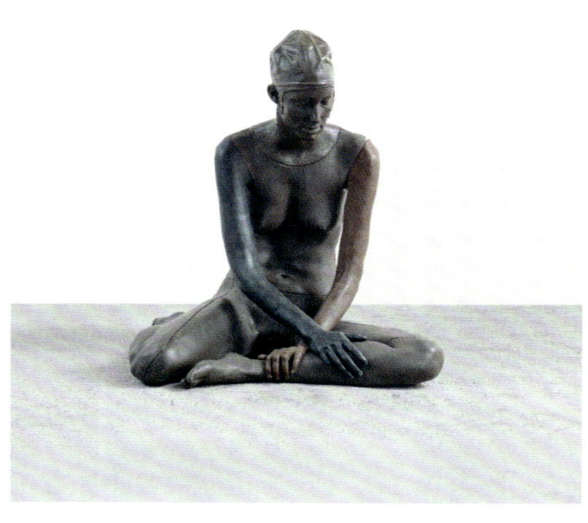

nude (xxxxxxxxx), 2011
wax, earth pigments
81 × 81 × 62 cm

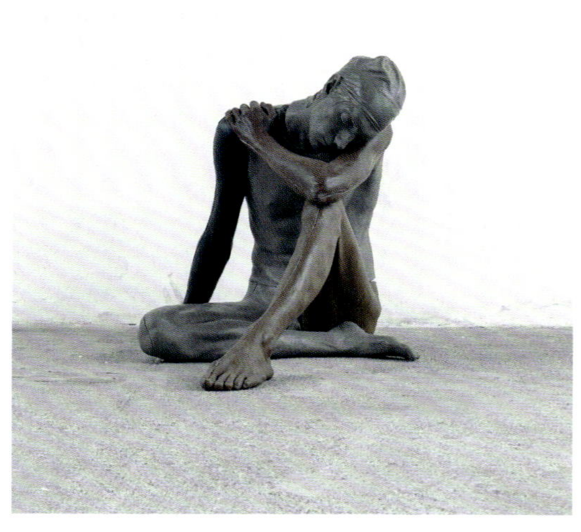

nude (xxxxxxxxxxx), 2011
wax, earth pigments
72 × 108 × 83 cm

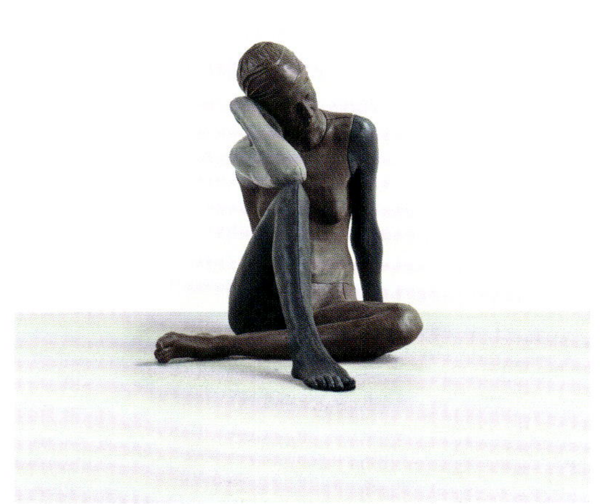

nude (xxxxxxxxxxxxx), 2011
wax, earth pigments
77 × 128 × 60 cm

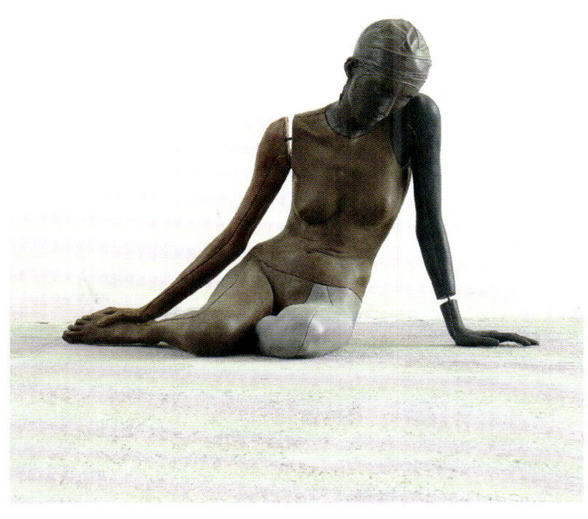

nude (xxxxxxxxxxxxxx), 2011
wax, earth pigments
74 × 109 × 64 cm

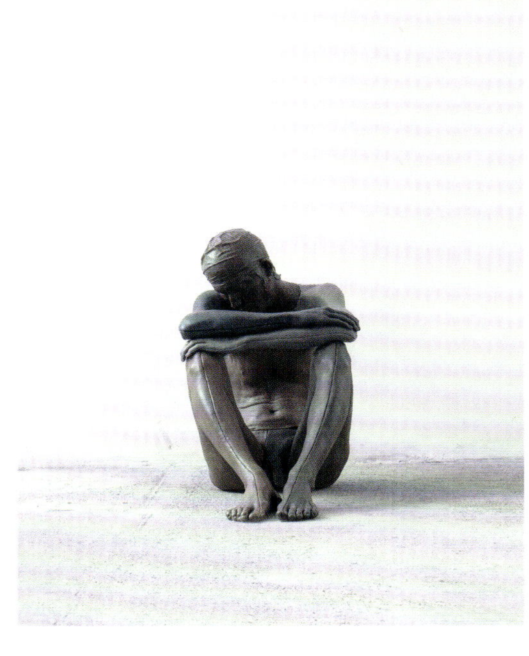

nude (xxxxxxxxxxxxxxx), 2011
wax, earth pigments
76 × 99 × 45 cm

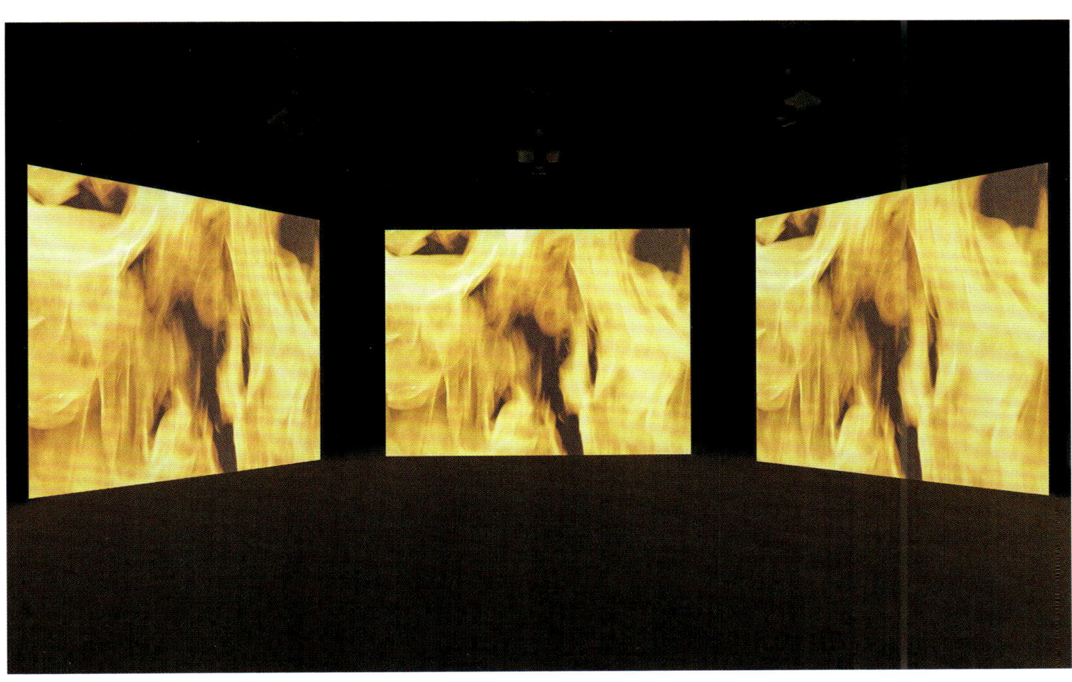

burn to shine, 2022
six screen synchronized video projection
dimensions variable

biography

ugo rondinone

1964
born in brunnen, switzerland

1986–90
studied at the hochschule für angewandte kunst, vienna

lives and works in new york

solo exhibitions

2023
one on one: ugo rondinone | louis eilshemius, the phillips collection, washington
galerija kula, split, croatia
burn to shine, fosun foundation, shanghai
i don't live here anymore, esther schipper, berlin
bright light shining, gladstone gallery, new york
the mask and the masked, the journal gallery, new york
sunrise. east, städel museum, frankfurt
milwaukee landscapes, the green gallery, milwaukee
the sun and the moon, storm king, new york
nuns + monks at the sea, gladstone gallery, brussels, belgium
when the sun goes down and the moon comes up, musée d'art et d'histoire, geneva

2022
the water is a poem unwritten by the air no. the earth is a poem unwritten by the fire, petit palais, paris
life time, schirn kunsthalle frankfurt
vocabulary of solitude, museo tamayo, mexico city
chuck nanney + joel otterson, curated by ugo rondinone, galerie eva presenhuber, zurich
nuns and monks by the sea, kukje gallery, seoul and busan
burn . shine . fly, scuola grande san giovanni evangelista di venezia, venice

2021
nude in the landscape, belvedere 21, vienna
vocabulary of solitude, auckland art gallery, new zealand
a low sun . golden mountains . fall, galerie krobath, vienna
sail me on a silver sun, the national exemplar, iowa city
still. life, tennis elbow, the journal gallery, new york
waterfalls and clouds, two person exhibition with pat steir, galerie eva presenhuber, zurich
ned smyth - life, curated by ugo rondinone, landcraft garden, mattituck
your age, my age, and the age of the rainbow, belvedere 21, vienna
a rainbow . a nude . bright light . summer, mennour, paris
chuck nanney + joel otterson, curated by ugo rondinone, martos gallery, new york
a yellow a brown and a blue candle, the national exemplar, iowa city
nuns + monks, gladstone gallery, new york
a sky . a sea . distant mountains . horses . spring, sadie coles hq, london
feeling the void and the rhone, kunsthalle marcel duchamp, cully
a wall. a door. a tree. a lightbulb. winter, skmu sørlandets kunstmuseum, kristiansand

2020
the monk, gladstone gallery, rome
nuns + monks, galerie eva presenhuber, zürich
nuns + monks, esther schipper, berlin
poetry, the national exemplar, iowa city

2019
medellín mountain, medellín modern art museum, medellín
thanx 4 nothing, gladstone gallery, new york
a wall . seven windows . four people . three trees . some clouds . one sun, kamel mennour, paris
everyone gets lighter, kunsthalle helsinki, helsinki
sunny days, guild hall, east hampton
thanx 4 nothing, carré d'art, chapelle des jésuites, nîmes
earthing, kukje gallery, seoul

2018
the true, laguna gloria, the contemporary austin
liverpool mountain, liverpool biennial, tate liverpool, liverpool
clockwork for oracles, phillips, paris
the marciano collection, marciano foundation, los angeles
the radiant, malta international contemporary art space, valetta
drifting clouds, gladstone gallery, new york
your age and my age and the age of the sun, fundación casawabi, puerto escondido

2017
vocabulary of solitude, arken museum of modern art, ishøj
moonrise. east. july, aspen art museum, aspen
good evening beautiful blue, bass museum of art, miami
flower moon, bristol hotel, paris
where do we go from here, the istanbul biennial, istanbul
i love john giorno, various institutions, new york
the sky over manhattan, sky art, new york
the world just makes me laugh, berkeley art museum and pacific film archive, berkeley
let's start this day again, contemporary arts center, cincinnati
winter moon, maxxi, rome
your age my age and the age of the rainbow, the garage museum of contemporary art, moscow

2016
every time the sun comes up, place vendôme, paris
two men contemplating the moon 1830, esther schipper, berlin
miami mountain, bass museum of art, miami
the sun at 4pm, gladstone gallery, new york
girono d'oro + notti d'argento, mercati dietraiano, rome

girono d'oro + notti d'argento, macro, rome
becoming soil, carre d'art, nîmes
seven magic mountains, art production fund and nevada museum of art / desert of nevada
vocabulary of solitude, boijmans van beuningen, rotterdam
primordial, gladstone gallery, brussels
ugo rondinone: moonrise sculptures, the institute of contemporary art (ica), boston
windows, poems, and stars, la caja negra, madrid

2015
i love john giorno, palais de tokyo, paris
mountains + clouds + waterfalls, sadie coles hq, london
feelings, kukje gallery, seoul
walls + windows + doors, galerie eva presenhuber, zurich
golden days and silver nights, art gallery of nsw, sydney
artists and poets, curated by ugo rondinone, secession, vienna
clouds, galerie krobath, vienna

2014
breathe walk die, rockbund art museum, shanghai
naturaleza humana, museo anahuacalli, coyoacán

2013
human nature, public art fund, rockefeller plaza, new york
we run through a desert on burning feet, all of us are glowing our faces look twisted, art institute of chicago, chicago
thank you silence, m museum, leuven
pure moonlight, almine rech gallery, paris
primal, esther schipper, berlin
soul, gladstone gallery, new york
soul, galerie eva presenhuber, zurich
primal, sommer contemporary art, tel aviv
poems, sorry we're closed, brussels
fatima center for contemporary culture, monterrey

2012
primitive, the common guild, glasgow
pure sunshine, sadie coles hq, london
nude, cycladic art museum, athens
wisdom?peace?blank?all of this?, kunsthistorisches museum, theseustempel, vienna
the moth poem and the holy forest, galerie krobath, vienna

2011
we are poems, gladstone gallery, brussels
new horizon, almine rech gallery, brussels
we are poems, lvmh, palais an der oper, munich
kiss now kill later, galerie eva presenhuber, zurich
we run through a desert on burning feet, all of us are glowing our faces look twisted, art basel, art parcours, basel
outside my window, peder lund, oslo

2010
nude, gladstone gallery, new york
ibm building, new york
turn back time. let's start this day again, fiac, hors les murs, jardins des tuileries, paris
clockwork for oracles, art basel, art unlimited, basel
sunrise. east, museum dhondt-dhaenens, deurle, belgium
die nacht aus blei, aargauer kunsthaus, aarau

2009
sunrise. east, festival d'automne à paris, jardin des tuileries, paris
how does it feel?, festival d'automne à paris, le 104, paris
nude, sadie coles hq, london
la vie silencieuse, galerie almine rech, paris
the night of lead, musac, museo de arte contemporáneo de castilla, léon

2008
clockwork for oracles ii, ica boston, art wall project, boston
turn back time. let's start this day again, galleria raucci/santamaria, naples
sunrise. east, frieze art fair, outdoor project, london
we burn, we shiver (with martin boyce), sculpture center, new york
moonrise. east, public art project, art basel, basel
twelve sunsets, twenty nine dawns, all in one, galerie eva presenhuber, zurich
dog days are over, hayward gallery, southbank centre, london

2007
big mind sky, matthew marks gallery, new york
wohnsiedlung werdweis, kunst und bau, zurich-altstetten
get up girl a sun is running the world (with urs fischer), church san stae, 52nd venice biennale, venice
our magic hour, arario gallery, cheonan
air gets into everything even nothing, creative time, ritz carlton plaza, battery park, new york

2006
giorni felici, galleria civica di modena, modena
on butterfly wings, galerie almine rech, paris
thank you silence, matthew marks gallery, new york
unday, galerie esther schipper, berlin
a waterlike still, ausstellungshalle zeitgenössische kunst, munster
my endless numbered days, sadie coles hq, london
zero built a nest in my navel, whitechapel gallery, london

2005
clockwork for oracles isr-centro culturale svizzero di milano, milan
sunsetsunrise, sommer contemporary art, tel aviv

2004
sail me on a silver sun, galleria raucci/santamaria, naples
long gone sole, matthew marks gallery, new york
long night short years, le consortium, dijon
clockwork for oracles, australian centre for contemporary art, melbourne

2003
la criée, théâtre national de bretagne, galerie art & essai, rennes

moonrise, galerie hauser & wirth & presenhuber, zurich
our magic hour, museum of contemporary art, sydney
lessness, galerie almine rech, paris
roundelay, musée national d'art moderne, centre georges pompidou, paris

2002
in alto arte sui ponteggi, centro culturale svizzero, milan
our magic hour, centre for contemporary visual arts, brighton
coming up for air, württembergischer kunstverein, stuttgart

1988, works on paper inc., los angeles
lowland lullaby (with urs fischer), swiss institute, new york
cigarettesandwich, sadie coles hq, london
the dancer and the dance, galerie krobath wimmer, vienna
no how on, kunsthalle wien, vienna
a horse with no name, matthew marks gallery, new york
on perspective, galleri faurschou, copenhagen

2001
slow graffiti, galerie schipper & krome, berlin
frac paca, marseille
yesterday's dancer, sommer contemporary art, tel aviv
dreams and dramas, herzliya museum of contemporary art, herzliya
kiss tomorrow goodbye, palazzo delle esposizioni, rome
if there were anywhere but desert, galerie almine rech, paris

2000
so much water so close to home, moma p.s.1, new york
love invents us, matthew marks gallery, new york
if there were anywhere but desert, mont-blanc boutique, new york
a doubleday and a pastime, galleria raucci/santamaria, naples
in the sweet years remaining, aarhus art museum, aarhus
hell, yes!, sadie coles hq, london

1999
guided by voices, galerie für zeitgenössische kunst leipzig, leipzig
guided by voices, kunsthaus glarus, glarus
moonlighting, galerie hauser & wirth & presenhuber, zurich
light of fallen stars, yves saint-laurent, new york
in the sweet years remaining, schipper & krome, berlin

1998
in the sweet years remaining, galerie joão graça, lisbon
the evening passes like any other, galerie almine rech, paris
so much water so close to home, galerie krobath wimmer, vienna

1997
stillsmoking, galleria raucci/santamaria, naples
moonlight and aspirin, galleria bonomo, rome
tender places come from nothing, cato jans der raum, hamburg
where do we go from here, le consortium, dijon

1996
dog days are over, migros museum für gegenwartskunst, zurich
le case d'arte, milan
heyday, centre d'art contemporain, geneva

1995
meantime, galerie froment-putman, paris
migrateurs, arc – musée d'art moderne de la ville de paris, paris
cry me a river, galerie walcheturm, zurich

1994
galerie daniel buchholz, cologne
galerie six friedrich, munich

1993
drawings, centre d'art contemporain de martigny, martigny
lightyears, galerie ballgasse, vienna

1992
pastime, galerie walcheturm, zurich

1991
far away trains passing by, galerie martina detterer, frankfurt
two stones in my pocket, galerie pinx, vienna
i'm a tree, galerie walcheturm, zurich

1989
galerie pinx, vienna

1987
raum für aktuelle schweizer kunst, lucerne

1986
sec 52, ricco bilger, zurich

1985
galerie marlene frei, zurich

artistic crew
ugo rondinone director
corinne castel art producer
fouad boussouf choreographer
blaise merlin music executive producer
dartagnan camara music director
luis armando arteaga director of photography & camera operator
céline croze camera operator
constance vargioni lead editor
edouard mailaender editor
nicolas becker sound designer
florian montchatre music recorder
luciano chessa music editor
gregory vincent sound effects recorder
olivier guillaume sound mixer
marie gascoin colorist & vfx

dancers
nadim bahsoun
mathieu bord
sami blond
julien boclé
filipa correia lescuyer
yanice djae
bryan doisy
justin gouin
maleo hernandez
pauline journé
jade lada
jocelyn laurent
julie laventure
johana maledon
mwendwa marchand
fanny rouyé
akciel regent gonzalez
céline thicot

musicians
dartagnan camara
bangaly bangoura
magali boucharlat
marta domingo
isabelle guidon
fabien kanou
sattar khan
issouf monkoro
clara noll
claude saturne
lisa taktouk
felipe veiga

burn to shine is produced by
studio rondinone & les volcans

support
sadie coles hq, london
gladstone, new york
mennour, paris
kukje gallery, seoul
galerie eva presenhuber, zurich
esther schipper, berlin

executive production
compagnie massala, france dance
l'onde & cybele, france music
james asher remix of send in the drums
jaja films, spain film shooting
lachaussée avocats:
assurance rubini et associés
cabinet comptable vincent baheux

thanks to the entire film crew

publication

production
ugo rondinone

design
ugo rondinone
francisco ramirez barrera
maeve o'regan

photography
stefan altenburger

texts
juliette singer
erik verhagen

translation
alix de la chapelle
laurie hurwitz
john tittensor

editorial coordination
alix de la chapelle
maeve o'regan

project management
sophie pechhacker

print production
thomas lemaître

reproductions
DruckConcept, Berlin

printing and binding
Printer Trento, s.r.l.

typeface
grotesque mt

paper
gardamatt art 170 gsm

imprint

this catalogue was published
on the occasion of the
exhibition:

ugo rondinone

the water is a poem
unwritten by the air
no. the earth is a poem
unwritten by the fire

18 october 2022 – 8 january 2023
petit palais – paris

a petit palais, paris musées
exhibition

exhibition curators
juliette singer chief curator
petit palais
erik verhagen professor of
contemporary art history

the exhibition and catalogue
were made possible
with the support of
galerie eva presenhuber
esther schipper
mennour
sadie coles hq
gladstone gallery
kukje gallery

acknowledgments

exhibition production
& installation
studio rondinone
petit palais
mennour, paris
artproject ithaque
cadmos

conservation
kunstbetrieb

press & communication
mathilde beaujard
david ulrichs
alexandra alexopoulou
maeve o'regan

thank you
anne-sophie de gasquet
executive director
paris musées
annick lemoine, director,
petit palais
juliette singer
erik verhagen
kamel mennour
jessy mansuy
alix de la chapelle
from mennour, paris
gilbert isermann,
architectural consultant,
zurich
corinne castel
fouad boussouf
eugène carrière estate
mattias herold
stuart mitchell
francisco ramirez barrera
chloe mcwhirt
ashlee baldwin
from studio rondinone

publisher

published by
Hatje Cantz Verlag GmbH
Mommsenstraße 27
10629 Berlin
www.hatjecantz.com
A Ganske Publishing
Group Company

printed in italy.

isbn
978-3-7757-5642-6

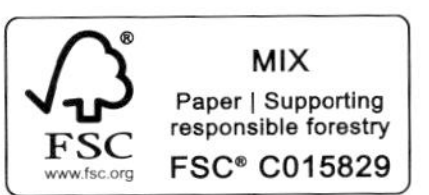

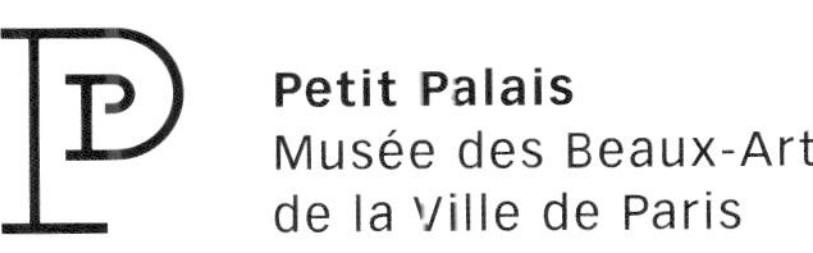

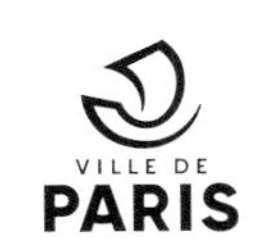

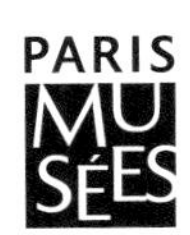

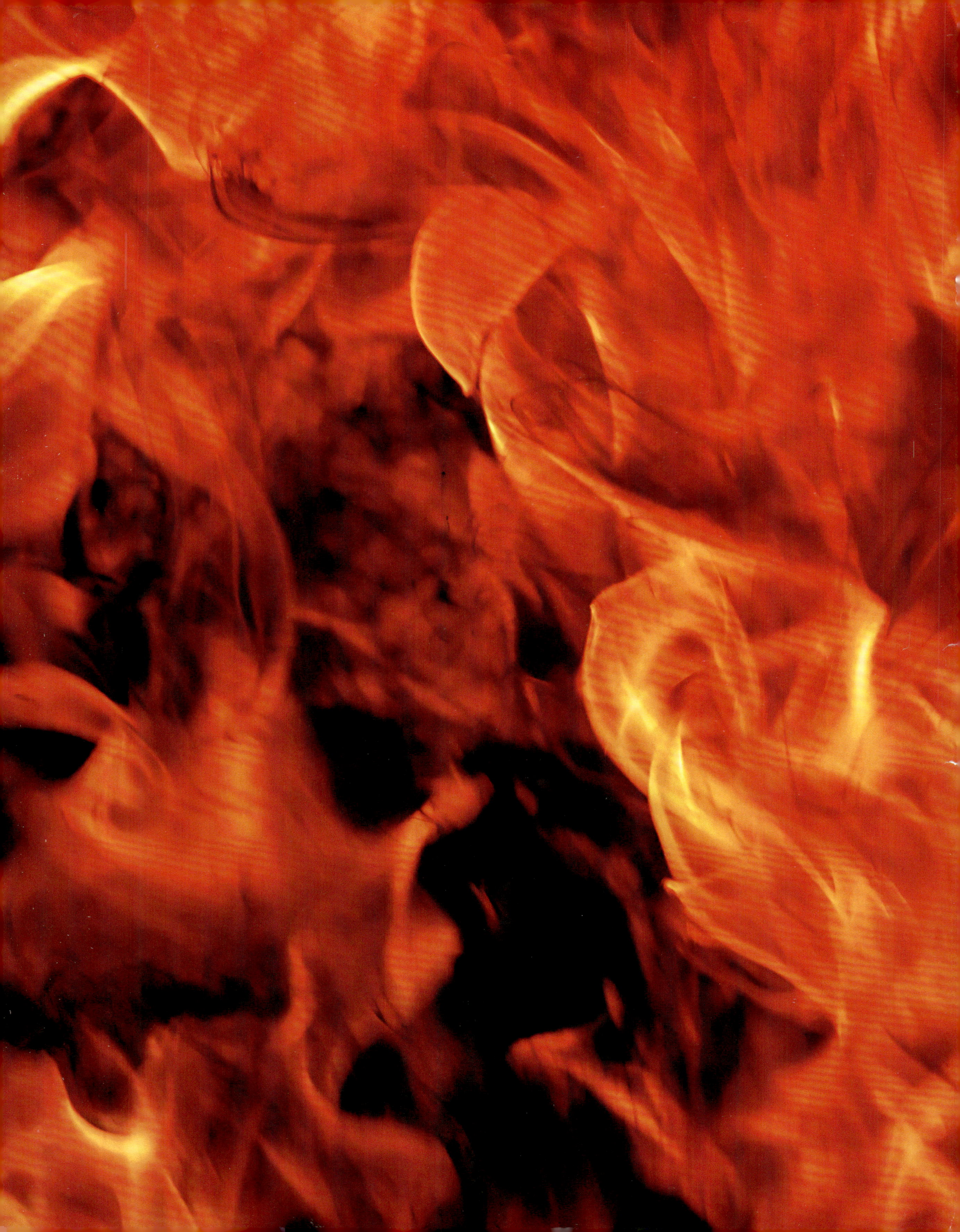